WHY I AM A ZIONIST
ISRAEL, JEWISH IDENTITY
AND THE CHALLENGES
OF TODAY

UPDATED EDITION

Gil Troy

ALSO BY GIL TROY

SEE HOW THEY RAN:
The Changing Role of the Presidential Candidate

MR. & MRS. PRESIDENT:
From the Trumans to the Clintons
(originally published as *Affairs of State: The Rise
and Rejection of the Presidential Couple Since World War II*)

MORNING IN AMERICA:
How Ronald Reagan Invented the 1980s

First printing, January 2002
Second printing, May 2002
Third printing, Updated Edition, June 2006

National Library of Canada Cataloguing in Publication Data

Troy, Gil
   Why I am a Zionist: Israel, Jewish Identity and the Challenges of Today

Includes bibliographical references and index.
ISBN 1-55234-648-X

1. Zionism. 2. Israel–Politics and government. I. Katz, Avi
II Bronfman Jewish Education Centre. III. Title.

DS149.T762001   320.54'095694   C2001-903632-9

To order contact: **Bronfman Jewish Education Centre**
                  1 Cummings Square
                  Montreal, Quebec H3W 1M6
                  Tel: (514) 345-2610
                  Fax: (514) 735-2175
                  e-mail: bjec@bjec.org

WHY I AM A ZIONIST

ISRAEL, JEWISH IDENTITY
AND THE CHALLENGES
OF TODAY

UPDATED EDITION

Gil Troy

BRONFMAN JEWISH EDUCATION CENTRE, MONTREAL

These two causes represent the two sides of modern Zionism, what the Israeli songwriter Naomi Shemer called *"hadvash vehaoketz,"* the honey and the sting. Even as we respond to the demands imposed by the continuing crisis in the Middle East, we need to articulate a positive vision that speaks to us and inspires us. In buying this book, dear reader, you are contributing to efforts to save Jewish bodies and Jewish souls which have been the twin aims of Zionism since it began as a modern movement just over a century ago.

DEDICATION

In memory of

Staff Sergeant Binyamin (Benny) Avraham, z"l

בנימן אברהם ז"ל

beloved son of Haim and Edna, cherished brother of Efrat and Dafna. Born January 1, 1980, he was murdered on October 7, 2000, along with Adi Avitan and Omer Souad, defending Israel's northern borders. Benny died not only defending his land, *Eretz Yisrael*, not only defending his country, *Medinat Yisrael*, but defending his people, *Am Yisrael*.

ושבו בנים לגבולם...

"And all the children shall return safely to their homes…"

REMEMBERING ZION

"By the rivers of Babylon, there we sat down, and wept, when we remembered Zion."

Psalm 137:1

"And Cyrus king of Persia said: the Lord, the God of heaven, has given me all the kingdoms of the earth; and He has charged me to build Him a house in Jerusalem…. Whoever among you of all His people is willing – his God be with him – let him go up to Jerusalem, which is in Judah, and build the House of the Lord…. And whoever is left, in any place where he lives, let the men of his place help him with silver, and with gold, and with goods, and with beasts to make a freewill-offering for the House of God which is in Jerusalem."

Ezra, 1:2-4

In 586 B.C.E. Nebuchadnezzar, King of Babylonia, conquered Jerusalem, razed the Jews' Holy Temple, and brought thousands of Jewish captives home with him. The pain of exile was searing. Despite finding themselves in one of the ancient world's most advanced civilizations, the Jews mourned for their lost homeland.

Less than fifty years later, a new ruler freed the Jews. Yet even as King Cyrus sent the Jews home to rebuild the Temple, Cyrus recognized that there would be many Jews "left" behind in Babylonia. Some estimate that a million Jews were exiled and only forty thousand returned to rejoin those Jews who had never left Israel.

Twenty-five-hundred years later, after a second, much longer, exile the Romans imposed, we Jews of North America are free to return to our ancient homeland. And like our Babylonian Jewish ancestors, many of us, too, have chosen not to return. Nevertheless, like the Jews who remained in Babylonia, we will not forsake our obligations, we will not forget our roots – we remain tied to our ancient homeland.

Zionism, the national liberation movement of the Jewish people, began in the nineteenth century as an attempt to redeem the Jews after nearly nineteen hundred years of exile. The movement produced one of the great miracles of the twentieth century, the establishment of the State of Israel in 1948. Unfortunately, at the start of the twenty-first century, Israel remains embattled – with far too many questioning the very legitimacy of the Jewish state and of Zionism, the movement which spawned it.

We Jews of the twenty-first century must relearn the lessons that many of our parents and grandparents learned. In defending Israel, in embracing Zionism, we are not only fulfilling some ancestral obligation. We are not simply reacting to our enemies. If we do it right, we can also use Israel, and Zionism, to redeem ourselves, as Jews, and as human beings.

CONTENTS

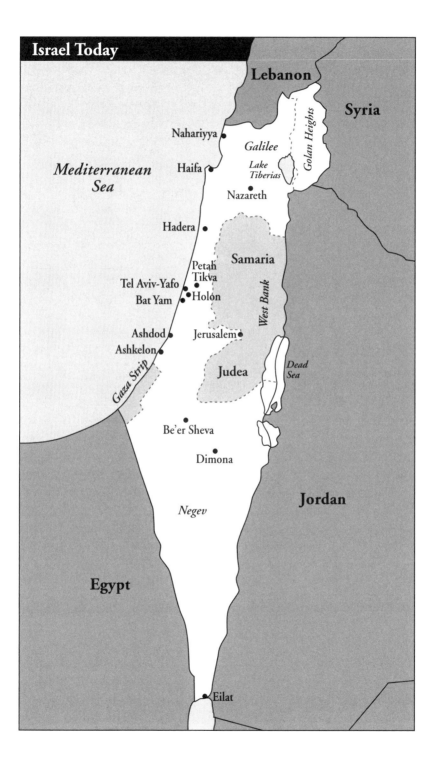

Israel Today

Lebanon

Syria

Mediterranean
Sea

Nahariyya

Galilee

Golan Heights

Haifa

Lake
Tiberias

Nazareth

Hadera

Samaria

West Bank

Petah
Tikva

Tel Aviv-Yafo

Bat Yam

Holon

Ashdod

Jerusalem

Ashkelon

Gaza Strip

Judea

Dead
Sea

Be'er Sheva

Dimona

Negev

Jordan

Egypt

Eilat

PROLOGUE
I AM A ZIONIST:
A TWENTY-FIRST CENTURY MANIFESTO

Today, more than half a century after Israel's founding, it remains all too tempting for friend and foe alike to define Israel, and Zionism, solely by the Arab world's hostility. To do so is to miss the normal miracles that occur in Israel daily, the millions who are able to live and learn, laugh and play, in the Middle East's only democracy. To do so is to underestimate the power of Zionism, a gutsy and visionary movement which has outlasted the twentieth century's grander and seemingly more permanent revolutions: Bolshevism, Nazism, fascism and communism.

The sad truth is that little more than a century after its founding, Zionism seems to be losing its luster. Arabs have demonized Zionism as the modern bogeyman, and many have clumped Zionists, along with Americans and most Westerners, as the Great Satans. The Palestinian attacks that began with renewed intensity in September 2000 have revived the United Nations libel equating Zionism with racism. In Israel, a small but influential group of intellectuals fancies themselves to be post-Zionists, while a negligible but voluble minority of Jews in the Diaspora please editorial page editors enamored of novelties by proudly proclaiming themselves Jewish anti-Zionists.

During these challenging times, Jews should reaffirm their faith and pride in Zionism, while the world should marvel at its achievements. Zionists must not allow their enemies to define and slander the movement. No nationalism is pure, no movement is perfect, no state ideal, but today Zionism remains legitimate, inspiring, and relevant, to me and to most Jews. A century ago, Zionism revived pride in the label "Jew"; today, Jews must revive pride in the label "Zionist."

I am a Zionist because I am a Jew – and without recognizing a national component in Judaism I cannot explain its unique character. Judaism is a world religion bound to one homeland, a people whose Holy Days are defined by the Israeli agricultural calendar, rooted in theological concepts, and linked with historic events.

I am a Zionist because I know my history – and after being exiled from their homeland more than 1900 years ago, the defenseless, wandering Jews endured repeated persecutions at the hands of both Christians and Muslims – centuries before this anti-Semitism culminated in the Holocaust.

I am a Zionist because Jews never forgot their ties to their homeland, their love for Jerusalem. Even when they established autonomous self-governing structures in Babylonia, in Europe, in North Africa, these were governments in exile yearning to return home.

I am a Zionist because those ideological ties nourished and were nurtured by the plucky minority of Jews who remained in the land of Israel, sustaining continued Jewish settlement throughout the exile.

I am a Zionist because in modern times the promise of Emancipation and Enlightenment was a double-edged sword, often offering acceptance for Jews in Europe only after they assimilated, yet never fully respecting them if they did assimilate.

I am a Zionist because in establishing the sovereign state of Israel in 1948, the Jews were reconstituting in modern Western terms a relationship with a land they had been attached to for 4,000 years, since the time of Abraham – just as India did in establishing a modern state out of an ancient civilization.

I am a Zionist because in building that state, the Jews were returning to history and embracing normalcy, a condition which gave them power, with all its benefits, responsibilities, and dilemmas.

I am a Zionist because I celebrate the existence of Israel, and like any thoughtful patriot, though I might criticize particular governmental policies which I dislike, I do not delegitimize the state itself.

I am a Zionist because I live in the real world of nation-states, and I see that Zionism is no more or less "racist" than any other nationalism, be it American, Armenian, Canadian, or Czech, all of which rely on some internal cohesion, some tribalism, some sense of solidarity among some historic grouping of individuals, and not others.

I am a Zionist because here in North America we have learned in this multicultural world that pride in one's heritage as a Jew, an Italian, a Greek, can provide essential and time-tested anchors in a world overdosing on materialism, consumerism, and the sensationalism of the here and now.

I am a Zionist because in our world of post-modern identities, I know that we don't have to be "either-ors", we can be "ands and buts" – a Zionist AND an American patriot; a secular and somewhat assimilated Jew BUT also a Zionist.

I am a Zionist because I am a democrat, and for the last two centuries, the history of democracy has been intertwined with the history of nationalism. Similarly, for the last century democracy has been a central Zionist ideal, despite being tested under the most severe conditions.

I am a Zionist because I am an idealist, and just as a century ago, the notion of a strong, independent, viable, sovereign Jewish state was an impossible dream – yet absolutely worth fighting for – so, too, today, the notion of a strong, independent, viable, sovereign Jewish state living in true peace and harmony with its neighbors appears to be an impossible dream – yet absolutely worth striving for.

I am a Zionist because I am a romantic, and the vision of the Jews rebuilding their homeland, reclaiming the desert, renewing themselves, was one of the greatest stories of the twentieth century, just as the vision of the Jews maintaining their homeland, reconciling with the Arab world, renewing themselves, and serving as a light to others, a model nation state, could be one of the greatest stories of the twenty-first century. Yes, it sounds far-fetched today. But, as Theodor Herzl, the father of modern Zionism, said in an idle boast that has become a cliché: "If you will it, it is no dream."

I AM AN ANTI-ANTI ZIONIST

In honor of Israel's fifty-third anniversary, on *Yom Ha'atzmaut* 2001, I wrote the above essay for the *Montreal Gazette* titled "Why I Am a Zionist." The article sought to return to basics during this difficult passage in Israel's existence. To our non-Jewish friends, I tried to explain why Zionism, which is Jewish nationalism, is no more racist than any other form of nationalism. And to my fellow Jews, I tried to emphasize the big picture beyond the messy and depressing complexities of 2001.

In this essay, I was very careful to avoid addressing the Palestinian question at all, beyond ending with a hope that just as in the twentieth century Israel made the Jewish dream of restoring a homeland a reality, in the twenty-first century Israel would figure out how to reconcile with the Arab world and make the dream of living in peace with her neighbors a reality.

Nevertheless, some respondents caricatured my essay in subsequent opinion essays and in letters to the editor as an attack on Palestinians and as a racist piece. These reactions made it very clear. Far too many of Israel's enemies see any affirmation of any kind of Zionism as an act of aggression against them.

Even more disturbing were some of the responses the *Gazette* chose not to publish. One pro-Palestinian organization defines itself as "Anti-Zionist, Anti-Capitalist, Anti-racism, Anti-US global hegemony, Anti-globalization!!" and "Pro-Hamas, Pro-Taliban, Pro-all Islamic resistance movements fighting occupation and oppression. AND MOST OF ALL PRO-ISLAM." The organization's Web site posted a letter sent to the *Gazette* saying "'Why I'm a Zionist' reminds me of other possible scenarios. Why I'm a KKK member. To be proud repressing others, feeling superior and a chosen people who deserve to kill, maim and torture…. God help us when we can allow people to stand up and say 'Why I'm [a] Terrorist,' 'Why I kill children,' 'Why I'm a Nazi,' 'Why I agree with State sponsored Terrorism,' 'Why I bulldoze families' home[s].'"

Perhaps most depressing was the letter that began with the by now knee-jerk (if conceptually paradoxical) free association of Zionism "with Bolshevism, Nazism and racism of the worst order." The man equated "the language the Nazis used to describe the Jews in Germany in the 1930s and 40s and the language now being used by the AshkeNAZI Jews to describe the natives of Palestine: snakes, sub-human, foreigners living on the land God gave us, etc."

As so many anti-Zionists do, the man then naturally segued into the ugliest forms of anti-Semitism, saying, "I understand why Herr Hitler rose to power and why the Jewish holocaust – a harsh reaction to the Jewish misdeeds – took place." Calling the "last Jewish holocaust" an "act of 'divine justice,'" he concluded, "You have, without realising [sic] it, given in your article fourteen reasons why the next holocaust is bound to occur…. Your article tends to support the view that I have heard about as a child that a Jew is born without a soul; he has no sympathy for anyone unless his own interest is involved in it."

These days, you do not need a Ph.D. to recognize that the Middle East is a very confusing place. And I would never do what my critics have done and tar all critics with the same brush. There is a lot of room for honest and critical debate about Israeli policy toward the Palestinians yesterday and today, and not everyone who questions any Israeli action in any realm is necessarily an Israel-hater or an anti-Zionist.

Nevertheless, I wish to thank my critics for imposing a certain conceptual clarity on the conflict. All Jews, all Americans, all Canadians, all people of good conscience throughout the world, should rise up and strike down this anti-Zionist venom that has seeped into daily political discourse. As the above examples indicate, such new-fangled anti-Zionism is often hard to distinguish from old-fashioned Jew hatred – no matter how many contrarian op-ed essays the few but loud anti-Zionist Jews may publish. We have seen anti-Semitism blur with anti-Zionism in the Syrian president's ugly anti-Jewish remarks when greeting the Pope; we have seen anti-Zionism blur into anti-Semitism with the surge in attacks on Jews throughout the world since the troubles began in Israel in September, 2000; we have seen anti-Zionism blur into anti-Semitism with the booklet of caricatures showing Jews with hook noses and fangs dripping blood some delegates distributed at an anti-racism conference in Durban, South Africa.

The former Soviet dissident, Natan Sharansky, offers a "3-D" test for modern anti-Zionists: If they demonize Israel, use double standards and delegitimize Israel or Zionism, they are anti-Semitic. Decades ago, the American civil rights leader Martin Luther King, Jr., put it more bluntly, saying, "When people criticize Zionists they mean Jews, you are talking anti-Semitism."

ANTI-ZIONISM:
UGLY RHETORIC WITH LETHAL CONSEQUENCES

For too long too many of us ignored the vitriol. We forgot that peace has to be made between peoples, not leaders, and that making nice to one another is an essential precondition for making peace. While Israelis were arguing about how to acknowledge Palestinian nationalism in their curricula, Palestinian curricula were fomenting anti-Zionism and anti-Semitism. Palestinian maps did not even acknowledge Israel's existence. There was also, we must admit, some liberal racism, some Western condescension, at work. Too many observers explained away Yasir Arafat's calls in Arabic for *jihad* (Holy War) against the Jews, as being necessary for domestic consumption, as simply the way "they" speak to each other over there.

Today, the intensity of the hatred, the ubiquity of the calls, has deadly consequences – and can no longer be ignored. What are we to make, for example, of this snippet from a sermon broadcast on official Palestinian

Authority television in the summer of 2001, which cried: "All weapons must be aimed at the Jews, at the enemies of Allah, the cursed nation in the Koran, whom the Koran describes as monkeys and pigs, worshippers of the calf and idol worshippers. Allah shall make the Moslem rule over the Jew, we will blow them up in Hadera, we will blow them up in Tel-Aviv and in Netanya in the righteousness of Allah against this riff-raff.... We will enter Jerusalem as conquerors, and Jaffa as conquerors, and Haifa as conquerors and Ashkelon as conquerors.... We bless all those who educate their children to *Jihad* and to Martyrdom, blessings to he who shot a bullet into the head of a Jew...." What are we to make of the final interview Faisal Husseini reportedly gave before he died of a heart attack that spring? Husseini, whom the Western world eulogized as a moderate, as a Palestinian dove, characterized Oslo as a Trojan Horse. "The Intifada itself is the coming down out of the [wooden] horse," he said. "The Oslo agreement, or any other agreement, is just a temporary procedure, or just a step toward something bigger... [which] is the liberation of all historical Palestine from the river to the sea." What are we to make of the fact that mainstream Palestinian press organs and leaders of the Palestinian Authority have accused Israel of spreading AIDS to Arab children, of disseminating Mad Cow disease in the West Bank, of "distributing food containing material that causes cancer and hormones that harm male virility and other spoiled food products in the Palestinian Authority's territories in order to poison and harm the Palestinian population"?

It is tragic and ironic that this resurgence of anti-Zionism comes almost a decade after the Oslo peace treaties, when, polls show, a majority of Israelis and a majority of Jews throughout the world began to acknowledge Palestinian nationalism. It is tragic and pathetic that these blood libels, new and old, come after Ehud Barak offered a sweeping set of concessions at Camp David in July of 2000. It is tragic and diabolic that these attacks on the right of Israel to exist are echoing throughout the world and affirming the choice many Palestinians made to resort to violence instead of peaceful negotiations.

We in the Jewish community need to focus on these fundamental issues, on the right of Israel to exist, and on the violent repudiation by so many Palestinians of Israelis' attempts at peace, even as we struggle with the political, strategic, moral, and existential challenges of today. We must not get so bogged down in apologias and defensiveness that we ignore the bigger picture. A quarter of a century ago, America's ambassador to the United Nations, Daniel Patrick Moynihan, rejected the infamous UN "Zionism is racism" resolution as "an obscene act." Moynihan later explained that he recognized more than "uninformed bigotry" at play, "it is conscious politics…. It is not merely that our adversaries have commenced an effort to destroy the legitimacy of a kindred democracy through the incessant repetition of the Zionist-racist lie. It is that others can come to believe it also."

The poisonous seeds Moynihan saw sown in the mid-1970s are bearing deadly fruit today. We cannot sit by idly and let these libels fester. We must as Jews and as proud citizens of great democracies like the United States and Canada stand up and fight. Just as the women's movement marched to "take back the night" from assailants, we Jews need to "take back" Zionism from its critics. Not only must we not let them define us, we also cannot let our reaction to them define us. Too much modern Judaism is defined by our enemies – of yesterday and today. In taking back Zionism, we need to articulate a positive vision that speaks to us – and inspires us.

Alas, the sad truth is that this renewed assault on Israel and on Zionism comes at an awkward time in Jewish history. As the next chapter will argue, despite all the speeches and rallies and essays generated after September 2000, despite all the "we are one" solidarity missions and statements, many North American Jews today remain ambivalent about Zionism and the State of Israel itself. Many say that the term "Zionism" makes them "uncomfortable," while others buy into the conventional wisdom that sets the Israelis as the colonialist "Goliaths" oppressing the Palestinian "Davids," or simply dismisses both sides as equally violent and barbaric. And even those who call themselves Zionist, who defend the State of Israel, often find themselves unable to articulate why – or to navigate around the complexities of Middle East politics.

THE AIMS OF THIS BOOK:
ZIONIST AND JEWISH RENEWAL

This book is an attempt to "take back" Zionism from its critics. This task is easier said than done. In today's politically correct world, it is far easier to damn a term than to redeem it. Many words have been banished from polite conversation, few have made the long journey back to respectability.

This book is also an attempt to "take back" Zionism from some of its fans. Zionist ideologues need to stop generating distractions with quixotic crusades trying to negate the Diaspora or limiting Zionism, meaning Jewish nationalism, to those who make *aliyah* (move to Israel). Zionist activists need to stop creating the misimpression that Zionism is a monolithic movement marching in lockstep with the Israeli policy of the moment. And Zionist leaders need to stop perpetuating an organizational culture that has many people marrying the word "Zionist" to sinecure or bureaucrat.

Friends and foes have done damage. Even Jews who accept the Zionist trinity, if you will, of peoplehood, history, and homeland, recoil at the use of the word – and shun the label. I am, however, an optimist. If Times Square can be reclaimed, Zionism can be, too. In fact, Zionists have to follow their own playbook. Much of the Zionist revolution of the late nineteenth century entailed resurrecting symbols, changing images, transforming negatives into positives. From the new cult of the Maccabees to the rediscovery of Masada, Zionists scoured Jewish history for new, physically assertive, powerful role models – and found them. Today, we need a similar reclamation project with the term Zionism itself.

In that spirit, the book is addressed to the many who may have forgotten – or never learned – just why Zionism began, and just why Israel needs to exist. It is addressed to the campus activist who told a reporter "Some people here can pull out all the Oslo details and pull all this knowledge out," while she was "trying to figure out just the basics." It is addressed to the college student who asked me how Israeli policy differed from apartheid. It is addressed to the counselor in a Zionist summer camp who asked me how I could support the Israeli "oppressors" – and her colleague who said, "I grew up in a Jewish day school, but I can't call myself 'Zionist' because I've only heard the biases of that side." It is addressed to the student leader who felt that the Israel advocacy day at a Hillel Student Leaders Assembly, while "rejuvenating," was "also kind of hard to swallow because it's so pro-Israel." It is addressed to the student leader who evenhandedly condemned "the uncompromising attitude both sides are taking." It is addressed to the many friends of mine who continued pursuing business as usual during this great crisis, and did not seem that disturbed.

However, this is not intended to be a defensive work – nor is it simply tied to the political needs of the moment. Rather, the book is an attempt to articulate a vision of Zionism that is rooted in the past, relevant to the present, and inspiring for the future. I believe that Zionism is more than simply pro-Israelism. I also believe that you don't have to sign off on every Israeli government policy and action to be a good Zionist. Finally, I believe that Zionism in the twenty-first century can be what it intended to be in the nineteenth century, and what it was for so many in the twentieth century – a solution to the Jewish problem, a way of solving some of our most pressing communal and individual needs.

Of course, the "problem" has changed – this generation needs Zionism to help revitalize Judaism, and not to protect us against anti-Semitism. This book, at the end of the day, is not simply about Gevalt or Crisis Zionism, about rallying around the blue-and-white flag during times of trouble. Rather, it is about what we might call Identity Zionism, about using this marvelous, mystical, and complex idea of Jewish nationalism to help make us better Jews, and better people.

"Aseh lechah rav," make for yourself a teacher; *"kneh lecha chaver,"* acquire for yourself a friend, *"Pirkei Avot,"* the *Ethics of the Fathers*, teaches. The distinction here suggests that while we seek out worthy teachers to absorb from them, we need to have a *"kinyan,"* an exchange, with a friend. If it is not mutual, it is not a friendship. So, too, our relationship with Israel is no friendship if it is only a one-way street. And the truth is that both of us, Israel and the Diaspora, need the friendship.

THE PLAN OF THE BOOK

This book is divided into 5 parts. Part 1, "How to be a Proud Zionist in Today's World," articulates an up-to-date affirmative ideology. It begins by diagnosing the current ills of North American Zionism. It then offers a different, more positive, vision of Zionism than what we usually get, arguing that Zionism, meaning Jewish nationalism, is essential to Judaism, whether you are secular or religious. It ends by focusing on three experiences that have shaped my personal Zionism but also illustrate how to revitalize Zionism and Judaism – attending Zionist summer camps, participating in group Israel experiences such as the birthright israel trips, and soaking in the magic of Jerusalem. Then Part 2, "History," provides some historical background. Without understanding our past, neither the Jewish tie to Israel nor the Jewish return to Israel makes much sense. In the face of a vicious assault on Israel's legitimacy, it is crucial these days to understand the depth of the Jewish attachment to Israel. The historical part stretches back to Abraham and culminates with an assessment of Israel today.

After this thumbnail historical sketch, Part 3, "Crisis Zionism," looks at some of the basic questions revolving around the current Israeli-Palestinian conflict, and the renewed assault on the legitimacy of Zionism and Israel. It features two new chapters, one on Israel's right to exist, and a second on the compatibility between Zionism and liberalism. Part 4,

"Identity Zionism," seeks to go beyond the depressing complexities of the Middle East and the propaganda war to explore this new positive Zionist vision for North America. Finally, the new, fifth part expands the original appendix which suggested how to win and sometimes avoid the fights that sprout like weeds around those of us who dare to support Israel. "Bumping into History" reflects the Zionist movement's ups and downs in the four years since the first edition. It explores modern anti-Semitism, suggests strategies for fighting the casual bigotry of the politically correct and anti-Zionist hatred, while keeping a positive Zionist vision on campus and throughout North America. It echoes Martin Luther King, Jr.'s call for "creative extremists," and ends upbeat, in the spirit of this work, promising *lo nafseek lirkod*, we won't stop dancing – and singing and celebrating and dreaming as Jews, Zionists, democrats, Westerners.

Two caveats at the start. This book is an introduction and a meditation. It is not an authoritative reference book. Anyone curious about my footnoting skills should read my American history works. This book is more survey course than seminar, uncovering ideas without covering everything. This book hopes to point in the right direction, but all readers must remember what the Passover Haggadah teaches *tseh ulmad*, go and learn!

Second, this book is a work in progress, hoping to trigger a dialogue in the Jewish world. I wrote it in August 2001, troubled by the defensive, demoralized, ineffectual way students in particular were responding to the renewed Arab onslaught. I added a last chapter – J'Accuse – shortly after September 11, to address what was already emerging as the modern blood libel blaming Jews for al Qaida's evil terrorist attacks. We published 5,000 copies, unsure anyone would notice. By May 2002, we released a second edition with 10,000 more copies, updated to incorporate the events of April 2002, when Israel finally started responding proactively to Palestinian terror. I thank the many readers who sent feedback.

Now, having sold 15,000 copies, I offer this major revision, adding six new chapters and tweaking to update as well. The argument remains untouched. The Zionist vision remains the same. The historical context has changed, and I have learned much more from readers, students, and audiences in the United States, Canada, Great Britain and Israel. I hope to continue revising this work for future editions. I welcome reader feedback, please send via email to me at bjec@bjec.org.

PART 1

HOW TO BE A PROUD ZIONIST
IN TODAY'S WORLD

We live in an age of multiple, and malleable, identities. We moderns juggle philosophies and switch personae in ways that would have dumbfounded our ancestors. We are indeed "free to be you and me" – and whoever else we choose to be. But our freedom is a double-edged sword. It invigorates us and it also makes us anxious.

For me, Zionism, meaning Jewish nationalism, meaning a passion about Jewish peoplehood and the Jewish homeland, has long been at the core of my being. This ideology anchors me. It is an ideology that has filled my life with meaning – and that has bonded me with many friends.

These are days of Zionist crisis, but these can also be days of Zionist renewal. The tea leaf readings are mixed. Even as many North American Jews distance themselves from the Jewish state and Jewish nationalism, thousands, especially young people, are discovering that through Jewish peoplehood, through engagement with Israel, we just might be able to find the recipe for Jewish renaissance.

CHAPTER 1

THE PROBLEM:
IS NORTH AMERICAN ZIONISM DYING?

By 2003, despite all the traumas in the Middle East, the organized Jewish community was feeling pretty good about itself. Solidarity with Israel was the order of the day. The "Jew versus Jew" fights over assimilation, intermarriage, and religious differences were yesterday's news. In the Diaspora, as in Israel, Jews could thank the Palestinians for forging a communal unity we could not otherwise achieve on our own.

Once again, Zionism was "in." After a decade of confusion, when Israel's greatest enemy became a Nobel prize-winning peace partner, when Federations discovered that "Israel doesn't sell" and shifted millions of dollars to local "needs," the Jewish community was back where it was comfortable – on a war footing defending the beleaguered Jewish state. The "crisis contributions" flowed more easily than the regular funds. As the United Jewish Communities campaign "talking points" distributed to canvassers put it: "What we need to do is to cry out in one loud voice 'We stand with you, Israel, as a strong unified Jewish community in your most desperate hours.'" Historically, 2000–2004 can now join the other years when Jews stepped forward and rallied for Israel, especially the Six Day War in 1967, the Yom Kippur War in 1973, and the Gulf War in 1991.

In the spring of 2001, news reports about the American Israel Public Affairs Committee (AIPAC) convention were practically giddy. The front page of the venerable New York Jewish newspaper, the *Forward,* proclaimed, "LOBBYING GROUP IN UP MOOD AT 1ST PARLEY OF POST-OSLO ERA." One AIPAC official rejoiced, "Membership is up, donations are up, and people feel charged."

As the old proverb warns, be careful what you wish for. The Jewish response to the Palestinians' anti-Oslo violence was disturbing. This apparent Zionist revival may have the opposite effect. It may have been a fatal fig leaf not just covering up North American Zionism in its death throes – but accelerating the process.

THE HEYDAY OF AMERICAN ZIONISM

Once upon a time, Zionism, meaning the support for Israel as a Jewish national homeland, was a powerful glue binding North American Jews with each other, with Israel, and with Jews throughout the world. After 1967, during the post-Six Day War euphoria, the plucky Jewish state was the apple of the American Jewish eye. This romance continued in the 1970s through the dark days of the Yom Kippur War and the Palestinian terror attacks, culminating with the grassroots movement to save Soviet Jewry by facilitating *aliyah*, immigration to Israel.

Forgetting how hesitant many had been to support the Jewish state before 1948, American Jews in the 1960s and 1970s embraced Justice Louis Brandeis's equation whereby "Zionism equals Americanism." Brandeis achieved this synthesis via progressivism, democratic liberalism, which gave Zionists and Americans a common language, and common ground. By focusing on the utopian and the communal aspects of the Zionist agenda, turning Zionism into a force for good around the world while saving oppressed Jews from benighted Europe, Brandeis at once legitimated and defanged American Zionism.

Half a century later, during the heyday of American Zionism after the Six Day War, even Philip Roth, *the enfant terrible* of American Jewish writing, could not resist the Israel of Moshe Dayan and Golda Meir, the Israel of the sabra and Jaffa oranges. Alexander Portnoy, Roth's perverse and perverted Jewish neurotic, finds the land of milk and honey the perfect salve, the healthy contrast to his smothering American Jewish ghetto, the land of guilt and money.

Toward the end of *Portnoy's Complaint* (1969), Portnoy runs away, runs "home," as it were, to Israel, and cannot believe what he sees. "My dream begins as soon as I disembark," Roth has Portnoy declare. "I am in an airport where I have never been before and all the people I see – passengers, stewardesses, ticket sellers, porters, pilots, taxi drivers – are Jews," he notes, as if scribbling down a dream, for "awake who ever heard of such a thing? The writing on the walls is Jewish – Jewish graffiti! The flag is Jewish…. These are (there's no other word!) the natives. Returned! This is where it all began! Just been away on a long vacation, that's all! Hey, here we're the WASPS!"

Portnoy Zionism was indeed a magical elixir. North American Jews in all their diversity could rally around the blue-and-white flag. Religious Jews, forgetting their grandfathers' anti-Zionism, fell in love with the state which had liberated the holy stones of Jerusalem. Secular Jews, grasping on to the heritage of their ancestors, fell in love with the unholy pragmatism of Tel Aviv. Liberals could laud the democratic socialism of the kibbutz and the monolithic *Hisdadrut* labor union, while conservatives could delight in the patriotic nationalism of the *Knesset*, the Parliament, and *Tzahal*, the Israel Defense Forces. When religious and secular, liberal and conservative, sang *Yerushalayim Shel Zahav*, each group could find idiosyncratic fulfillment while reveling in their common devotion to Jerusalem of Gold.

THE GROWING DIVIDE

Alas, in the intervening decades, Israel has changed, and so has North American Jewry. American Jews became more fully American, and more likely to posit their gleaming suburban castles as healthy contrasts to their Israeli cousins' cramped proletarian apartments. Looking back on it, in many ways, Zionist activism served as an Americanizing agent, allowing the Jewish community in North America to find a loud, assertive and comfortable political voice that now most often is directed to more secular and careerist pursuits.

Moreover, Israel itself became less universally popular. The war in Lebanon – "Israel's Vietnam" – cooled the ardor of many American Jewish baby boomers who so proudly protested their own country's Vietnam. Israel's economic boom and transition to capitalism disappointed many American Jewish liberals whose commitment to capitalism is limited to their own family's economic advancement. And somewhere along the way, Israel not only lost its status as victim in the Middle East conflict, but began to be perceived as the aggressor, the colonizer, the occupier.

This delegitimization of Zionism, and growing sympathy for the Palestinians, resulted from a combustible combination of Israel's own mistakes, the Israeli elite's harsh self-criticism, the reality of Israeli power and prosperity, the contrast with Palestinian powerlessness and poverty, the West's newfound politically correct romance with indigenous peoples, and the successful quarter-century-long propaganda campaign to demonize Zionism as racism. All this culminated with the 1987-1988 "Intifada" when Woody Allen, the bad boy of American Jewish celebrity, snarled at Israel: "My goodness! Are these the people whose money I used to steal from those little blue-and-white cans after collecting funds for a Jewish homeland?"

As a result, today, Israel's reputation as a country is heavily at odds with tenets central to the ideology of many secular North American Jews.

To the extent that most North American Jews remain politically liberal, most Jews are uncomfortable with intense patriotism, religious fundamentalism, and militarism – yet Israel is often caricatured as committed to all three. Moreover, whereas once Israel may have united religious and secular Jews in their Zionism, today the religious-secular story is one more flashpoint. Yes, a century ago, the religious community was overwhelming non- or anti-Zionist, and Zionism was the special province of some secular Jews. By contrast, today, the religious community – except for the most extreme – is overwhelmingly Zionist, and it is secular Jews who are increasingly agnostic about Israel.

Tragically, the Oslo Accords, the grandiose gamble to achieve a lasting Mideast peace, only intensified the divisions. Throughout the Oslo years, from 1993 to 2000, as the Jewish community became more polarized over the peace issue, researchers noted that "America's doves on the whole did not care about Israel nearly as deeply as did its hawks." As Samuel Freedman reports in *Jew vs. Jew* (2000), "in specific measurements of the bond – multiple trips to Israel, study in Israel, friendships with Israelis, Hebrew fluency – the liberals showed far less connection than the conservatives."

THE RISE OF IDENTITY ZIONISM

Of course, some secular liberal Jews recognized that Israel and Zionism could help revive the Jewish community. These Identity Zionists harked back to the ideological roots of the movement, and posited Israel and Jewish nationalism as the solution to contemporary Jewish problems. As the Israeli dove and Zionist activist Yossi Beilin notes in *His Brother's Keeper* (2000), Israel is "proof that secular Jews can survive as Jews. It is one of the only places in the world – if not the only one – where a secular Jew is not worried about whether his or her grandchildren will remain Jewish." Eschewing schmaltz for social science – language that would appeal to ethnically-oriented secular Jews – researchers confirmed that simply visiting Israel, let alone living there, could renew a modern Jew's identity. Noting a "positive association between a visit to Israel and measures of Jewish identification, community affiliation and religious practice," academics argued that "the identity-enhancing effect of a visit to Israel for North American Jews may be independent of prior socialization." Such insights were the basis for the birthright israel initiative and many other educational enterprises that build on Israel as the spiritual and ideological center of world Jewry.

The latest violence threatens the important conversation these Identity Zionists have triggered, as well as the essential reconceptualization of Israel-Diaspora relations that needs to take place. For some, resources spent on soft Jewish identity projects take a back seat to harder ADL and AIPAC lobbying initiatives. For others, the crisis is a welcome short cut to stronger Jewish identity. "When you mobilize a generation of Jewish students on campuses today to defend Israel, that's Jewish renaissance," Martin Raffel of the Jewish Council for Public Affairs told the Jewish Telegraph Agency in September, using the new community buzzword (Jewish survival became Jewish continuity and is now Jewish renaissance). Raffel observed that "war and Intifada and violence" pleases no one but many leaders believe it did work in the past, given that "a lot of middle-aged people came to greater Jewish awareness" through the 1967 Six Day War and the 1973 Yom Kippur War.

It is only natural for pressing security, political, diplomatic, and financial needs to eclipse identity building and theorizing. And given how North American Jews respond to negative stimuli and bathos, it is quite predictable for leaders to try to base a Jewish revival on this unfortunate situation. But the terror could, at the end of the day, distance most North American Jews even further from Israel and Zionism.

"WE ARE ONE" ... OR ARE WE?

For starters, all the "we are one" rhetoric contradicts the reality. It papers over serious divisions and it rings hollow. The sad truth is that even as the North American Jewish community rallied around Israel en masse, individual Jews abandoned Israel in droves. When Arabs target Israel, American Jews change their vacation plans. After 2000, tourists all but disappeared from the country. Bar and Bat Mitzvah trips were cancelled, longstanding school programs postponed, summer tours deserted. In a depressing historical inversion, in the spring of 2001, many parents seemed unconcerned about sending their teenagers to Auschwitz for the March of the Living Program but feared sending them to Jerusalem. In perhaps the most distasteful yet telling move, parents at one day school in Brooklyn, New York, voted to send the school's seniors to Disney World instead of Israel.

Furthermore, these trip cancellations stemmed from the CNN-*New York Times* view of Israel as a country under siege. Diaspora Jews have become true "mediots," media idiots, when it comes to Israel. If all we experience about Israel is the latest CNN lead, and the latest *New York*

Times headline, we are bound to see Israel as awash in turmoil, paralyzed by crisis. CNN offers footage of bombs bursting in air, not Israelis commuting to work or going to school. The *New York Times* reports troop movements and terrorist attacks, not youth movements and scientific breakthroughs. Even as we recognize it, we succumb to the steady drumbeat of news – 99 percent of it negative – as our major Israel information lifeline. Visits to Israel, correspondence with Israelis, reading Israeli newspapers on the internet, all these can paint a broader and fuller picture of a society which is under stress, but is still growing, earning, living, learning. Without these alternative perspectives, and with all the talk about what Israelis "need" from us, it is impossible for us to think about what we might need – or simply gain – from them.

The harsh realities of the current conflict, the Palestinian Authority's embrace of violence instead of diplomacy, the bloodthirsty murders of two lost reservists, of five members of a single family eating in a pizzeria, of twenty-one night-clubbers, shifted the community to the right. Some on the left exacerbated the problem by demonizing the settlers, excusing the Palestinians, blaming Israel, and delegitimizing Zionism with promiscuous analogizing, attacking Israel for creating "bantustans" and comparing the IDF to the Gestapo. As a result, the Jewish establishment is back to its old tricks, preferring to squelch dissent rather than engage it. Dismissing dissenters as "self-hating Jews" is an approach which substitutes cheap psychology and a long established demonology for informed and critical debate. Clumping Zionist and non-Zionist critics together ignores serious ideological challenges to Diaspora-Israel relations while shortsightedly and narrowly identifying Zionism as unquestioning support for the Israel government of the moment.

BEWARE FOUL WEATHER AND FAIR WEATHER FRIENDS

Such a polarization creates an unhealthy dynamic. Foul weather friends beget fair weather friends by obscuring the real reasons for a friendship. Foul weather friends and fair weather friends both make what should be a three-dimensional relationship unidimensional. If the foul weather friends rally to the cry "My country right or wrong, take it or leave it," the fair weather friends simply leave it. Few American Jewish liberals rejected the United States itself during Ronald Reagan's terms in office – and few Canadian liberals abandoned their country during the Brian Mulroney years. So why do they repudiate the Jewish state when Benjamin Netanyahu or Ariel Sharon becomes the democratically elected temporary steward of Israel?

This all-or-nothing approach to our Jewish homeland is most unfortunate. Many of Israel's harshest critics are Israelis themselves. They understand that criticism can also be an expression of love, that they can fight fiercely for their state's right to exist, even as they fight fiercely against one policy or another, one tactic or another. Stateside, someone like Mark Seal, the Executive Vice President of the Jewish Reconstructionist Federation, recognizes the special obligations of critics to distinguish between opposition and apostasy. "There is so much to do and progressive Jews must become involved," he wrote in the Spring 2001 issue of *Reconstructionism Today*. "I support Israel and therefore I demand peace, justice and equality. The right wing and the Orthodox within both Israel and the organized American Jewish community cannot be allowed to define the parameters of Zionism." All too often, the fair weather friend simply walks away; the foul weather friend, when mobilized, blasts the Israeli internal critic as a traitor too, perpetuating a stereotype of our community as narrow-minded.

A politicized and hysterical relationship simply will not work. It alienates too many independent souls during times of crisis, and distances the majority when things are good. The "I love Israel" resurgence of 2000-2004 after a decade of drift and tension in Israel-Diaspora relations makes the pathology all too clear: when Israel is tasting peace and enjoying prosperity, many North American Jews do not know what to do with it; but when Israel is victimized and attacked: "We Are One."

In short, while yesterday's tactics may once again serve us well today, they may make it harder for us tomorrow. The twentieth century was indeed punctuated by crises for world Jewry; let us hope that the same will not be true in the twenty-first century. In the late twentieth century,

American Jews were eager to compete with other oppressed minorities in the victimology sweepstakes. Let us hope that American ethnic and gender politics will mature a bit in the twenty-first century. To prepare for better times, we must change our tactics and reevaluate our ideologies. Gevalt Zionism with its diet of schmaltz and guilt, leavened by the occasional crisis, is very thin gruel indeed.

FRAYING BONDS: INDIFFERENCE AND IGNORANCE

In fact, a closer look reveals that there was a brittleness underlying the community actions since September, 2000 as well. Ambivalence and ignorance lurked behind the affirmations of solidarity. Jewish day schools scheduled sessions for parents on "How to deal with the Israel crisis" – and had to cancel them because no parents showed up. Some rabbis reported being asked why their Hebrew schools were teaching *"Hatikvah."* The *Jerusalem Post* reported that Hebrew University fundraisers objected strenuously to a proposed slogan that "Hebrew University is the future of Jerusalem." The fundraisers said Jerusalem "would be a bad selling point," the university's president Menachem Magidor reported.

At first, leaders in New York City, the capital of Jewish North America, struggled to pull together a major solidarity rally. In New York in June, 2001, a "pluralistic coalition" of over one hundred rabbis joined the Federations in the tristate area in what was billed as a "consensus rally." After nine months and nearly ninety deaths, the leaders were careful to emphasize the rally's nonpartisan, nonpolitical, and "transdenominational" nature. Some of the rabbis organizing the event told the *Jerusalem Post* that so few rallies had been mounted during the previous eight months due to a "fear that demonstrators will simply not show up." Even though, as "luck" would have it, the rally took place two days after the slaughter of twenty-one young Israelis at the Dolphinarium night club in Tel Aviv, only ten thousand people attended the rally – out of two million Jews in New York's metropolitan area.

It is in fact quite difficult to mobilize troops for a rally defined by what it is not – nonpartisan and nonpolitical. The skittishness about being "political" reflected the fragility of the alliance and the deeper crisis. One person's solidarity gesture is another's person's political statement. One rally organizer, Bruce Block, a Reform rabbi, reported to *The Jewish Week* that he was confronted while fundraising for armored ambulances and buses. "This borders on the political," he was told. Shocked, Block responded: "Saving a life 'borders on the political?'"

Survey data confirmed the shift. The Jewish Agency's 2004 National Survey of American Jews found broad-based community support for Israel, overall, but close analysis detects an increasing distance, and growing doubts. Only twenty-six percent of American Jews consider themselves "very" emotionally attached to Israel, with thirty-eight percent "somewhat" attached. Viewing this in context, sixty-nine percent of all Americans in a February 2005 Gallup Poll reported feeling "favorably" toward Israel. The 2004 poll found one third – thirty-seven percent – of American Jews "often disturbed by Israel's policies and actions," while two-thirds – sixty-three percent – had never even visited Israel. In a 2001 survey the United Jewish Communities commissioned, nearly half of American Jews polled believed that "the Palestinians had their land taken away from them unfairly when Israel was created" and more than a third – thirty-seven percent – believed that "Israel is overreacting by shooting live bullets at Palestinian demonstrators who are throwing stones."

A new generation has arisen that knows not the Zionist verities of the past. This is the generation of parents sending Jewish kids to day school now or giving them no Jewish education at all. This generation, is post-*Exodus*, post-Six Day War, post-Yom Kippur War, post-Entebbe. This is the generation of the Invasion of Lebanon and the first "Intifada," more likely to see Israel as a powerful (if sympathetic) aggressor than a powerless victim. While some of that is good – or at least reality based – this is a generation much more likely to abandon Israel than were previous generations.

The growing doubts about Israeli policy and the Israeli state are accompanied by widespread ignorance. It is fashionable to lament that many Jewish students know their Eminem from their REM – rock trivia – but do not know their 1948 from their 242 (the year Israel was established versus the U.N. Resolution passed after the Six Day War). More disturbing are their parents. In the 2001 United Jewish Communities survey, five percent of American Jews admitted to being unfamiliar with Israel, and six percent said that they "don't know" how they feel about the Jewish state. Even more disturbing than the twelve percent or so who admitted to being ignorant on many questions, thirty percent of American Jews did not even know that Israel had given control of any land to the Palestinians, and fully eighty-five percent came nowhere close to estimating just what percentage of land Israel had already effectively relinquished before the troubles began (over two thirds of the territories).

Moreover, English has replaced Hebrew as the lingua franca of the Jewish people – and even of the Zionist movement. Most times when Israelis and Diaspora Jews meet, even in Israel with mostly Israelis present, people speak English not Hebrew, without even thinking about it. Most Israelis are fluent in English, and begin learning English at school before they begin learning Arabic. In the Jewish Agency's 2004 survey, only two percent of American Jews reported fluency in Hebrew, thirty-five percent said they did not speak Hebrew at all, forty-three percent said they knew a few words and forty-nine percent were not even interested in learning any Hebrew. Jewish day schools and afternoon schools which once were so committed to the conversationally-oriented "ulpan" method that they were called "Hebrew" schools, have evolved away from emphasizing Hebrew. So, now, much of even the small minority that bothers getting any Jewish education learns minimal Hebrew.

This shift reflects the arrogant unilingual approach of most Americans combined with a major reorientation among Jews away from a central Zionist tenet. The Bible scholar Shalom Paul calls Hebrew "the DNA of the Jewish people." The stories, values, teachings and rhythms of Jewish life are encoded in the Jewish people's mother tongue. Knowledge of Hebrew is indeed the key to unlocking much of the Jewish past, present and future. Being fluent in Hebrew helped my wife compensate for the rudimentary Jewish education she received when young. Hebrew fluency allowed her to communicate with her Israeli friends and relatives, to become familiar with modern Israeli society and to understand traditional prayer, once she became interested. Without a working knowledge of Hebrew, Israel becomes a foreign country, and most synagogues become alien terrain too. Even worse than the problem itself is the fact that most North American Jews do not even recognize their linguistic ignorance as a problem, so insulated and self-satisfied are we.

My grandfather, living in the South Bronx for decades, loved his Hebrew-speaking club and his weekly Hebrew newspaper. My father, raising us in Queens, New York, insisted on speaking to his children in Hebrew. Will their grandchildren and great-grandchildren master the language of the Jewish people as well as they did, and if they do, will they have anyone outside of Israel with whom they can chat?

SOME BRIGHT SPOTS

There have been some bright spots on this otherwise bleak horizon. Attendance soared at New York's annual Salute to Israel Parade, with some estimating a jump from twenty thousand in 2000 to one hundred thousand a year later. Birthright israel continued sending thousands of eighteen to twenty-six year olds to Israel. They came as pilgrims, not missionaries, to learn and not to demonstrate. At the same time, Rabbi Nathan Laufer of the Wexner Heritage Foundation challenged many community leaders visiting Israel on missions, when he called on the United Jewish Communities "to encourage one thousand of its top leaders to purchase a piece of real property in Israel over the next twelve months." Such "demonstrative collective action" would "hearten the people of Israel" and lay a new, more vital foundation for the North American friendship with Israel.

The bloody events of March 2002, culminating in the slaughter of 30 Israelis enjoying their Passover seders in Netanya, finally galvanized the Jewish community. In one remarkable week in April, over a quarter of a million Jews in the United States and Canada celebrated Israel's birthday with huge solidarity rallies. At the same time, the United Jewish Communities launched a massive fundraising campaign and the Jewish community responded. One event in Montreal raised ten million dollars. Such scenes evoked comparisons with the generous outpouring of funds at the start of the Yom Kippur War in 1973, when Jews went home from the synagogues to break their fasts, then returned with their checkbooks just hours later.

Still, critics wondered what had taken the community so long. North American Jewry mobilized only after Palestinians had murdered 450 Israelis in an eighteen-month campaign of terror. Why was the Palestinians' decision back in September 2000 to turn from negotiations to terror not enough? Why wasn't Hezbollah's illegal kidnapping of three young soldiers on the border with Lebanon enough? Why wasn't the lynching of two reservists in the fall of 2000 or the bludgeoning to death of two thirteen-year-olds that spring enough? Why weren't the Dolphinarium disco killings or the Sbarro Pizzeria murders enough? Why wasn't Durban enough? Or the September 11 slaughter or the Daniel Pearl homicide or the daily sniping at commuters enough to wake up the Jewish community? Why did it take over 12,000 terrorist incidents in eighteen months, with mass murders of young and old in cafes and buses, inside bat-mitzvah parties and outside synagogues culminating in 131 Israeli deaths in March 2002 for most Jews to mobilize?

In truth, some communities were sufficiently shocked by the overall apathy to begin reconceptualizing the approach to Israel. In Montreal, for example, one hundred and five community organizations united in an unprecedented solidarity initiative, raising a dollar for each Jew in the community – $100,000 in total – to support medical trauma facilities in Jerusalem. At the same time Montreal's Bronfman Jewish Education

Centre held a day-long seminar for more than forty teachers in the Jewish day school system. Central to the initiative, as articulated in a statement of principles, was the commitment "to teach our students about the multidimensional nature of the Jewish people's relationship with the land of Israel, and the State of Israel. Israel should not be thought of simply as the central headache of the Jewish people, but as the historical, ideological, intellectual, and emotional epicenter of our people. We must teach *ahavat yisrael* (love of Israel), not simply the Arab-Israeli conflict."

In fairness, these are difficult times. The viciousness of the anti-Israel rhetoric, the brutality of the terrorist attacks, the ease with which Arab leaders' anti-Zionism descended into anti-Semitism, has unnerved most Jews. Jews throughout the world must rise to the challenge. We must march, fight, donate, protest. But at the same time, we must resist the temptation to wallow in cheap emotion or to be deluded by a false sense of unity. We need to lay the groundwork for a renewed relationship between Israel and the Diaspora, or risk making the growing number of Zionist agnostics downright atheists.

PATRIOTISM: NOT THE FEAR OF SOMETHING, BUT THE LOVE OF SOMETHING ELSE

Here then, is the broader challenge the community must tackle even while duking it out with the Palestinians and their cheerleaders in this bizarre, post-modern media war: can we build a relationship with Israel that is an ongoing and mutual friendship, rather than a periodic stewardship? Can we be true *Ohavei Tzion*, Lovers of Zion, and not simply *Ohadei Yisrael,* supporters of Israel? During the McCarthy era in the United States, the patron saint of American liberalism and two-time Democratic candidate, Adlai Stevenson, said that "Patriotism is not the fear of something, but the love of something else." We have, alas, much reason to fear these days – a strong, vibrant relationship with Israel in the future depends on finding something to love.

CHAPTER 2

ZIONISM: NOT JUST JEWISH NATIONALISM BUT ESSENTIAL TO JUDAISM

When I was seventeen and living in Israel for a year, I nicknamed my peppery, blonde Hebrew teacher Jordana Ben Canaan. She was, after all, a dynamic "sabra" straight out of Leon Uris's blockbuster book and the Paul Newman movie "Exodus" – Jordana was Paul's high-spirited sister. Toward the end of the year, when I answered a question in a clever but ambiguous way, "Jordana" snorted: "That's typical, coming from Mr. *lo basar v' lo chalav*," (Mr. Not-Meat-and-Not-Milk – an allusion to the strict separation Jewish dietary laws maintain between the two types of food and the neutral, "pareve" state in between them). With this put-down, this aggressively secular Israeli used a fundamentally religious concept to highlight the difference between the bold, physically vital Jew flourishing in her old-new homeland and the neutered, neither-fish-nor-fowl, compulsively moderate, intellectually constipated Jew languishing abroad.

To committed Zionists like "Jordana," those Jews who do not live in Israel are not merely scattered in the "Diaspora," they are physically or psychically imprisoned in *Galut*, exile. As an American historian swept by the vagaries of the job market to Canada, I wallow in ambivalence, fearing that I am earning "Jordana's" nickname. Many Jews who, like me, take Zionism seriously but live in *"Galut"* are similarly abashed. Our passion for Israel and Jewish nationalism is muted by Zionist guilt for choosing "exile" over "redemption." As a result, we, the people most likely to revitalize Zionism, to develop a new Zionism that addresses the challenges of modern Diaspora life, are silenced. The field is thus left to Gevalt Zionists, political supporters of Israel who easily call themselves "Zionist" because they do not understand the dynamic dimensions of the ideology, and to Israelis, most of whom do not understand Diaspora life. This book is a call for a *"Galut"*-based Zionism to revitalize Diaspora Judaism, a Zionism emerging from abroad that recognizes the charms and perils of contemporary "exile."

ZIONISM AND THE JEWISH PROBLEM

Zionism began as an effort to solve "the Jewish problem." The Jewish problem in late nineteenth and early twentieth-century Europe was clear: Despite living in Europe for centuries, the Jews remained a people apart, a stateless people, tolerated at best, oppressed at worst. By 1948 the two parts of the problem, European anti-Semitism and Jewish statelessness, had been solved. Adolf Hitler's mass murder campaign had shrunk the scale of the Jewish problem in Europe. And the founding of the State of Israel in 1948 meant that, finally, after two thousand bitter years, there was at least one place on earth which welcomed persecuted Jews.

Of course, after World War II, Israel was not the only place on earth where Jews found safety. Yes, thousands of survivors, "the last remnant," as they were called, streamed "home" to Israel. But thousands of others found new homes in the United States, in Canada, in Australia, in Argentina. Two blessings, the miracle of Israel's rebirth and the miracle of Western democracy, combined with the horrors of war to shift the Jewish center of gravity. In 1940, as in 1840, as in 840 B.C.E., Jewish life centered around the Mediterranean; every major Jewish center, Israel, Babylonia, Egypt, Spain, Ashkenaz (roughly medieval France and Germany), Poland, Russia, Morocco, radiated from the Mediterranean Sea. Ten years later, in 1950, Jewish life centered around the Atlantic Ocean, with two new poles in Jewish life: Israel and North America.

The North American Jewish experience was as precedent-shattering as the Israeli experience. In the United States of America especially, millions of Jews found a homeland as well as a home. On the whole, American Jews were and are an extraordinarily proud, prosperous, happy, free, and settled people. By the 1950s, the Jewish problem of Europe seemed as distant to the Jews of North America as it did to the Jews of Israel. If anything, the Jews of Israel still retained the European Jews' sense of precariousness, while American Jews did not. Life for a Jew in the Middle East, like life for a Jew in Tevye's fictional Anatevka, was as shaky as life was for a fiddler on the roof. On the other hand, in America, Jews fiddled, or more typically, especially for that generation, played piano, in comfortable if somewhat over-decorated, *"ungepatchked"* parlors.

This, then, is the central challenge to North American Zionism. Most American Jews love America, most Canadian Jews love Canada, and have no desire to leave. They believe, as did the Russian idealists in 1883 who founded the *"Am Olam"* pro-American emigration movement, that in America the Jewish people can find "emancipation from slavery and… a new truth, freedom and peace." As a result, an anti-Semitism-fueled Zionism is bound to fail, as is an *aliyah*-based Zionism, a Zionism requiring moving to Israel.

Yet, at the same time, American Jews have discovered a sense of spiritual if not physical precariousness. More and more Jews worry about the future of Judaism in North America. Jewish lives are not endangered, Jewish life is. And many of the proudest, richest, happiest, freest and most settled American Jews still identify with their *"Am Olam"* or Eternal People. It is that sense of peoplehood that is the essence of Zionism. And it is that sense of peoplehood that can save Diaspora Judaism.

A CONTENTIOUS BUT FLATTENED-OUT NORTH AMERICAN JUDAISM

North American Judaism needs to be fixed on two levels, ideologically and experientially. Ideologically, North American Judaism is edging ever-closer to the Protestant sectarian model as tensions between the branches of modern Judaism intensify. Too many of us are "Orthodox" or "Conservative" or "Reform" or "Reconstructionist." We use those terms as nouns, states of being, forgetting that they are supposed to be adjectives modifying the word "Jew." The result is a contentious but flattened-out Judaism, a one-dimensional religion rooted more in nineteenth-century Enlightenment ideology, defined largely by a modern North American agenda, and less faithful to our four-thousand-year-old tradition.

Think of the typical American Jewish experience. Most American Jews FEEL Jewish but DO little about it. They will, of course, cry at "Schindler's List" and bristle if anyone makes cracks about Jews, Israel or the Holocaust. But the average American Jew spends more time in a typical week working, eating, sleeping, commuting, shopping, watching television, talking on the phone, surfing the net, cleaning the house, walking the dog, than doing anything Jewish. Judaism is an occasional visitor to the modern Jew's life, not a daily or even weekly presence. Kids endure seven years of desultory afternoon Hebrew schooling to have a splashy Bar Mitzvah. Adults show up at High Holiday services just in case the mumbo-jumbo of the Book of Life is true, and sit *shiva* and occasionally say *Yizkor*, the memorial prayer, to pay homage to the dead. Is it any wonder that thousands of young Jews find the whole package farcical?

Much of the problem stems from our surroundings. Much of what we experience as "Judaism" is in fact "North American Judaism," which is distinct from the Lithuanian or Polish or German or Moroccan or Iranian Judaism of our great-grandparents, let alone from the Israeli Judaism of our transatlantic cousins. Ironically, it is often the most American aspects of the Judaism we experience that are least appealing. Last year, before *Rosh Hashanah*, I asked some Jewish students what they loved and what they hated about what they saw at the High Holidays. The things they most hated – the fashion show, the gossiping, the superficial engagement of people who rarely attended synagogue – were the most American aspects of the experience. What they loved – the family time, the timeless tableau of the cantor and rabbi up on the *bimah*, the communal prayer – were the most traditional, the most authentically Jewish, aspects.

Modern America, especially modern cosmopolitan America where most American and Canadian Jews live, is not hospitable to any kind of religion. Jews are concentrated in the areas where North Americans are most likely to dismiss religious leaders as fundamentalists and fanatics, to be far more career-oriented than God-centered, and to find more intense emotional release in sex, sports, video games, television watching, movie-going, friendships, or family vacations, than they do in any religion. Those Americans who own pets are far more likely to feel more intensely about their dog or their cat than they do about their priest, minister or rabbi.

And yet, in the last two decades in particular, Americans have come to feel more passionate about their respective subcultures. Ethnicity is in. Multiculturalism is hot. The only issues that seemed to spur any excitement in the 2000 presidential campaign had to do with identity politics: women and abortion, gays and marriage, African-Americans and the affirmative action debate. North of the border, Canadians are more instinctively multicultural, and the threat of Quebec separatism, the passions of the language debate, still shape Canadian politics.

These issues are the public manifestations of the rainbow of subcultures currently thriving in America and Canada. On campuses, the first generation of special programs, such as Women's Studies, begat a second generation of requests for other specialized identity programs, such as Queer Studies. Among people of color, the shift away from being called "Black" represents a broader shift away from integration and toward an embrace of "African-American" culture, whether expressed by celebrating the winter holiday, Kwanza, or finding a boutique in Macy's department store specifically dedicated to African-American clothing, trinkets, books, and icons.

Ironically, as women, blacks, gays, Latinos, have embraced particularistic identities more intensely, Jews have become more generically American. Now, it is true that there is much that is shrill and unappealing in the current mania for diversity. It often appears that superficial symbols are more important than real values, that public postures predominate and tear at the American national fabric even as everyone at home buys the same Nikes and eats the same junk food. The nineteenth-century Enlightenment formula that many Jews embraced: "Be a Jew in your home and a man in the street" has been inverted, often with politically disastrous results, as we all become uniformly enslaved to consumerism at home, but take to the streets with angry, divisive, chip-on-the-shoulder particularistic agendas.

PLACING PEOPLEHOOD AT THE CENTER

A new Zionism can be the modern North American Jew's entry into the identity sweepstakes, hopefully in a constructive way. Zionism, the movement of Jewish national liberation, places peoplehood at the center of the Jewish experience. What we call "religion" is obviously an essential part of the Jewish experience, but it is not the starting point. Peoplehood is. To the Zionist, belonging comes before belief, or at least comes with it simultaneously. The national character of Judaism rather than its religious character provides the essential framework. Thus Orthodox JEWS, or Reform JEWS, are expressing some aspects of their religious practice in different ways but there is much that unites them – from a common past and a common fate, to a host of traditions, ideas, and symbols which transcend these temporary, sectarian interpretations or divisions. Jewish history is not "Orthodox" or "Reform." The story of Passover or Israel or our ethical code cannot be "Conservative" or "Reconstructionist."

Zionism does not negate anything we normally associate with Judaism today, from synagogues to seders. Zionism does, however, view Judaism from a different perspective and thus offers different emphases. To the alienated Jew who doubts God's existence or cannot find an acceptable synagogue, Zionism says: "You're still Jewish, find another way in, find another way to express your belonging." To the religious fanatic who deems this kind of Jew or that kind of Jew "unJewish," Zionism says: "We are one."

Zionism can work in North America because it harnesses the deep feelings of belonging which all but the most alienated Jews have. Thanks to multiculturalism, and multiple generations of successful life in North America, young Jews often feel very comfortable acknowledging that they are Jewish. Although previous generations of Jews often had richer Jewish identities, more Jews tried to "pass" as non-Jews, as "normal" people. For a long time, at Harvard, at McGill, I liked the fact that my name "Gil Troy" did not tip off teachers or students. I did not hide being Jewish, but I was raised not to flaunt it either. By contrast, when Monica Lewinsky was flirting with the President of the United States, the fact that she was Jewish was in play, part of her charm, despite the superficial quality of her Judaism. Among her gifts to Bill Clinton was a book of Jewish jokes, *"Oy Vey: The Things They Say."*

Modern Jews also remain deeply tribal. If you doubt it, ask Jews who have introduced a non-Jewish spouse to their seemingly progressive parents. Or ask a non-Jew who asked one of those "Why do you people…" kinds of questions to a Jewish friend. Zionism can give the tribalism transcendence. By using the broad and deep American Jewish sense of belonging as a way into the many splendors of Jewish life, Zionism can help mature what too often is a defensive instinct into a positive identity.

Today, the Holocaust lies at the center of the modern Jewish tribal identity. When all other rationales for remaining Jewish fail, too many parents, too many leaders, invoke Auschwitz. In the last two decades, the Jewish establishment has invested tremendous resources to make the Holocaust the central modern Jewish experience. It is memorialized in monuments and museums from coast to coast, from Miami to Montreal, from New York to Los Angeles. Holocaust books sell. Holocaust movies reap Academy Awards. Holocaust courses are the only Jewish studies classes on campus that draw students by the hundreds, not by the fives and the tens.

It is, of course, important to remember the six million. It is also essential to honor and respect the survivors who endured this unspeakable experience.   But making the Holocaust the central preoccupation of modern Judaism distorts Judaism from a life-affirming creed into a death-obsessed one. It fosters a tribalism that is closed and defensive, consecrated by guilt and obligation. It encourages a politics of "do it to them before they do it to you."

Imagine what would happen if the Jewish community invested the same emotional, intellectual, and financial resources it does in commemorating the Holocaust into celebrating the State of Israel. Intellectually, one can certainly make the case that the reestablishment of the Jewish state after two thousand years is as compelling. Emotionally and ideologically, we could foster pride instead of guilt, optimism instead of pessimism, joy instead of mourning, exuberance instead of despair, love instead of rage.

Of course, it is possible to construct an Israel-based identity fueled by guilt that we are not there, pessimism regarding prospects of peace, mourning for the military martyrs, despair over the myriad problems Israel faces, and hatred for the Arabs. And some do. But a renewed Zionism has to accentuate the positive – and it is not that big a stretch. The pride comes from the success of the Zionist ethos of self-help. The optimism comes from the many miracles that have already occurred, ranging from simple survival to those peace treaties that have held with longstanding enemies such as Egypt and Jordan. The joy, exuberance, and love come from tapping into a Zionist and Israeli culture that is affirmative and inspiring, that instinctively takes ancient ideals and gives them a modern beat. It is more than cosmetic, and it is not delusional. A liturgy which tapped into the Zionist spirit, which used the Israeli beat rather than Eastern European dirges, would revolutionize Judaism.

ZIONISM IS JUDAISM WITH A TWIST

In addition to viewing Judaism differently, a new Zionism would emphasize different Jewish experiences. To foster a sense of peoplehood more than religious expression, camp is more important than Hebrew school; an Israel experience is more important than a Bar Mitzvah; community involvement is more important than synagogue attendance. Any kind of Jewish camp, be it Orthodox or left-wing Zionist, offers an opportunity for 24/7 Jewish living, where all aspects of Judaism can be integrated into one's daily life, and where being Jewish is normal. Making a group trip to Israel in one's early twenties followed by a year of working, volunteering or studying there, as universal a Jewish rite of passage as the Bar or Bat Mitzvah would introduce young Jews to their homeland at a crucial time of life and show how some of the Jewish life lessons learned in the summer can extend beyond the artificial camp environment. And community involvement teaches the essential Zionist lesson of self-determination, of taking personal responsibility for the Jewish people's future.

This formulation sets up false choices when in fact this approach to Zionism can let Jews have their kosher cake and eat it too. More involvement with camps can only enhance the Hebrew school experience – and perhaps prod these all too often failing factories which produce alienated Jews into more dynamic educational approaches. Bar and Bat Mitzvah's should continue – but perhaps the Zionist lessons of community and discipline might encourage less elaborate "bars" and more meaningful "mitzvahs." And community involvement in synagogue is essential if we are to free ourselves from the Christian model of rabbis as the only full-time Jews in the community, as if they were Jewish priests, and instead all become more involved Jews.

Some might claim this is pick-and-choose Zionism, an idiosyncratic culling of my favorite characteristics. Some might also wonder why we should bother injecting Zionism into this discussion at all, when the term makes so many Jews uncomfortable today. After all, anything that is Zionist is Jewish, so why not call it a new-style, pick-and-choose Judaism?

"Zionism" is the appropriate term because it is the historically accurate one. Zionism set out in the late nineteenth and early twentieth centuries to solve the Jewish problem. Zionism did not reject modernity but sought to create a new and workable synthesis between Judaism and worldliness. The result was an ideologically rich debate filled with many perspectives that can address some of our woes today. More than that, the specifics of Zionist ideology, the emphasis on peoplehood, community, activism, history, homeland, and self-determination all suggest that even in North America in the twenty-first century, Zionism can be a path to personal, communal, and even universal fulfillment.

CHAPTER 3

ZIONIST LABORATORIES FOR JEWISH LIVING: CAMPS AND ISRAEL EXPERIENCES

ZIONIST LABORATORIES FOR JEWISH LIVING: WHY CAMPS WORK

I was chasing my two children around Montreal's Dorval airport, killing time as we waited to fly to New York. At customs I thought I recognized a woman from the Zionist camp I attended for many years, Camp Tel Yehudah. But this was Canada, after all, and I never run into people from my past here. Ten minutes later, I followed her into the candy shop and made eye contact. Indeed, it was a former fellow staffer, Michelle, who was flying through Montreal. After we exchanged pleasantries, Michelle burst out: "I miss camp so. I have never found another community prayer as spiritually fulfilling!"

It was a doubly odd statement. Normal campers and counselors remember friendships, songs, campfires, wacky moments, nighttime raids, a first kiss. Few focus on spirituality. Also, this was a Zionist camp we attended, not a "religious" camp. We were supposed to remember the *chevra* (the community), the *ruach* (the spirit), the *medurot* (the campfires), as well as our own wacky moments, nighttime raids, and first kisses. But spirituality? That was for Ramah, the Conservative camp, Massad, the Orthodox camp, even Kutz, the Reform camp, not ours.

But Michelle was right. I, too, have yet to find a community or a prayer so spiritually fulfilling, especially on Friday night. As in Israel, the whole rhythm of the week was attuned to *Shabbat*, the Sabbath. Friday lunch was hot dogs outside, so representatives from each bunk could help mop the floor of the *chadar ochel*, the dining hall. Most *chugim*, or groups, met late Friday afternoon to reflect on what had occurred during the week. There was then a mad dash for the showers during *Shabbat* prep, the slowpokes having to endure cold water once the hot water ran out. While not everyone dressed in white, everyone dressed up, or at least cleaned up. Then each group would rendezvous at its regular meeting point, and, hand-in-hand walk down together to the *t'fillot*, or prayers site, singing a *Shabbat nigun*, or tune.

In truth, not everyone had God on their mind during *Shabbat* prep or the walk down to *t'fillot*. On one level, the entire camp was preparing for a huge, elaborate mating ritual. On Friday night and throughout all of *Shabbat*, the rules relaxed, there was more free time. This camp was a teen camp, and Friday night was the night for romancing or at least for trying. Two of my best friends, who now have four children, began their romance on the first Friday night at camp one year.

Each week a different group would be responsible for preparing a song and dance for *kabbalat Shabbat*, to receive the Sabbath. The songs were usually modern Israeli songs celebrating peace, rest, or the *Shabbat*, and the dances were Zionist folk dances. Everyone knew that the *kabbalat Shabbat* had to start on time, just enough before sundown so the guitars, microphones, and tape decks could be turned off before sundown and the start of *Shabbat*.

Two or three representatives of the group of the week lit candles, said the prayers, and then the prayers began. A sense of tranquility, of warmth, would settle over the crowd.   On warm nights we would be outside, facing each other in a semi-circle of wooden benches. The prayers would start with a *nigun*, a magical wordless *Hasidic* tune that all could sing, and climax very quickly with *"Lecha Dodi,"* the welcoming of the Sabbath written by the 16th century Safed mystics. With each verse, with each repetition of the chorus, the singing grew louder. Two-thirds of the way through, reenacting a classic tableau of Jewish history, we would shift into a more mournful tune for one verse, to mark the destruction of the Temple. Then the tempo would pick up and become more joyous, culminating with the *"Boee Kalah,"* the "welcome bride" verse, when all two hundred campers and counselors and drivers and kitchen workers would stand as one, turn around to the imaginary entrance in this open-air synagogue, and bow, to welcome the Sabbath Queen.

THE MAGIC OF BEING NORMAL

Of course this was a Jewish moment, a religious moment. But it was also a profoundly Zionist moment, one in which the Zionist elements of the camp enhanced the Jewish ritual. The egalitarian nature of the community, the counter-cultural values, the widespread participation, the intimacy fostered, the common language and common bonds forged, the consecration of Jewish time and Jewish space, the mixing of Israeli and Jewish culture, all added to the magic, all generated excitement.

More than excitement, life at camp generated a sense of great fulfillment. Many of us thrived in an atmosphere where to be Jewish was to be "normal" – which of course was one of Zionism's initial aims. The sense of being normal, of not having to shift gears between being Jewish and being a "regular" person, was one of the glues that bonded us together, and made camp the source of so many life-long friendships. Moreover, through that experience I learned that Zionism is more than pro-Israelism, that it can be an ideology fostering humanism, communalism, a commitment to social criticism, and an idealism that questions modern materialism and conventionalism.

The power of the camp experience resonated throughout the year because this was a movement camp. In fact, the camp was simply the summer home of the Young Judaea Zionist Youth movement. And both the camp and the movement were so appealing because that ideology was bold, ambitious, all-encompassing. The movement advanced a critique of modern society, not just of the Jewish world. And the movement experience was fueled by ideas and emotions. We in the movement believed in the power of ideas to shape the world and relished our feeling of belonging in a warm, values-oriented community of friends that offered a contrast to the "real world's" stiffness and formality.

Recently, I had an email exchange with a fellow camp alumnus who worried that our shared desire to experience another *Shabbat* like our camp *Shabbatot* and other such moments was "immature." He wondered whether we were as stuck in time as some retro Princeton alumnus who still marches around in black and orange or some Harvard alumnus wrapped in crimson who sings Harvard fight songs every chance he gets. I disagreed. Seeking to recreate great experiences like the camp *Shabbat* struck me as more akin to the university graduate who continues reading great books, as my friend does, or who, like me, is so taken by the life of the mind he becomes a scholar.

I acknowledge that not everything can be recreated. The intense experiences each group shared during the week, the friendships forged, the Zionist movement thing, formed an essential backdrop to the camp *Shabbat*. It is not realistic to expect one's co-workers to end the week together by joining in exuberantly in a Friday night service – though wouldn't that be great? Still, I prefer to look at these summer camps as Zionist laboratories for Jewish living, and I strive to find ways to make some of those wonderful experiments work under real world conditions. It rarely works – but it is worth the effort.

In 2000, Hadassah, which sponsored Camp Tel Yehudah, commissioned a team of sociologists to assess the Jewish identity of those who shared such experiences in our youth. By any criterion of Jewish success – marrying a fellow Jew, lighting *Shabbat* candles weekly, working in the community – TY alumni, like the alumni of other Jewish camps, are dramatically more successful as Jews. And the deeper one's involvement in camp as a youth, the richer the Jewish life was ten, twenty, thirty years down the line. When I spoke at the Hadassah conference where they announced these results, I said: "Boy, you could have saved a ton of money. Had you paid me a tenth of what you paid these pollsters, my friends and I could have told you the same thing."

ZIONIST LABORATORIES FOR JEWISH LIVING: WHY THE ISRAEL EXPERIENCE WORKS

Every now and then, if you are really lucky, experience confirms your fundamental prejudices. Accompanying the first delegation of two hundred young Montrealers to Israel as part of the birthright program was one such experience for me. In its first year, this bold two-hundred-million-dollar initiative to send young Jews on all-expenses-paid organized Israel tours blossomed.

Almost all of the six thousand eighteen to twenty-six year olds who went claimed to have been "blown away," "overwhelmed," "amazed" — the superlatives flowed. "I've never felt so proud of my Judaism," said one. "I realized a part of me was missing," said another. "I didn't feel very complete…. I felt I was Jewish in name only. Now that I've experienced Israel, I feel I'm Jewish at heart." "Everything moved me," said Lee Poulin, a religion major and record store employee. Poulin, twenty-one, could be a poster child for the type of Jew birthright is angling for, with his tattoos, streaked blond hair, and multiple body piercings.

In truth, when I first heard about the program I was skeptical. The money was not the issue. Critics always assume that the program detracts from Jewish day schools or from feeding the poor; none ever calculate how much money Jews fritter away each year on synagogue decor, building funds, or catering. My concern, as I wrote in a *Moment* article in April, 1999, was that Zionism might not speak to modern American Jews, especially the kind of Zionism preached in Hebrew schools and on typical Israel trips. I wrote that without "a new understanding of Zionism and a more relevant vocabulary" about Israel and Jewish identity, birthright would be yet another expensive magic bullet that missed its mark. Charles Bronfman, Michael Steinhardt and company "are offering young Jews the equivalent of free hardware," I wrote. "Jewish educators in Israel and the Diaspora must now develop the right software to make the Israel experience compatible with the realities of Jewish life, to allow Jews to process their Israel experience in a vital and meaningful way."

In classic Jewish community style, the organizers co-opted me. They invited me to chair the Montreal launch, implicitly saying, "Okay, big shot, put your money where your mouth is and help make the program succeed." I agreed to help because I wanted us skeptics to be proven wrong. I wanted this maniacal, unconventional gambit to work. I wanted Zionism to be a solution to our North American Jewish problems. I wanted modern Israel to speak to today's Jewish youth. I wanted to see if it was possible to escape our community's instinctive defensiveness: rather than fighting assimilation, I wanted to see young Jews embracing Judaism; rather than linking Israel with the Arab conflict, I wanted to see young Jews linking Israel with the joys of Judaism.

We spend too much time worrying about Israel – and far too little time enjoying it and learning from it. We in the Diaspora have ossified our approaches to Judaism which too often emphasize the individual rather than the community, the synagogue over society, special holidays not daily commitments, beliefs and feelings more than practices and actions, a private Judaism rather than a public Judaism.

Somewhere between the external wars and the internal tensions, Diaspora Zionism lost its way. It became "Federationed," concerned with supporting Israeli positions, raising money, and enforcing community unity, rather than building a new kind of Jew and a new kind of Judaism. Diaspora Jews were so busy defending the Jewish state, we forgot how to dream, how to criticize what is and envision what could be.

BACK TO FIRST PRINCIPLES WITH BIRTHRIGHT

Simply by turning to Israel to solve our modern identity problem, birthright returned Zionism to first principles, addressing the problem of modern Jewish identity by criticizing the Jewish and the secular status quo. Let's face it. On a certain level, North American Judaism is failing. Thousands of young Jews are voting with their feet, and rejecting Judaism. Birthright is a white flag, an admission of community failure. But it is also a battle standard, a call to arms. By offering alternatives, by exposing participants to a different style of Judaism, I believed birthright could trigger a much needed critique, and a burst of creative Jewish energy.

Still, had I not seen it and felt it myself, I would not believe it: the reactions were simply too uniform and too fervent to be believed. Had I scripted a birthright propaganda movie, I would not have dared to write the heartfelt, pro-Jewish, and deeply Zionist sentiments the participants articulated. Even a skeptical professor like myself who missed his family could not stand by as the participants danced wildly at the Wall on *Leil Shabbat,* barely eight hours after they had arrived, or partied exuberantly until 3 a.m. in the basement of a hotel in Arad. True, not everyone was swept up. There were some who went to the Wall, who climbed Masada, and afterwards felt bad because they "felt nothing." There were occasional gripes. But the tone from start to finish was exhilarating, from the first activity (riding Jeeps in the Judean desert), to the finale when, after I spoke briefly in an ancient alleyway in Jerusalem's Cardo, a

hundred of us moshed together in a furious whirl singing *"Am Yisrael Chai"* (the Jewish people live). In truth, my words rarely have that effect on people.

When they first arrived, many birthrighters fell in love with the romantic Israel of yesteryear – Israel as a "Jewish Disneyland," as one student put it: a fun and meaningful Jewish theme park. It was a superficial first impression, and first love easily fades. But it was heartening to see that at the start of the new millennium, Israel, the complicated, frustrating, polarized, schizophrenic, high-tech behemoth that it is, could still dazzle a bunch of North American pagans. In less than 24 hours the participants went from the blinding white snow of the Canadian winter into the dazzling yellow of the desert sun; from the hurly-burly of a modern city to the rich, rocky, Biblical emptiness of the Judean wasteland; from secular time to Jewish time: we rushed to make *Shabbat* at the Western Wall rather than rushing for classes or work. Despite having lived their entire lives in the New World, many talked about feeling at home, feeling connected.

Israel, the image and the reality, remains a compelling alternate universe to any Westerner. Few can resist the exotic beauty of the land, the lure of a young country located in a place where history is counted in millennia, not decades, the bizarre juxtaposition of the sacred and the mundane. Consider: rappeling the same cliffs that Abraham once contemplated; entering trendy clubs via cobblestone courtyards; folk dancing on *Shabbat* to Biblical songs with Zionist melodies in front of the electric lights of the Ben & Jerry's ice cream shop on Tel Aviv's beach.

Being transported to such a universe in mid-semester inspired many to examine their core assumptions, to think critically about their identities and ambitions. To put it simply, place matters. Speaking with a business student about why there is more to life than "making money" has a different impact on a rocky ridge in the Negev than it would during office hours. In the desert, the whole world just seems a lot more open. That, too, is the genius of the program: helping individuals free themselves from their own private ruts, by traveling somewhere so foreign, yet so familiar.

JUDAISM ON ITS HOME TURF

And by seeing Judaism on its home turf, our odd, complicated, religious-ethical-national hybrid begins to make sense. Only by standing in the desert, by seeing what Abraham saw, can we begin to understand the triangular relationship among Jews, God, and land that has sustained our people for millennia. By walking the ancient alleys of Jerusalem, by following David's footsteps, by seeing the site of Solomon's Temple, young Jews, many of whom do not believe in God, can begin to understand how history consecrates our tradition, whether or not a supernatural deity does.

Paradoxically, the overwhelmingly secular participants, who admitted feeling put off by "the religious" back home, felt embraced by "the religious" at the Wall. The Wall's chaotic but skilled three-ring Jewish circus showcased an edgier but deeper Judaism than their orderly, square homegrown variety.

While most participants felt the connection immediately, and responded to the Jewishness of the Jewish state, it took them longer to accept Israel's secular character. Even as they enjoyed clubbing in Jerusalem's Russian Compound late Friday night, some were disappointed to see stores open and cars flowing in Israel on *Shabbat*. Like so many North American Jews, many implicitly, unthinkingly, rejected the Zionist aspiration to be normal. They wanted Israel to be a twenty-four-hour-a-day Jewish museum. However, as we left the cocoon of Jerusalem's Jewish quarter on *Shabbat,* as we traversed the country, the participants began to appreciate the richness of the Israeli secular identity – and realized that Judaism combines both national and religious expressions. There was a kind of "gee whiz, they disco and they're Jewish" quality to the reaction; even a "gee whiz, they push and shove and they're Jewish" quality – traits which lose their charm when exhibited by Israelis on Fifth Avenue or Rodeo Drive.

JUDAISM AS AN OREO COOKIE – NATION AND RELIGION

During the three orientation sessions in Montreal, we had emphasized that Judaism was not just a religion, and that Israel was a real country, not just a Jewish tourist site. Echoing one of my teachers, I compared Judaism to an Oreo cookie: an Oreo requires the cookie part AND the creme; so, too, Judaism combines national AND religious components. Passover is a holiday of religious deliverance and a moment of national liberation; the Torah itself, in the most traditional terms, is God's word and our people's story. Similarly, in Israel, we showed how the religious and secular wires often crossed: "Is Masada a secular site or a religious site?" we asked. We answered "yes." We approached this mountain of martyrdom in our everyday tourist wear. It represents a turning point in Jewish history and an important Zionist symbol. But many "religious" people were there paying homage to this holy site of Jewish self-sacrifice. The same could be said about the Mount Herzl Israeli military cemetery, or our archaeological dig under the moonlight at Bet Guvrin. Was this pre-Hasmonean village a holy site? No. But poking around 2300 year-old ruins – harking back to the days before the Maccabees, seeing a Mikvah, a ritual bath, finding a perfume bottle – these were profound national and religious moments, spiritually fulfilling times regardless of where you stood on the Jewish spectrum.

Of course, it's easy to cross these wires, to integrate the "Jewish" and the "human" under the artificial conditions of a ten-day tour. In the

Diaspora, Jewish moments are too often special moments: departures from regular society, from normal life. Understandably, most of us prefer to live our regular lives like everyone else. We find it exhausting and often disappointing to work so hard seeking Jewish moments. In Israel, there were no gears to shift. Going to clubs, rappeling, and tending to one's skin at the Dead Sea Spa did not entail having to choose between being normal and Jewish. That full-time, round-the-clock normalcy was exhilarating for many.

Moreover, without reading Zionist ideology, without fancy theorizing, many participants felt integrated in Israel. They felt that Israel and their Judaism could unite all their identities rather than fragment them further. After the trip, one participant emailed his fellow bus members: "I feel as if a spiritual void has been filled. This outcome has been, for me, the most confusing growth I have undergone. Prior to the trip I was content being an anglophone, a male, a friend, a Canadian, a student, a traveler, a skier, a son, a restaurant employee, an athlete, a boyfriend, and all the other elements of which my identity was composed. However, as the trip hurled me into Jerusalem during *Shabbat*, I could not help but to feel a sense of unity that I have never felt anywhere else. I have always felt welcome in my community, but never before have I found a place for my center of being." Others responded to Israel's energy, its intensity, its idealism, its bubbling mixture of the old and the new, and found that the country inspired them on a human level, beyond whatever Jewish awakening they experienced.

A JUDAISM OF JOY AND SPIRIT, OF SONG AND DANCE

As they hopped on and off buses, as they bought souvenirs by day and boozed and caroused into the night, many participants experienced the re-Jew-venation the sponsors desired. But the Judaism they experienced in Israel is unlike the Judaism they experience at home. It was a Judaism of joy, of spirit, of song and of dance.

Most of these participants experienced North American Judaism as pallid, as pedestrian, as stiff and as square. They don't want to dress up to pray in a mournful, incomprehensible, and inaccessible Eastern European liturgy. They don't want to walk into a synagogue feeling underdressed, undereducated, and unwelcome. They loved the *nigunim*, the little wordless soulful ditties their tour guides taught them. They relished the informed and informal chaos they watched at the Wall, the warm, family-centered *Shabbat* meals some shared with their guides' families. They wanted to be welcomed, to participate, to feel at home – which, alas, many rarely had before.

And they even felt at home in places where they might not have expected to feel welcome. The first Shabbat, twenty participants joined a *Seudah Shlishit*, a final evening meal, at a "hippie" *shul* located behind Jerusalem's Mahaneh Yehudah Market. The synagogue was in a small cramped space. Its *mechitza* (divider) split the room horizontally – the front for the men, the back for the women. I was sure this was going to trigger a feminist revolt, but I was wrong. The women walked away as jazzed as the men, because they, too, had been able to dance with the Torah – and dance and sing deliriously. Rather than feeling excluded, the women felt included by the dynamic service – in a way they rarely felt in their more egalitarian congregations back home.

These positive Jewish experiences, on Israeli soil, enhanced by the atmospherics of Israel, help explain why it is necessary to send people six thousand miles away to improve their Jewish identity at home. Too often, while acknowledging Israel's centrality to Judaism, Diaspora Jews experience Israel as the biggest Jewish headache – thanks to the endless headlines about the Arab-Israeli conflict, the pleas for money, the guilt for not giving more. Going there, seeing the country in all its ancient and modern contradictions, in all its shabby and glistening glory, puts it all in context. By experiencing the panoply of Jewish identities in our homeland, young Jews can find new role models who break the typical American Jewish molds.

I have faith in Israel as a "product" – as a rich, complex, inspiring, multifaceted phenomenon that speaks to Jews on many levels. I have less faith in North American style Judaism. American Judaism is rarely sexy, exciting, intense, or normal. The community remains too wedded to its institutionalized and fossilized forms of expression and identification. It is not ready to change.

Birthright has given the Jewish community a wake-up call. It has shown that we need to think creatively about our Judaism. We need a Judaism that is not synthetic. Without reforming Judaism into something it isn't, we need to forge a new traditional Judaism for the twenty-first century. We also need a new Zionism that speaks to today's concerns in modern idioms – that addresses questions of who we are and where we are at, instead of focusing on our enemies and whether we shall be saved.

Of course, life is not a free Israel trip with peers, and Judaism is no picnic. Much of birthright cannot be replicated or transported: It functions as a point of entry. And yet, many of the most successful characteristics of birthright suggest necessary ingredients to revitalizing Judaism.

HOW TO FALL IN LOVE WITH ISRAEL... AND JUDAISM

The romantic view of Israel suggests that we need to start rebuilding our myths, to fall in love with Israel anew, even from afar. Birthright reminds us what Israel should be – a beacon of modernity and of tradition, humanity and vitality, the best of Judaism and the best of the West. Birthright suggests that a revitalized relationship with Israel can revitalize Diaspora Judaism. Encounters with Israel can help us reorient our study of the past, from a chronicle of holocausts to a history of heroes, of thinkers, of prophets.

Encounters with Israel can help us redefine what it means to be "a good Jew." Typically, our "good Jew" is either an Orthodox rabbi who appears ethereal or a Conservative rabbi who desperately tries to prove that he or she is "with it." Israel offers a different model: a non-professional but full-time Jew who lives a normal life filled with Jewish details, enhanced by Jewish values and traditions, taking place in a Jewish place that runs on Jewish time, following our calendar, with our people, in our land.

Imagine, if a typical American Jew met someone who speaks Hebrew fluently, who can quote Jewish sources extensively – and often throws ancient idioms into modern speech – who does not work on *Shabbat*, always has Friday night dinner with the family, does not eat bread on Passover and will eat cheesecake on *Shavuot*, the Feast of Weeks that most American Jews have never heard of. Most American Jews would consider that person "religious." In fact, that describes the behavior patterns of the overwhelming majority of secular Israelis.

For four millennia now, Jewish identity has been about covenants, commitments, and compulsion. Most Jews were Jewish not because they wanted to be but because they had to be. In the twenty-first century, Jewish identity is voluntary. Most Jews are free to be whoever they want to be. North American society in particular is a wide open souk hawking a thousand and one different identities. Too often the Jewish community has responded to the threat by trying to find a new set of compulsions, internal if not external. As a result, our community, and especially our community leadership, has become addicted to a theology of guilt and a politics of fear. Birthright recognizes that Judaism will thrive in the twenty-first century only if it is affirmative, if it is relevant, if it works in the here and now and for me, rather than the once-upon-a-time and for someone else – even if that someone else is a *bubbe*, a *zayde*, a mommy or a daddy.

Of course, birthright is so generous that it is sui generis. Few programs can match its sex appeal, and most initiatives will feel like pale imitations in comparison. Still, the Jewish community needs to get beyond the alluring package and build on the fundamentals: the sense of community fostered, the quest for meaning advanced, the centrality of Israel acknowledged, the awareness achieved that a positive Jewish identity is not in opposition to one's humanity, and in fact can answer contemporary and eternal human questions.

The challenge for the rest of the community is to follow the best of the birthright example; to begin to craft a joyous Judaism of meaning and goodness that elevates and roots, that excites and fulfills. A renewed relationship toward Zionism is a key first step in that journey.

BUILDING A NEW JEW

Once upon a time, Zionism was about building a new Jew – a proud, virile, vital Jew who could wield a hoe and a rifle as necessary. Today, Diaspora Zionism needs to build a different kind of new Jew – a proud, literate, and exuberant Jew who can function in the modern and Jewish worlds as necessary.

Recent studies have confirmed that this vision is no dream. To the surprise of many educators and rabbis, camps and Israel experiences have proven more potent than day schools and synagogues in keeping non-Orthodox Jews Jewish. The Jewish community has deployed an army of statisticians in search of the essential catalyst to positive Jewish experience a North American kid gets from camp or from Israel.

To each his own buzzword. Each expert will find his or her own secret ingredient – pride, community, intensity, exuberance, belonging, ownership, peoplehood. I call it Zionism. At the end of the day, the American Jewish camp experience, regardless of the camp ideology, is a product of Zionist collectivism and counter-cultural values; the Israel experience is partially collective, partially nationalistic, and partially religious. These are the forces that must be harnessed – not to fight intermarriage, that is far too defensive a goal – but to forge a positive, joyous, powerful, and useful Jewish identity, one that not just "works" in the twenty-first century, but absolutely soars.

CHAPTER 4

IF I FORGET THEE O JERUSALEM –
THE ETERNAL CAPITAL FOR THE ETERNAL PEOPLE

About fifteen years ago, I had *Shabbat* dinner in Jerusalem with a retired radio reporter. He had spent three decades covering Israel for America's old Mutual Broadcasting Network. I forget his name – but I will never forget his story.

His was a typical Israeli apartment, a bit too small, overflowing with a few too many books. The furniture was simple but not shabby, with a picture of an officer in uniform dominating the living room wall-unit.

He was a typical journalist, well-educated, wide-ranging, brimming with great stories. "What was your greatest moment in journalism," I asked him, whereupon he left the table, cued up an old reel-to-reel tape machine on his wall unit, and said "Listen."

The tape was from the morning of June 7, 1967. My host had set out early that morning, and ended up at an Israeli command post on Rechov Strauss, in the center of Jerusalem, with a commanding view of the ancient walled city. As my friend set the scene, I tried to picture tanks and soldiers, half-tracks and stretchers, amid the tacky souvenir shops and pungent shwarma stands of today's Jerusalem. The tape began, describing the efforts of Mota Gur's paratrooper brigade to reach the Old City.

The reporter's dispassionate, descriptive, professional tone sounded to the ears of this spoiled American like the play-by-play of a well-paced basketball or hockey game. Only this time, the roar of ammunition replaced the roar of the crowds.

Then, from his perch, the reporter sees the paratroopers pierce Lion's Gate and enter the Old City. All of sudden, he bursts out: "After 2,000 years, the Jewish people have liberated Jerusalem! Jerusalem is ours once again!" Hearing this man shift from playing the objective reporter to being a proud Jew gave me goose bumps. His sense of history, the way he felt the past in the present, instinctively echoed the stirring battle orders handed to the troops that morning, which read: "final objective: the Temple Mount, the Western Wall, the Old City. For two thousand years our people have prayed for this moment. Let us go forward *(kadimah)* – to victory."

over six hundred times in the Bible, it was the city of David the heroic, who conquered it, and of Solomon the wise, who built the first of the two Holy Temples there. During the many centuries of exile, Jerusalem symbolized both the glorious past of the Jewish people – and their hopes for the future. Much of Jewish prayer, in fact, entailed reflecting on what once was in Jerusalem as a way of conceptualizing what again might be there.

The fate of the Jewish people seemed tied directly to the fate of Jerusalem. As the great philosopher Martin Buber noted in 1934, "When Jerusalem ceased to be a Jewish city, when the Jew was no longer permitted to be at home in his own country – it is then that he was hurdled into the abyss of the world. Ever since, he has represented to the world the insecure man." Most Zionists understood that only if Jerusalem were redeemed could the Jews be redeemed as well.

Jerusalem was such a vital symbol during the exile that it both inspired and repelled early Zionists. In the early throes of the Zionist revolution against Rabbinic legalism, some zealots discounted the centrality of Jerusalem. Hoping to build a new Europe in their ancient homeland, some young rebels felt compelled to reject the way Jerusalem had been used to anaesthetize the Jews. To them, the Jerusalemite was a hostage to fate, awaiting the Messiah in prayerful silence while relying, in the meantime, on the next best thing – a handout from abroad.

Labor Zionists, in particular, sought a Nietzschean "transvaluation of values," to transcend the passivity, the scholasticism, the arid rationalism of the Diaspora Jew and the pious Jerusalemite. Ultimately, however, Jerusalem was so central to the Zionist's material and spiritual world that the idea had to be updated and reconfigured, but not rejected. Even in 1882 – a decade before Herzl – the pioneers of "Bilu" waxed nostalgic about their "celestial Temple." Establishing a modern, international movement, they chose an ancient city for their head office – Jerusalem. Conflating seemingly "religious" and "secular" symbols, they amended the *"Shema,"* the most basic prayer, to read: "Hear, O Israel, the Lord our God, the Lord is one, and our Land, Zion, is our one hope."

A CITY DIVIDED, A NATION DEPRESSED

Unfortunately, when the state finally emerged, in May, 1948, war tore apart the city of peace. David Ben-Gurion, who had expediently but broken-heartedly accepted the United Nations' 1947 partition plan, read the Declaration of Independence from Tel Aviv. Many "secular" Zionists preferred Tel Aviv, a refreshing city of the future, a Zionist city lacking Jerusalem's historical baggage. But two weeks later, when the Old City fell, the secular and the religious mourned together.

How odd it was. After two thousand years, the Jews had a state. They controlled most of the city of Jerusalem. But without *Har HaBayit*, the most purely religious part of the city, without the site of the Holy Temple and the Jewish quarter, the State of Israel was not whole. The divided city came to symbolize the great costs of maintaining a state – while also becoming a potent national-cultural symbol for secular Zionists.

In 1949, when the United Nations voted to internationalize the city, Prime Minister Ben-Gurion, the secular Zionist prophet governing from Tel Aviv, told his colleagues "pack up. We're all moving to Jerusalem tomorrow." On January 23, 1950, the Israeli Parliament, the *Knesset*, proclaimed Jerusalem would "always" be "the capital of the Jewish nation." Since July 1950, diplomats have presented their credentials to Israel's president in Jerusalem.

During those frustrating nineteen years, as the Jordanians desecrated synagogues and cemeteries, turning sanctuaries into stables and headstones into cobblestones, Jews throughout the world learned just how important Jerusalem was to them. By 1967, the songwriter Naomi Shemer had captured the Jewish yearning for a united capital in her stirring *"Yerushalayim Shel Zahav."* Shemer's Jerusalem is a golden city that delights the senses, stirs the soul, fills the heart and engages the mind. It is an eternal city, a city deeply tied to the Jewish people, where time stands still, where ancient markets still bustle, where twentieth-century moderns become time-travellers wandering from reminders of one milestone in Jewish history to another.

JERUSALEM OF GOLD AFTER 1967

The 1967 victory – secured by modern weaponry but appropriately celebrated with the blowing of the *shofar*, the venerable ram's horn – initiated modern Jerusalem's golden era. The battle-hardened, deeply secular kibbutznik soldiers who wept unashamedly at the newly-liberated Western Wall underscored the nationalistic significance of the Holy Temple's ruins. With that rumpled genius, Mayor

Teddy Kollek, at the helm, the city banked its future on preserving its past. Putting millions of Diaspora dollars to good use, Kollek and his Jerusalem Foundation polished one architectural diamond after another – creating a dazzling tiara of old-new beauty in the reunited capital of Herzl's *"Altneuland."* Developers built upward, transforming the venerable skyline, balancing gleaming skyscrapers against golden towers. At the same time, an army of archaeologists burrowed deep into the city's core, adding new dimensions, literally and figuratively, to the Jews' relationship with their capital as they uncovered material proof of the Jews' time-honored love for the city.

The result is a magical mix of the *Kotel* and the *Knesset,* the old and the new, the secular and the divine, the East and the West. To the east, in the Old City, a museum with remnants from Second Temple times displays the earliest representation of a menorah, the seven-handed candelabra, while to the west, in the New City, a large menorah stands sentry outside Israel's parliament, testifying to the modern state's ancient but vital roots. To the east, the refurbished Cardo, the ancient shopping arcade, once again hums with merchants and shoppers, while to the west a huge mall offers kosher Burger King and exclusive boutiques to Arabs and Jews united, albeit temporarily, in consumerism. To the east, donkeys, cars, and pedestrians crowd the narrow cobblestoned alleys, while to the west, sporty sedans whiz across the superhighway. To the east, muezzins chant, rabbis pray, mystics meditate, artists paint, vagrants beg, merchants haggle, while to the west, rock stars perform, politicians posture, scholars study, computer scientists program, pedestrians jaywalk, and businessmen haggle.

As the Jerusalem of earth and stones thrived, so, too, did its inhabitants. For nearly twenty years – until the outbreak of the Intifada in 1987 – Jerusalem, the city of peace, offered a remarkable example of Arab-Jewish cooperation. Yes, there were tensions lingering and traumas aplenty, but there were also business arrangements formed and warm friendships made. Jews wandered the back alleys of the Old City freely, respectfully, relishing the exotic warmth of the Arab casbah – relishing the Middle Eastern character of their modern state. Many Arabs, despite their frustrations, enjoyed the relative autonomy Mayor Kollek secured for them. Even as many bristled under the occupation, many prospered, and all were freer in Kollek's Jerusalem than were almost all of their brethren in the rest of the Arab world.

"JERUSALEM LETTERS"

Today, the beauty of Jerusalem still entrances but the passions roiling the city evoke terror. In the imagination, Jerusalem's romantic landscape sketched in gold coexists with a memorial scroll etched in blood. A geography of loss has been superimposed on the map of magic. The crowded chaos of Mahaneh Yehudah, the open air market, attracts tourists and terrorists. Warm memories of rich smells and exotic foods collide now with the memories of too many dead and wounded from too many bombs planted there. Similarly, Sbarro's Pizza in the heart of the city represents economic progress as American franchises opened kosher branches in the Jewish capital, and devastating loss.

In the Middle Ages, Christian pilgrims proudly sported "Jerusalem letters," crosses or other symbols tattooed on their bodies to commemorate their visit to the Holy City. Alas, today, too many Jews bear scars attesting to their devotion to this city. Far better for the modern "Jerusalem letters" to be metaphorical, and positive.

The battle for Jerusalem has begun – or continues in a new, bloodier, phase. Unfortunately, many secular Israelis, and many North American Jews, have allowed themselves to overlook the centrality of this city to our people. Now that we have it all, too many of us take it for granted. References to Jerusalem are so ubiquitous in Jewish lore, we become momentarily inured to the potency of the symbol. We may sing "Next Year in Jerusalem" at our *Seders*, we may even participate in a community "March to Jerusalem" every year, but we often fail to take that extra moment to savor our connection to the city. Even more disturbing, as many Palestinians demand that Jerusalem serve as their capital, too many Jews blithely cede Jerusalem to them. Some extreme secular Israelis disdain the fuss made over a "bunch of stones," while too many American Jews just don't know why there is a fuss at all.

To the extent that this abdication reflects a desperate yearning for peace, it is at least well-meaning; to the extent that it reflects the dry, clinical, excessively rationalistic approach too many sophisticated Jews take to contemporary Judaism and Zionism, it is pathetic. A century after the Zionist revolution began against the Rabbis' dry, clinical, excessively rationalistic approach, we have come full circle. It is the modernizers who now risk deforming the Jewish soul.

Hopefully, some diplomatic wizardry will be able to satisfy the Palestinian desire for Jerusalem while protecting the Jewish stake in the city. During the July 2000 Camp David negotiations, Prime Minister

Barak and his aides floated various proposals for sharing this multi-dimensional city, on different planes. Some recognized the centrality of Jerusalem to the Jewish soul, others did not do that sufficiently. And even if part of Jerusalem is ceded for the sake of peace, no one should underestimate how important Jerusalem is to the Jewish people and the Jewish state, something the good people of Jerusalem reminded the world during Yasir Arafat's wave of terror.

In fact, for their endurance, Jerusalemites should be inducted into history's hall of fame honoring heroic mass resistance by average citizens. Like Londoners during the Nazis' World War II Blitz, and Berliners during the Soviets' Cold War Blockade, Jerusalemites from 2000 to 2004 demonstrated the extraordinary courage it takes sometimes to maintain ordinary routines. Israelis, especially the citizens of the country's oft-targeted capital, weathered Palestinian terror with aplomb, teaching the world how to cope with the defining challenge of our times.

Soldiers, security guards and citizens made heroism commonplace. When Palestinian terror peaked in 2002, ads announced "The Lions are Coming." Peugeot of Israel, whose symbol, like Jerusalem's, is a lion, spent $200,000 sponsoring local artists who placed 80 sculptures of lions throughout the city. Many of these creatively conceived creatures still dot the city, a warm reminder of a pleasing distraction during trying times.

The democratic civility, restraint, generosity and ingenuity which kept Jerusalem functioning – and once kept London and Berlin functioning - show that Vitamin D, democracy, remains the secret to Israel's success in resisting a grave threat. As Palestinian nationalism degenerated into nihilism, Israel's liberal democratic values ennobled Jewish nationalism, emboldening Israel's citizens to face unprecedented challenges with dignity, grit and an unyielding commitment to the poetry and prose of everyday life.

COSMIC NATIONALISM

Forgetting the unhappy experiences when Jordan ruled, overlooking the practical difficulties of sharing the same territories, neglecting the Jewish people's unique and enduring relationship to the city, are foolhardy and dangerous. We already learned in the 1950s and 1960s how central Jerusalem is to the Zionist enterprise. Jerusalem is not simply a piece of real estate that can be subdivided easily; it is the touchstone of Zionism and the State of Israel. "There is a cosmic element in nationality which is its basic ingredient," the Zionist thinker A.D. Gordon explained.

"That cosmic element may best be described as the blending of the natural landscape of the Homeland with the spirit of the people inhabiting it. This is the mainspring of a people's vitality and creativity, of its spiritual and cultural values. Any conglomeration of individuals may form a society in the mechanical sense, one that moves and acts, but only the presence of the cosmic element makes for an organic national entity with creative vitality."

I first discovered Gordon's "creative vitality" at the Young Judaea camp Tel Yehudah. I have since become reacquainted with it through my experiences with birthright israel. And I find the cosmic element renewed again and again when I wander around Jerusalem, even when the city is haunted by terrorism and tension. These three experiences have shaped my Zionism profoundly – and make me optimistic about the Jewish future. These three experiences convince me that we have a "product" that can still "sell" in the modern world.

In February 2000 I danced in the *Shabbat* with a group of birthrighters at the Western Wall. As our "lah, lahs" resonated in my ears, I heard from behind me a muezzin's sonorous call inviting Muslims to pray; in front of me, and across the valley, I heard church bells ringing. Today, these might sound like discordant notes fighting for primacy. But back in the days of Oslo peace and prosperity, I heard the three musical expressions as a symphony of synergy, as a chorus of coexistence. I do not know why great beauty and great tragedy are so often linked, but I reserve the right to hope that in Jerusalem, and elsewhere, the beauty will trump the tragedy very soon.

"Im eshkachech Yerushalayim, tishkach yemeeni": If I forget, if I FORSAKE, you O Jerusalem, may my right hand lose its cunning, may my tongue cling to the roof of my mouth. If we abandon Jerusalem, we betray the essence of our being, that which makes us human, our hands and our mouths, our bodies and our souls. Jerusalem reminds us of the passion Zionism should evoke; Jerusalem transcends today's often overstated dichotomy between the religious and the secular in our Zionism, in our Judaism.

Over many centuries, across many cultures, Jerusalem has signified a corner of the earth offering a taste of heaven, or at least the heavenly. Every Thanksgiving Americans remember how the Pilgrims came to the New World seeking a New Jerusalem. As Jews, we are blessed by a connection with the old, real Jerusalem, but we also can create new Jerusalems. I found a taste of Jerusalem at camp, summer after summer. I found a taste of Jerusalem on one birthright bus after another. I still find the taste of the real Jerusalem enriching, inspiring, ennobling. We need more Jerusalem in our lives.

PART 2

HISTORY

"Those who forget the past are condemned to repeat it," the old saying goes. Despite spending my professional life as an historian, I do not believe that insight always holds true. What I do believe is that those who forget the past are condemned in a different way; they are robbed of their identity, distanced from traditions and memories that ground us as individuals and as groups.

Unfortunately, we live in a society of amnesiacs, a society committed to the here and now, not the tried and true. However, if we are to understand where we are today, who we are, and where we want to go, we need to look backwards. In discovering our origins, we learn about ourselves.

CHAPTER 5

ORIGINS

WHY ISRAEL? THE JEWISH PEOPLE'S LOVE AFFAIR WITH THEIR HOMELAND

It is a generational phenomenon. When most Jews in their sixties, seventies, and eighties sing *Hatikvah*, the Jewish national anthem, they snap to attention, their eyes sometimes glaze with tears. *"Kol od balevav, penima, nefesh Yehudi homiya"* – Deep within the Jewish heart, the Jewish spirit still sings, they belt out proudly, profoundly, just a tad defiantly. By contrast, many younger Jews don't know what to do with themselves when the Jewish national anthem begins. Some shuffle. Some slouch. The more comfortable ones might link together, arms over shoulders, and sway. Their eyes simply glazing over, faking the words, they mutter: "Go old Beelzebub, Panama...."

It is ironic yet also typically human. One of the first generations in two thousand years to grow up with a thriving Jewish commonwealth takes the Jewish state for granted. Many of their grandparents remember what it was like to live in a world without Israel, without a Jewish state. For the older generation, this initial longing still shapes their love for Israel, intensifying the feeling of connection. The new generation, blessed with a vital Israel, has to find new ways to carry on the Jewish people's ancient and enduring love affair with *Eretz Yisrael*, the land of Israel, the Jewish people's homeland.

BACK TO ABRAHAM, 2000 B.C.E.

The relationship with the land began, as the Jewish people themselves did, four thousand years ago, with Abraham. *"Lech lecha meartzecha, memolodetcha...."* "Get yourself out of your country, and from your homeland, and from your father's house, to the land that I will show you," God commands in *Genesis* 12, verses 1 and 2. "And I will make of you a great nation, and I will bless you, and make your name great." The Torah defines a three way relationship among God, the people, and the land – Abram, the first Jew, cannot fully be a Jew, cannot become Abraham, until he moves to *Eretz Yisrael*. Israel is where the Jewish chronicle will unfold, Israel is where God's covenant with Abraham and the Jewish people is to be fulfilled.

Over the next two thousand years, Israel becomes ground zero for the Jewish people, it is the stage, the focal point, the holy land. Many of the greatest Jewish heroes strut their stuff in their homeland: Joshua the liberator, David the poet and warrior, Solomon the sage and builder, Elijah the prophet. The Torah lovingly details the beautiful vessel built to carry around the word of the Lord, the *Mishkan* or tabernacle. Jewish history climaxes when that transient structure finds a permanent home. The Temple of Solomon, gleaming, majestic, magical, is the jewel in the Jewish crown, a mark of Jewish piety – and a result of Jewish power in Saul's and David's kingdoms.

Many of the six hundred and thirteen mitzvot, commandments, require residency in Israel and service in the Temple to fulfill. The *Shalosh Regalim*, the three festivals mandating pilgrimages to Jerusalem, the sacred feasts of *Pesach* (Passover), of *Shavuot* (Weeks), of *Sukkot* (Tabernacles), are tied to the land. As agricultural festivals, they celebrate the timetable, the harvests, of the ancient Judean farmer. As walking festivals, they celebrate a particular walk, a pilgrimage, bearing gifts to the Holy Temple in Jerusalem.

In *Shemot, Exodus,* Chapter 13 verses 3 to 5, Moses tells the people: "remember this day, in which you came out of Egypt, out of the house of bondage; for by strength of hand the Lord brought you out from this place; no leavened bread shall be eaten. This day you go forth in the month of *Aviv* (spring). And it shall be when the Lord shall bring you into the land of the Canaanite, and the Hittite, and the Amorite, and the Hivite, and the Jebusite, which He swore unto your fathers to give you, a land flowing with milk and honey, that you shall keep this service in this month." What a mind-boggling concept. Regardless of what one may think about the origins or accuracy of the Bible, it is quite amazing that we're still avoiding leavened bread, commemorating an event that took place approximately three thousand seven hundred and fifty years ago! And that the land flowing with milk and honey to which Moses refers is the land today flowing with Maccabee beer and humus.

The flow of time is so vast. Dividing the chronology into more digestible chunks helps. Estimate 2000 to 1750 B.C.E. as the era of the forefathers – actually it was four mothers, Sara, Rebekah, Rachel and Leah, and three fathers, Abraham, Isaac, and Jacob. (Note that many say Before the Common Era rather than Before Christ, for obvious reasons).

Estimate 1750 to 1400 as the years in Egypt and in the desert. Act Three, conquering the land, establishing a Jewish kingdom, building the Temple and the division, degeneration, and ultimate destruction, covers from 1250 to 586 B.C.E.

The Jews were first ruled by prophets – Moses, Deborah, Samuel. But the people, not for the first time and not for the last, wanted to be more like other peoples. They demanded a king. The prophet Samuel obliged by anointing Saul, who was succeeded by the lyrical, heroic David, the fair-haired boy of early Biblical history. A charismatic, passionate, energetic and virile redhead, David is a child star – he defeats the giant Goliath. He forges a friendship with Saul's son Jonathan that sets a standard for selflessness. When he is not fighting Philistines, seducing women, expanding and unifying his kingdom, David writes devotional poems, Psalms, celebrating his love for God. In the highlight of his career, David is the one who conquers what is now known as Jerusalem, what was known as *Ir David*, the city of David, and establishes it as the capital city – and the emotional epicenter of Jewish life. But he is not pure enough to build the Holy Temple, for, as a warrior, his hands are stained with blood.

BUILDING THE BEIT HAMIKDASH, THE HOLY TEMPLE, 950 B.C.E.

Thus, in *First Kings*, Chapter 6, verses 11 to 14, the Lord turns to David's son and successor Solomon saying: "As for this house which you are building, if you will walk in My statutes and execute my ordinances, and keep all My commandments to walk in them; then will I establish My word with you, which I spoke to David your father; in that I will dwell there among the children of Israel, and will not forsake My people Israel." The text concludes: "So Solomon built the house, and finished it."

The building of the Temple is a national undertaking. The Jews contribute the finest gold, the smoothest silks, the tallest cedars from Lebanon, to build as worthy a house as humans can construct for their Lord. But Solomon the wise, Solomon the pious, will not allow the Temple to be merely a monument to materialism. Legend has it that he enlists the poorest people to help his project as well. Lacking money, jewels, finery to contribute, they give what they have – their time and their skills. The result is the wall that today represents the Jewish people's endurance, the Western Wall.

Unfortunately, the building of the Temple is the high point of early Jewish history. Not only was it a magnificent structure, but things began to deteriorate shortly thereafter. In fact, the cost of building, the high taxes required, strained the kingdom. The united Davidic kingdom would soon split, North versus South, into the Kingdoms of Israel and Judah. The Assyrians would conquer the North in 721 B.C.E. and the Babylonians would destroy the Temple and Judah less than two centuries later in 586 B.C.E.

Despite the tragic ending, the Temple lasted long enough to cement itself in the national imagination, pilgrimage by pilgrimage, year after year. Ancient Judaism was a much more literal Judaism, a Judaism of sacrifice in a particular place at particular times. Jews relished these moments. Not only did most enjoy the rare opportunity to eat meat, but only through sacrifice could they cleanse themselves of their sins. This notion of walking around in the unbearable state of not being cleansed is incomprehensible to most moderns, who have simply washed away the notion of sin and evil from our lives.

While allowing your imagination to soar, imagining a glorious shrine to God gleaming with gold and cleansing the soul, don't forget that it was also a sophisticated but quite smelly abattoir, a slaughterhouse that had to choreograph the sacrifice of animals, moving the terrified bleating livestock to the appropriate place, completing the ritual properly, draining vast amounts of blood efficiently. The stench must have been overwhelming, especially considering how heavy Jerusalem's air can be so many months a year – no wonder the Temple had to be built in the hills.

Judaism would, thankfully, evolve into a more abstract phenomenon. Rabbinic Judaism's great innovation would be in finding a way to redeem sinners without Temple sacrifices. And, as the next chapter will show, the connection between the people and the land would sometimes be physically tenuous. But Israel would remain inscribed in the Jewish heart, it would preoccupy the Jewish brain. Israel would never stop being the Jewish home.

ISRAEL IS A KEEPER

Is this story hip enough, now enough, moving enough, to speak to modern Jews? Can this story of Abraham from 2000 B.C.E. speak to us in 2000 C.E.? Can this story of animal sacrifice at the Holy Temple speak to a generation used to praying in dignified silence at Holy Blossom Temple? I believe it can. For starters, it is ours. In a world so free many often feel rootless, Israel belongs to all Jews, whether we live there or not.

Despite all the hype about secular and religious tensions, Israel remains the focal point of the Jewish people – and a place with a remarkably high quality of Jewish life. A Bar Ilan University Poll published just before Passover 2002 found that 91 percent of Jewish Israelis intended to eat matzah, 79 percent intended to participate in a traditional seder, and over half, 52 percent, expected to avoid eating unleavened foods entirely during the week-long holiday. In a characteristic scientific understatement, Dr. Zvi Zohar observed: "the poll seems to support the hypothesis that living in a country with a Jewish majority and a generally Jewish-oriented culture and calendar has the effect of involving a high percentage of people in Jewish customs and way of life." Especially considering that one fifth of the sample represents highly assimilated Russian Jews Dr. Zohar found it "reasonable to conclude that life in Israel has a significant counter-assimilationist effect."

In truth, Israel is not just a great Jewish story, it is a great human story. Even amid the horrors of 2002, Israelis continued to live one of the great modern miracles, characterized both by the prosaic rhythms of daily life and by their singular achievements. The high tech revolution continued. The pace of medical and pharmaceutical breakthroughs intensified. While earning worldwide acclaim for treating wounded Jews and Arabs equally and humanely, Hadassah Hospital made headlines for collaborating with the Weizmann Institute in developing a new vaccination to arrest juvenile diabetes. Servicing the other end of the age spectrum, Tel Aviv University helped set the pace in the Israeli rush toward a cure for Alzheimer's disease. Israeli companies also took the lead in voice recognition and other cyber technologies of particular relevance after September 11. And Israel's first astronaut, Air Force Colonel Ilan Ramon, kept training for his first flight with the Columbia space shuttle.

Moreover, the movement to improve the quality of Israeli life persisted. During a mayhem-filled March, Ra'anana became the first municipality in Israel to be recognized for having achieved an international standard ISO-14000, a mark of the city's success in minimizing the harmful effects of development on the environment. The *Jerusalem Post* reported that five years earlier Ra'anana had qualified for another international standard ISO-9002 that recognizes the high quality of the city's public services.

Furthermore, this Jewish and human epic is ancient and enduring. In a world filled with ephemeral toys, fleeting sensations, fragile family bonds, Israel is a keeper. So even for those who do not believe that this covenant is sanctified by God, history offers its own sanctification. If in the antique business, a four thousand-year-old jug is infinitely more precious than a four-day-old cup; if in sports, a hitting or winning streak becomes exponentially more significant with each passing plateau, so, too, has our relationship with Israel, and with Judaism, deepened, multiplied, intensified over the millennia. And over the last two thousand years, with so much of Jewish life taking place away from ground zero, the Jews learned an essential lesson: you don't have to be Israeli to love Israel, you don't have to live in the Jewish homeland to love it and draw spiritual sustenance from it.

CHAPTER 6

EXILE
LIFE IN GALUT:
THE CURSE – AND BLESSINGS – OF EXILE

We are a peculiar people. Think of the top tourist sites in the United States, then think of the top tourist sites in Israel. Instead of the Washington Mall, Jerusalem offers the Western Wall. Instead of the spic and span artificiality of Disney World, Israel offers the dusty ruins of Masada. Instead of the Statue of Liberty and Ellis Island, monument and museum to the inspiring ideal of freedom, Israel offers Yad Vashem, monument and museum to the ugly tragedy of the Holocaust.

Yes, every visit to Israel goes beyond this Jewish *Via Dolorosa* or Way of Suffering. But this trinity of Jewish tragedy is particularly fascinating because all three sites illustrate just how indelibly the pain of exile has marked the Jewish homeland. With the cycle of destruction and redemption having repeated itself again and again, the Jews learned how to remain centered on their home even when in exile. Yet, at the same time, Jews cannot forget the impact of exile even when at home.

FIRST EXILE: SLAVERY IN EGYPT 1750-1400 B.C.E.

Unfortunately, from the start, the story of the Jewish people and the land was not simple. Just as *Bereisheet, Genesis*, roots the Jewish people in their homeland, *Bereisheet* uproots the Jewish people from their homeland. This first book of the Bible climaxes and closes with Jacob's tearful reunion with his lost son Joseph. Driven out by famine, saved by the brother they themselves exiled, Jacob's sons move to the land of Goshen, in Egypt, voluntarily abandoning their homeland.

This departure, of course, backfires. When a new Pharaoh arises who knew not Joseph, this foreign people living among Egyptians is enslaved. So begins a central motif in Jewish history. Even before the Jews receive the Ten Commandments, even before the Torah is completed, the Jews suffer in exile and yearn for redemption. In this first exile in Egypt, as in all subsequent exiles until ours in the late twentieth and early twenty-first centuries, the dream of the return would never waver. If anything, the dream intensified as a return to the land became the hope for redemption. Thanks to the Egyptians, the Babylonians, and, finally, the Romans, Jews became experts in the world of long-distance national romance; they learned to love *Eretz Yisrael* ever so intently from afar.

Exile, then, was clearly a curse. Again and again the Jews would both suffer persecution and be prevented from fulfilling all their commandments. But the repeated exiles, the pattern of banishment and redemption, honed certain skills, intensified certain patterns, and like it or not, shaped the Judaism we know and see today.

Mourning the exile, the pain and pathos of displacement, is an essential part of Jewish psychology, liturgy, literature, ritual, and ideology. After the Babylonians destroyed Solomon's Temple in 586 B.C.E., and the Jews were sent into their second exile (albeit the first involuntary one), the Jews let out a wail that still resonates. *"Im eshcachech Yerushalayim, tishkach yemeeni"*: If I forget you O Jerusalem, may my right hand lose its cunning. We cannot forget Jerusalem without losing ourselves.

Exile shook up Judaism and the Jewish people, for better and for worse. To keep Judaism alive without the Holy Temple, smaller temples had to be established. Judaism had to become transistorized, made more flexible, more transportable, and, ultimately as a result, more endurable.

Jews and Judaism also became more cosmopolitan. Many Jews tasted the fruits of the world outside, and liked the taste. Less than fifty years later, when the Jews were free to return, their Persian benefactor King Cyrus himself recognized a key reality, when he ordered that those who did not return should still help rebuild the Temple from afar. The voluntary exiles were charged with a task very familiar to modern American Jews, who also have chosen not to return home despite being free to do so. Those remaining in Babylonia should "help… with silver, and with gold."

AVOIDING A TEAR-STAINED JEWISH IDENTITY

Thus, for at least 2500 years exile has not been just a permanent condition but occasionally a voluntary one. Miraculously, withstanding a

Tsunami of massacres, murders, decrees, injustices, and insults, Jews have not only survived but have thrived. We must never forget our ghastly past. And yet, we cannot become so embittered that we grant our oppressors posthumous victories: we cannot let them define our Judaism. The great historian Salo Baron repudiated the "lachrymose" – tear-stained – approach to Jewish history. The greater challenge is to avoid a tear-stained Jewish identity, one built on the perverse refusal to let the murderers win rather than on an exuberant embrace of our values, rituals, and ideals.

In fairness to the Cassandras of today and yesterday, it has been hard to accentuate the positive and eliminate the negative. The period of the Second Temple proved as tumultuous as the period of the First Temple, though longer. As civilization developed, as empires spread, Israel, at the crossroads of the world, became the world's doormat. The rise of the Greeks, then the Romans, might represent progress on the universal stage, but it was not good news for the Jews.

HEDONISM VERSUS HELLENISM AT HANUKKAH, 168 B.C.E.

The classic struggle between traditional Judaism and modern values, between Torah and Temple on one side, and hedonism and Hellenism on the other side, occurred during the Maccabean Revolt around 168 B.C.E. Today, suffering from a case of Christmas envy, North American Jews have made Hanukkah a major holiday on the Jewish calendar. Every Jewish kid – who has eaten latkes, spun dreidels, and, most important of all, reveled in eight nights of candlelighting and presents – knows the story. Hanukkah celebrates the victory of the virtuous Maccabees against the conquering Greeks. Judah Maccabee, the leader of five heroic brothers, defeated the Greek tyrant Antiochus Epiphanes, and cleansed the Temple of the Hellenistic influences.

What fewer American and Canadian Jews note – or care to acknowledge – is that Hanukkah was not just a war of liberation, it was a civil war. And to the extent that it was a civil war, the Maccabees were most like the ultra-Orthodox today – fundamentalists rejecting modern seductions such as non-Jewish names, a pagan worship of the body, visits to the gymnasium, violations of the dietary laws. You could argue that most of us, most modern Jews, are more like the bad guys in the story. The point is not to make most of us feel guilty. Rather, even as we celebrate the Maccabean victory, we need to acknowledge that the victory was fleeting, and that the challenges of assimilation, of identity, continually assert themselves, from generation to generation.

The Hasmonean dynasty which the Maccabees established eventually degenerated into precisely the Hellenistic, pagan, corrupt, impious monarchy that Antiochus sought to impose. The great symbol of this is the Hasmoneans' Rome-backed successor, the maniacal Herod, a Henry the Eighth-type king who in his paranoia killed off children as well as wives.

Herod was a master builder who expanded and renovated Jerusalem and its surroundings. Ironically, as hateful as Herod was, many of the sites we see today, many of the ancient stones modern Jews most cherish, represent Herod's handiwork.

By the time Herod reigned in the first century before Jesus was born, Rome had replaced Greece as the empire of the moment. Alas, even Herod's massive stoneworks could not withstand the Roman assault. The Jews held out valiantly against the Romans – skirmishing for decades against the world's most powerful empire. Do the math. Jesus of Nazareth is born and dies under the shadow of Roman rule. The Romans lay siege to Jerusalem and raze the Second Temple in 70 C.E., almost four decades after Jesus's death. The Bar Kochba revolt would occur 62 years later in 132 C.E.

70 C.E.: THE END OF JEWISH HISTORY?

Still, the black letter day in the Jewish fight against the Romans is the 9th of Av, 70 C.E. On the same calendar day that the First Temple was destroyed, the second one fell, too. On that date the nearly two-thousand-year-long exile began. That is the event that caused the martyrs of Masada to hole up in the Judaean desert – and that is the event that suggested to them that the Romans would mistreat them once Masada fell.

With Jerusalem destroyed, with the Temple in flames – you can still see charred remains from the conflagration in Jerusalem today – many Jews believed that the end of Jewish history had come. And had every Jew followed the model of Masada, indeed the journey that began two thousand years earlier with Abraham would have ended. That is why, until modern Zionists resurrected it as a model of grit, the mass suicide at

Masada was largely forgotten. The Rabbis feared the model and suppressed the memory.

Throughout the centuries of exile the Rabbis celebrated a different character and a different image. They taught that during Jerusalem's siege, the students of Rabbi Yohanan Ben Zakkai snuck their teacher out of the city in a coffin. The Rabbi met with the Roman general Vespasian and arranged to establish a *yeshiva* at Yavneh, considerably north of all the trouble in Jerusalem. Some cultures would denigrate Ben Zakkai as a coward. But the Rabbis celebrated him as the Scarlett O'Hara of the Jewish world, a visionary spirit who played by the conqueror's rules to keep alive a defeated civilization.

However, while in "Gone With the Wind" Scarlett learned to worship what the hated Yankees worshiped – money – Ben Zakkai's *yeshiva* offered an alternative to Roman values. As a result, Jewish history was saved but reoriented. The milestones of Jewish life in the twelve hundred years before Jesus's birth were mostly political – the unification of the kingdom, building the Temple, the division, the destruction, the return, the revolt, the renovating, followed by the destruction once again. By contrast, the milestones in the millennium after Jesus were more theoretical, theological, intellectual.

Note, both the mass suicide at Masada and the ideological reorientation at Yavneh take place in Israel after "the exile." The location of these two symbolically powerful events demonstrates that throughout the millennia of exile, communities of Jews remained in the land of Israel. The connection between the Jewish people and their homeland was not simply abstract, it remained concrete, and vital.

Remarkably, in the first centuries of the exile, after the most devastating defeat, the Jews produced a tremendous achievement – the compiling of the Talmud, dozens of volumes transcribing rabbinic commentary on the Mishnah, itself a commentary on the Torah. These commentaries on the commentaries are a breathtaking source of information on Jewish law, Jewish ritual, Jewish attitudes, Jewish thought, Jewish history, Jewish life, as well as contemporary mores and medicine, knowledge and knowhow. But in a sad sign of the Jewish political crisis, there were two Talmuds, the Jerusalem Talmud which was completed around 390 B.C.E., and the Babylonian Talmud, completed over a century later. Today, we can visit villages like Tsipori in the Galilee and Katzrin in the Golan that thrived during this Talmudic period. Still, the Babylonian Talmud, the product of exile, is the more authoritative.

This indicates just how far Jerusalem had fallen – and just how dramatically the Jewish world had changed.

1000 C.E.: THE PAIN OF EXILE,
THE YEARNING FOR ISRAEL

The Talmud represents our ancestors' indomitable will to survive, as individuals and as a people. A quick tour through the past centuries of exile suggests there is much to appreciate, much to contemplate during the long, depressing period when some Jews could still live in their homeland, but sovereignty proved elusive. From village to village, from empire to empire, Jews discovered how to survive and how to maintain Judaism while functioning in and often benefiting the outside world.

One thousand years ago the Jews were a people in exile, scattered around the Mediterranean Basin. Most lived under Moslem rule, but the Arab caliphate was crumbling and Christianity's domain was expanding. The spiritual heart of the Jewish people remained *Eretz Yisrael*, even though Babylonian Jewry had dominated for centuries, Spanish Jewry was thriving, and the communities of Ashkenaz – roughly contemporary France and Germany – were growing.

Banned from Islamic villages and the elaborate feudal structure of Christian Europe, Jews tended to live in towns. The *Kehillah*, the community, served as the Jews' guild, offering an independent corporate structure that provided an identity. Jews had a whole range of jobs, but were renowned for their network of trading ties, their talents in administering imperial outposts, and their money-lending.

Despite the pain of exile, despite the yearning for *Eretz Yisrael*, few Jews doubted God, or God's special relationship with the "chosen people." Along with this faith, Jews shared a sense of national destiny and peoplehood. Their daily rituals and the outside world's hostility both reinforced this sense of community. Yet Jews, for all their insulation, were embedded in the world around them. The earliest sketch of a medieval Jew – found in the margins of the Forest Roll of Essex England – caricatures a Jew's bushy hair, hooked nose, and thick lips. The Jew wears a badge shaped like the two tablets, a reminder that many medieval communities forced Jews to wear some symbol – despite the canard that they all looked alike. At the same time, this supposed stranger wears a medieval cloak like everyone else, testimony to his and his people's adaptability. This sketch, then, illustrates a central theme of Jewish history, the tension between otherness and belonging, as Jews struggled to remain distinct and join the world, just as their neighbors alternately welcomed and rejected them.

In Ashkenaz, the traumatic Crusades and the periodic expulsions fostered a cult of martyrdom, emphasizing the value of dying *al kiddush hashem,* to sanctify God's name. And the Jews' powerlessness would breed an instinctive obsequiousness and sense of resignation. But even as the crusading thunder clouds gathered, some rays of light shone with brilliant scholarship, good deeds, innovative ideas. Rabbis continued their ancient dialogue with the Bible, weaving commentaries, addressing contemporary dilemmas through responsa, and issuing *Takkanot,* ordinances. Rabbenu Gershom ben Judah (960-1028), "the Light of the Exile," outlawed polygamy and decreed – or is credited with decreeing – that a husband could not divorce his wife unilaterally. These far-reaching decisions harmonized the Jewish way of life with the Christian environment and solidified the monogamous family as the building block of Ashkenazi Jewry.

Ashkenazi culture would become renowned for its piety, its scholarship, its morality, its prosperity. This was a community led by great rabbis and fed by resourceful merchants. The leading rabbi of the time, and, perhaps, of this millennium, the prolific and profound Rabbi Solomon Yitzhaki (1040-1105), known by the acronym Rashi, lived in Troyes, France. Today, when we comment on Rashi's nearly-thousand-year-old commentaries about our even older Bible, we span the millennia and engage in the critical colloquy so central to Judaism. That, and not some fancy program generated by the local Federation, is Jewish continuity!

MEDIEVAL JEWRY: FROM MUSLIM TO CHRISTIAN RULE

The rise of Ashkenazi Jewry shifted the Jewish center of gravity toward the Christian world. Harsh Christian anti-Semitism made Islam's attitude toward Jews seem benign. Moslems deemed Jews dhimmis, protected but inferior. As fellow "people of the book," the Jews at least were not infidels subject to the sword. The Jews established an elaborate communal hierarchy, with the Exilarch the only Jewish authority Moslem rulers recognized. Under Islam, *yeshivas* thrived, and many Jews prospered, despite constant oppression, perpetual second-class status, and occasional riots.

The Jews of Muslim Spain did exceedingly well. They were poets, physicians, traders, military advisers, administrators, and courtiers. The poetry of Rabbi Yehudah HaLevi (1074-1141), who sighed "My heart is in the East (in Israel), but I am in the West," still casts its spell – and defines many contemporary Jews' predicament. Unlike most of his descendants, HaLevi actually forsook the riches of the Diaspora for the Holy Land, symbolizing the enduring ties the exiled Jews cultivated with their homeland.

Even while declining militarily, the Islamic world crackled with intellectual energy. The great Jewish philosopher, and court physician, Moses ben Maimon (1135-1204) was a product of the Islamic world. Maimonides tried to reconcile his venerable faith with the Greek philosophy he and other Islamic scholars studied. Maimonides' rationalist approach provoked great controversy at the time, yet still shapes Jewish thought today. Nearly eight hundred years after his death, his thirteen attributes of faith – commemorated in the *Yigdal* – and his eight steps of charity continue to color what we believe, and how we behave.

Amazingly, such lasting intellectual achievements emerged despite the fragility of medieval life. Life-spans were short. Disease was rampant. The Black Death of 1348-1349 ravaged Europe, and devastated the Jews who were scapegoated for this epidemic. This turning point in medieval Jewish history would result in mass expulsions from the Western lands. Many of the Jews of Ashkenaz would drift eastward toward the Kingdom of Poland and the Duchy of Lithuania, the next great center of Jewish life.

The Black Death also doomed the Jews of Spain. Life in Christian Spain was less golden than life under the Moslems, though still good. But the Bubonic plague emboldened the Jews' enemies, who spread lies about Jews poisoning the wells (in addition to desecrating the host and harvesting the blood of young Christians). This upheaval eventually spawned the infamous Inquisition and expulsion from Spain in 1492. Alas, as with the Jews of Poland in the twentieth century, the tragic final chapter would eclipse positive memories of centuries of creativity, prosperity, even power.

Some of the Jews fleeing the Inquisition sailed for the New World – presaging the rise of another great Jewish center. But most of the Sephardim, Spanish Jews, ended up living in the expanding Ottoman Empire, which in 1517 would conquer Eretz Yisrael. The fact that Jews in mid-millennium found refuge in the relatively "backward" East from the supposedly more civilized West further illustrates that, tragically, progress has not always been good for the Jews.

THE SHULCHAN ARUCH, 1555: PRIVATE ACTS OF JEWISH LIVING

Painting broad, even gross, brush strokes of major migrations, large communities, leading figures, neglects the fact that life was lived on a small scale, in intimate settings – most people rarely ventured more than five miles from their birthplaces in their entire lives. And in this pre-nationalist era, Jews defined themselves by their hometowns more than by their regions or "countries." To do real justice to Jewish life then (as now) we would need to etch fine portraits of anonymous Jews who regularly set the *Shabbat* table, lit candles, prayed in shul, and who went to the market, worked for a living, raised a family. This was the period in which the Jewish people not only kept the *Shabbat* but the *Shabbat* kept the Jewish people, emphasizing the interconnection between what we would now artificially distinguish as Judaism's religious and nationalist components. Unlike us, most Jews lived Jewish lives. They yearned for what we take for granted and often resent – "boredom," meaning safety, stability, regularity.

The *"Shulchan Aruch"* offers a lasting public symbol of these private acts of Jewish living. Hebrew for the "set table," this digest of Sephardic customs reflects the fullness and timelessness of the *Halachah*, Jewish law. Compiled in 1555 by Joseph Caro (1488-1575), the book remains the authoritative source for Jewish ritual practice. Rabbi Moses Isserles (c.1520-c.1572), the chief rabbi of Cracow, Poland, catalogued the contrasts between Ashkenazi and Sephardi ritual using Caro's work as his standard. The resulting *"Mappah,"* or tablecloth, spread over the *Shulchan Aruch*'s "table," acknowledged Caro's primacy, and was incorporated into subsequent editions for Ashkenazim.

Caro's adopted home, the holy city of Safed, in the Galilee, flourished under Ottoman rule. Other communities in *Eretz Yisrael* languished, depending on the monies emissaries from Israel collected from Jews around the world. But not Safed. Safed became a center for textiles and for the mystical counterattack against Maimonidean rationalism. Kabbalists, mystics, such as Rabbi Isaac Luria (1534-1572), contemplated the mysteries of creation, of exile, of redemption, while emphasizing good deeds, asceticism, and intense prayer. For Ha'ari, the "Lion," as Luria was known, and his mystics, *Shabbat* was the weekly attempt to set the world right. Bedecked in white, they would beckon the Sabbath Queen amid the glorious green hills of the Galilee, singing "Come my beloved," *Lecha Dodi*, "Welcome to the bride," *Boee Kalah*.

SHOCKS IN THE SEVENTEENTH CENTURY

Just as we do today, the Kabbalists grappled with the mystery of Jewish suffering, while seeking what moderns might call an authentic Judaism. Whatever successes Jews enjoyed, whatever autonomy their individual *kehillot*, communities, secured, whatever influence *shtadlanim* or intercessors held, all could vanish in a flash, due to forces beyond the Jews' control. When Catholicism underwent its own internal crisis, during the Catholic counter-reformation of the sixteenth century, the Jews of Venice ended up in a ghetto, a new and ugly invention. One hundred and thirty years later, in 1648, when Bogdan Khmelnitski led a populist Cossack Revolt against Polish nobles in the Ukraine, he massacred the local Jews. Jews wanted answers, which is why some turned to Kabbalah; they yearned for salvation, which is why some turned to false messiahs, most notably Shabbatai Zevi (1626-1676), who dazzled the Jewish masses until he betrayed them by converting to Islam in 1666.

The twin shocks of Khmelnitski and Sabbateanism shattered the Polish-Lithuanian community. This tranquil community of scholars and merchants enjoyed great autonomy. The local governing structures of the *Kehillah*, the community, institutionalized rabbinic authority, collected taxes, enforced order, maintained schools and synagogues, looked out for the widowed, the orphaned, the sick, and the poor. During long stretches, throughout many lifetimes, the Jews of Poland and Lithuania led lives governed more by *Halachah* than by secular law, lives surrounded by fellow Jews and often lacking much contact with the outside world, although this varied depending on one's livelihood.

These communities buzzed with the characteristic sing-song of *yeshiva* learning, but many, alas, became intellectually sterile. As the Renaissance, then the early Enlightenment, supplanted the Dark Ages, new ideas swirled through Europe. Protestantism nurtured the seeds of individualism, humanism, and rationalism – and improved the Jews' lot in the Netherlands and England. As modern thought centered on man, not God, Jews would enjoy more freedom – and more pressure to jettison their faith. One of the first Jews to embrace this intellectual and political revolution was Baruch Spinoza (1632-1677), a Sephardic exile living in

Amsterdam. In rejecting Jewish society – and being rejected by it – this creative thinker did not adopt another religion, he became what so many of his descendants would try to be, a man of the world.

MODERN WINDS – AND LIGHT

By the eighteenth century, with modern seductions just beginning to beckon, with Eastern Europe's insulated Jewish communities withering intellectually and spiritually, a civil war of words rather than swords ensued. A charismatic folk preacher, Israel ben Eliezer of Miedzyboz (1700-1760) sought to purge Judaism of its elitism, its casuistry, its stiffness. This "Master of the Good Name," the Baal Shem Tov, entranced the Jewish masses with a revivalist *Hasidic* movement that was ecstatic, populist, often deliciously primitive. Opposing the *Hasidim* were the *Mitnagdim*, led by the brilliant Elijah of Vilna, the Vilna Gaon (1720-1797), a rationalist polymath who revitalized Talmudic study, making it less pedantic, and more informed by secular sciences and logic.

For all the bitterness between the *Hasidim* and *Mitnagdim*, both remained rooted in tradition. Yet more and more Jews were able to flourish in the outside world, in part because the capitalist revolution prized economic skills rather than religious beliefs. In the 1760s the Rothschilds began a financial and philanthropic dynasty that would symbolize to friend and foe alike the Jewish role in building the new economic order.

Many of the Jews who prospered in this new world wanted to enlighten their benighted people. Fortunately, the first great Jewish figure of the Enlightenment, Moses Mendelssohn (1729-1786), shared that passion for renewal without the condescension. Enlightenment in Hebrew is *Haskalah*, which emphasizes thought rather than light. Hailed by his own people as the third great Moses in a chain of genius with Maimonides and Moses the lawgiver, Mendelssohn earned praise from the parlor sophisticates of Berlin as the "Jewish Socrates." A *Maskil* and an Orthodox Jew, Mendelssohn recognized the great intellectual promise of enlightenment. He was, however, less cognizant of the secular temptations which could bewitch his people and his own family. Mendelssohn's balancing act was idiosyncratic and not enduring. Two generations later, his grandson Felix, the Romantic composer, was raised as a Christian.

Throughout it all, even as the Jews became a people of exile, they continued to venerate their homeland, and Jerusalem most of all. Three times a day, every day, Jews prayed for a return from the four corners of the earth, back to their beloved homeland. And the all-important Passover *seder*, that ritualized socio-drama reliving the pain of exile and the joy of redemption, climaxes with the prayer, "Next year, in Jerusalem."

In the eighteenth century in Morocco and in Moldavia, in Poland and in Prussia, Jews continued to dream as they always had. Who would have imagined that in the coming centuries, as the world rapidly modernized, they would endure their greatest of nightmares, while also fulfilling their greatest dream, all within the space of a decade?

CHAPTER 7

AWAKENING:
MUGGED BY MODERNITY–
THE CRISIS OF EMANCIPATION AND
THE RISE OF ZIONISM

For centuries the Jews of Europe were locked in their ghettoes and shtetls, largely frozen in time. Insulated from outside influences by rampant anti-Semitism, Jews enjoyed a great deal of autonomy. As long as the community paid taxes and followed the laws, Jews could establish their own rabbinical hierarchy, schools, social services, and community funds. They could be ethnically, nationally, ethically, and religiously Jewish. In fact, their Judaism was so coherent, so integrated, that they did not even have a word for "religion" – the modern Hebrew word for religion, *dat*, is of Persian origin.

The Enlightenment, a Western movement celebrating man's rationality, centrality, and equality, helped melt some of the ice encasing – both imprisoning and protecting – the Jews. The resulting Emancipation offered Jews freedom and equality as citizens, usually on one condition: that they free themselves from their ancient heritage.

NAPOLEON'S SANHEDRIN AND
THE FRAGMENTATION OF JEWISH IDENTITY

One moment dramatizes this complicated and traumatic clash between traditional Judaism and the forces of Enlightenment and Emancipation. In 1806 Napoleon convened an Assembly of Jewish Notables throughout his Empire. Christening them with the name of the venerable Jewish tribunal, the Sanhedrin, Napoleon asked his ad hoc council twelve questions. The questions seemed innocuous. They asked where Jews stood on intermarriage, polygamy, divorce, usury. But underlying them was a challenge: were they Jews first or Frenchmen first? How could they reconcile their loyalty to an ancient set of laws uniting a people scattered around the world and their loyalty to a nation offering its citizens liberty, equality and fraternity?

Naturally, the French Jews told the great emperor just what he wanted to hear. All the Jews were cowed, although many of the notables were quite anxious to embrace their emperor and their country. Defining themselves as "Frenchmen of the Mosaic persuasion," hair-splitting and somersaulting their way out of the situations in which Jewish custom or law contradicted French law, these Jews ripped Judaism from its moorings. Rather than a complicated creed and a people's way of life, Judaism became just another religion. It was still true, as the German Jewish convert and poet, Heinrich Heine, wrote, that "Baptism" remained the "ticket of admission" into European civilization. But in taking the Jewish nationalism out of Judaism, Napoleon's Sanhedrin began preparing Judaism for its respectable entry into the West, especially in America.

"BE A MAN ON THE STREET AND A JEW IN YOUR TENT"

Six decades later, when Enlightenment and Emancipation began to transform the Eastern European Jewish masses as well as the French and German Jewish elites, a Russian Jewish poet articulated the great enlightened dream. "Awake my people! How long will you slumber?" Y.L. Gordon asked in 1863. "The night has passed, the sun shines bright," he insisted, thanks to the Enlightenment. "This land of Eden [newly emancipated Russia] now opens its gates to you... [so] Raise your head high, straighten your back, And gaze with loving eyes open" at your new "brothers." To achieve this equality, Gordon offered an essential formula: "Be a man on the street and a Jew in your tent." This then, became what millions of Jews in the first phase of Enlightenment yearned for: a vital, updated yet traditional Judaism at home, but complete acceptance, even anonymity, on the streets of Europe, be it Napoleonic France or Czarist Russia.

THE RISE OF ANTI-SEMITISM AND
THE DEATH OF ENLIGHTENMENT

Look at the modern Jewish world. Almost all the major movements, institutions, and dilemmas that define Jewish life today are rooted in the nineteenth century. The three major branches of contemporary Judaism, Reform, Conservative and Orthodox, emerged in the first few decades of the century. The Reformers tried to revolutionize Judaism; the Conservatives took a step back from the Reform efforts and tried to help

Judaism evolve within the boundaries of the *Halachah,* Jewish law; and the Orthodox rejected these radical changes. In the 1700s no one spoke about being "Orthodox" – although we would define most of the Jews at the time as such.

Similarly, Zionism and Bundism – a harbinger of today's proud, liberal, non-religious ethnicity – emerged in the last few decades of the 1800s. The nineteenth-century clash between Judaism and Enlightenment forged most of the tools we use to balance our Jewish lives and our secular lives, our synagogues, schools, camps, and organizations. And only in the nineteenth century did the two biggest centers of contemporary Jewry, Israel and the United States, begin to attract Jews en masse.

More than transforming the Jewish world, the nineteenth century largely invented our modern world as we know it. It was an age of isms – rationalism, secularism, liberalism, Socialism, Communism. It was also an age of great optimism that inspired many talented European Jews. Only by understanding these hopes can we fathom just how devastating it was to see the Enlightenment, their very source of salvation, also breed a new, virulent, and racial form of the age-old Jew hatred, anti-Semitism.

Anti-Semitism, alas, had roots in the ideological ferment and in the social change among the most forward-looking thinkers and among the most backward-looking bigots. Sadly, both a dedication to Enlightenment and an aversion to it spawned anti-Semitism. As a result, Jews were caricatured as both modernizers and traditionalists, as conspirators trying to sneak through Christian defenses by hiding in the Trojan horse of Enlightenment, as well as conspirators seeking to keep society in the dark ages.

KISHINEV, 1903 – CITY OF SLAUGHTER

Anti-Semitism was particularly embittering to Enlightened Jews because it left them doubly deprived. Losing faith in their new secular god did not restore faith in the ancestral God – or in those folkways and rituals they repudiated. Nowhere was this sense of loss captured more powerfully than in the great Russian Jewish poet Chaim Nahman Bialik's heartbreaking *"Ir HaHareigah,"* City of Slaughter. Appointed to a commission to investigate the bloody Kishinev pogroms in Russia, in 1903, an embittered Bialik wrote an epic poem describing what he had seen.

"City of Slaughter" vividly recreates the terror and brutality of the Cossacks who wantonly raped mothers and daughters, dead or alive. But Bialik also turns his attention to the victims' cowardly menfolk. Not only did they cower in the corners, praying for their own salvation while watching the unwatchable, but those who were *Cohanim*, descendants of the high priests, ran out of the house when the pillaging was finished, burst into the Rabbi's study and asked: Is my wife now permissible to be touched or unclean? In attacking their timidity, in attacking their pedantic, soulless legalism, Bialik speaks for a whole generation that repudiated the desiccated ways of the rabbis.

But where could someone like Bialik turn? The harsh anti-Semitism of the nineteenth century made manifest the Jewish problem that was latent throughout the century. Even if a young Viennese journalist Theodor Herzl had not stumbled onto an anti-Dreyfus rally in France that turned anti-Semitic, there were many people at the turn of the century who understood that the Jewish problem required creative solutions.

THE ZIONIST SOLUTIONS

Many movements have founding moments, dramatic epiphanies supposedly launching the great initiative. Modern feminists often point to the publication in 1963 of Betty Friedan's *The Feminine Mystique* as the start of their movement. Similarly, Zionists point to Theodor Herzl's epiphany. Herzl, a cultivated and assimilated Middle European with a distinguished black beard, was a playwright and journalist covering the divisive treason trial in 1894 of a French Captain, Alfred Dreyfus. Herzl's Jewish identity awakened – and Zionist vision emerged – when the crowds shouted "Death to the Jew" rather than "Death to the Traitor," a descent into Jew-hatred exacerbated by the fact that Dreyfus was not even guilty. He had been framed. Two years later, in 1896, Herzl published his manifesto, *Der Judenstaat, The Jewish State.*

Of course, Herzl's epiphany, like Friedan's, was only the tip of the iceberg – both movements had been building for decades. The nineteenth century spawned the Zionist revolution, and Herzl's metamorphosis. It was a century of intellectual chaos, of fragmenting identity, of great hope and deep despair. Zionism, at its most sweeping, wanted to fix both of Bialik's problems – protect Bialik and his co-religionists from anti-Semitism by making them "normal," giving them a state, and in so doing revitalize Judaism, sweep away the legalistic commitment to mental gymnastics rather than real life. The founders of the Kibbutz movement, among others, also saw the new Jewish state as a vanguard for worldwide change. Many thinkers believed that the chaos of the Jewish world mirrored the bedlam of the outside world. At their most grandiose, they hoped to save the world as well as save the Jews. Theodor Herzl, whose political Zionism is now remembered as pragmatic and unromantic, did promise that with a Jewish state: "We shall live at last as free men on our own soil, and in our own homes peacefully die." But his imagination also soared when he beheld the Switzerland in the sand he hoped to build. "The world will be liberated by our freedom, enriched by our wealth, magnified by our greatness," he gushed. "And whatever we attempt there for our own benefit will redound mightily and beneficially to the good of all mankind."

While rooting itself in God's covenant with Abraham, while inhaling Herzl's utopian yet conventionally European spirit, Zionism was also radical. Zionists demanded what Nietzsche called a "transvaluation of values," an ideological overhaul. In the early 1900s, Micah Joseph Berdichevski reflected Zionism's rootedness in tradition and its radicalism when he recalled the Rabbinic teaching: "Whoever walks by the way and interrupts his study to remark, How fine is that tree, how fine is that field – forfeits his life!" Berdichevski insisted that Israel will "be saved" only "when another teaching is given unto us, namely: whoever walks by the way and sees a fine tree and a fine field and leaves them to think on other thoughts – that man is like one who forfeits his life!" Berdichevski cried: "Give us back our fine trees and fine fields! Give us back the Universe!"

This cry is more than a plea to return to the land. This is a call to reevaluate your personal life and your environment. This is a call for purifying, electrifying revolution.

The Zionist revolution defied the twentieth-century trend toward individualism and the Jewish trend toward sectarianism. Zionism was communitarian, and it sought to resurrect a more integrated, authentic Judaism and Jew. In the second decade of the twentieth century, Jacob Klatzkin rejected the Enlightenment's ideological hairsplitting. "To be a Jew means the acceptance of neither a religious nor an ethical creed," he insisted, dismissing the false choices we still use to distort Judaism. "We are neither a denomination nor a school of thought, but members of one family, bearers of a common history." And it is no coincidence that *Hatikvah*, the national anthem, THE one, ancient enduring Hope, like so many Jewish prayers, speaks of abstractions as singular, but the people as collective: It is THE Jewish spirit that still sings and it is THE eyes that seek out Zion, but "OUR" hope of two thousand years, to be a free nation in OUR Land.

As an enlightened movement that disdained much of ghetto Judaism, Zionism is best remembered for repudiating Judaism's religious dimension. At its most extreme it offered a mirror image of the Napoleon Sanhedrin solution and the approach of some Reformers, stripping away everything but the national identity. For some Zionists, rather than being Frenchmen or Englishmen or Russians of the Mosaic persuasion, the goal was to be Jews of the European persuasion. Theoretically, once freed of the specter of anti-Semitism, the Jew could flourish as a cultivated human being, meaning a European, away from Europeans. The most infamous example of this was Theodor Herzl's consideration of the British offer of a homeland in Uganda. But the most significant lesson from that episode is how roundly that idea was repudiated – how deeply Jewish, what we should call, on some levels, religious, most Zionists were. "Judaism is fundamentally national," the Russian-born cultural Zionist Ahad Ha'am insisted, "and all the efforts of the 'Reformers' to separate the Jewish religion from its national element have no result except to ruin both the nationalism and the religion."

YOU CANNOT TAKE THE ZION OUT OF ZIONISM

Zionism was a typically schizophrenic product of the typically schizophrenic nineteenth century wherein rationalism and romanticism competed and coexisted. Zionism in part was as abstract as the *Wissenschaft*, the intellectual German Jewish initiative to study Jewish history systematically. Each movement reflected a different combination of the epoch's rationalist, liberal, scientific, and nationalist sentiments. But Zionism was also fundamentalist and spiritual, which was essential to its success. Zionism was a passionate, romantic, religious movement – even at its most secular.

And in fact, most secular Zionists could not take the Zion out of Zionism. Their nationalism was deeply Jewish, and thus incontestably religious. (Similarly, today's "secular" Israelis, for all their hostility to religion, are far more tied into the Jewish religious calendar, the holy language, the sacred Jewish texts, than many of their most pious American cousins).

Among the first Zionist pioneers, the "Biluim" were characteristically secular. Rejecting the *"sha-shtill"* quiescence of their parents and rabbis, appalled by what Judaism had become, they moved to Israel in 1882 – a decade before Herzl's epiphany. Yet these gruff pioneers called themselves Bilu (BYLU), an acronym based on the Biblical verse – *"Beit Yaakov Lechu V'Nelcha"*– House of Jacob, arise and go forth. Their manifesto rejecting the false dream of "assimilation," turning Eastward not Westward, was written in Biblical language and appealed to "thine ancient pride," remembering that "thou wast a nation possessing a wise religion, a law, a constitution, a celestial Temple, whose wall [the Western wall] is still a silent witness to the glories of the past."

STATE-BUILDING AND MYTH-MAKING

Thus began a glorious exercise in state-building, and, yes, in nationalist myth-making. The hearty *chalutzim*, the heroic pioneers, came to the land *"livnot u'lhibanot bah,"* to build it and be rebuilt. They drained swamps, paved roads, founded kibbutzim. They revitalized old cities, such as Jerusalem and established new cities, such as Tel Aviv, the refreshing "hill of spring." There were fiascoes along the way. Many individuals, thrust from the Russian winters into sizzling hot summers, withered. Some of the land that the pioneers meticulously purchased in good conscience was sold by absentee Arab landlords, which made for very disgruntled – and displaced – Arab neighbors. A few generations later, modern scientists would even discover that the sweeping Eucalyptus trees that helped drain the swamps were environmentally problematic. Nevertheless, it was an heroic and revolutionary endeavor. These people were translating ideas into action, these people were shaping the future of Israel, and the Jewish people.

Forty years after the Biluim, and many failures and successes later, the great poet Chaim Nahman Bialik offered a similar tribute to the rationalism and passion, the nationalism and revitalized religionism, the modernism and the traditionalism, so central to most Zionism. January 4, 1925 marked a great moment in the development of the fledgling nation-state – the founding of the Hebrew University in Jerusalem. The opening of this university testified to the rationalist, scientific side of Zionism, and also to a certain comfort level – if you can stop draining swamps and toiling in the field to study, you are well on your way to building a sophisticated nation-state.

Bialik, who made his reputation with his poetry of oppression, of misery, of exile, now offered some prose of liberation. Standing on Mount

Scopus with its breathtaking view of Jerusalem's cobblestone alleyways and ancient walls, Bialik played on the notion of this new university joining a long line of "nationalist schools in all its forms" – the *heder* (a one room Torah school for young Eastern European boys), the *yeshiva* (a grand institution of Torah study), the *bet midrash* (smaller study houses, often linked with synagogues). As in his poem "City of Slaughter," the Enlightened poet again used Biblical language, this time to celebrate this modern "festival," and to synthesize the rough-hewn pioneers with their pale, intellectual cousins, to link the secular workers with the religious dreamers. Speaking of the pioneers, and invoking the traditional Jewish concept of the Jerusalem on high and the Jerusalem below, he cried:

"Let those youths build the Earthly Jerusalem with fire and let them who work within these walls build the Heavenly Jerusalem with fire, and between them let them build and establish our House of Life. 'For thou, O Lord, did consume it with fire, and with fire Thou will rebuild it.'"

CONTENDING SCHOOLS OF ZIONIST THOUGHT

In some ways, Bialik's address is misleading, it marked a precious but rare moment of compatibility between religious and political Zionism, a cease-fire from the factionalism endemic to the movement then and now. But one of the hallmarks of Zionist vitality, and perhaps, one of its keys to success, was its many clashing schools of thought. Zionist denominationalism was passionate, divisive, but also strangely constructive. It allowed many different people to find a foothold in this vast nation-building project. The key to Zionism's future popularity was its relative universality – like the Torah it offered many ways in, many paths to understanding and fulfillment. And, at a certain point, it became "apple pie," a sentimental rallying point and unifying point.

Still, it is worth taking a guided tour of the major Zionist denominations with two goals in mind, first, to see what ideas ultimately united them all; and second, to see how the divisions animated the debate and may offer models for our own times.

POLITICAL ZIONISM is the Zionism of Theodor Herzl, of the European scientist Chaim Weizmann and the American jurist Louis Brandeis. Its primary focus was securing a state to save Jewish lives – but in emphasizing Jewish normalcy, it sought to allow Jews to cultivate their enlightened and traditional selves.

LABOR ZIONISM is the Zionism of the kibbutz and the moshav, of rebuilding the Jewish self by reconnecting with the land – and grounding the excessively intellectual European Jew in the challenging practicalities of agriculture. While deeply secular, Labor Zionism fostered an enduring love for Eretz Yisrael, the land of Israel, and turned thousands of kibbutznikim into Bible-quoting amateur archaeologists – a passion it is hard to believe would have sprouted in Uganda.

SOCIALIST ZIONISM harnessed the messianic tradition, the commitment to *Tikun Olam*, fixing the world by fostering justice, to build a vision of Israel as a Socialist vanguard. Like the secular Marxist Bundists, Socialist Zionists were too realistic about the unpopularity of the Jewish people in Europe – and the particular needs of Jews – to expect class consciousness to unite all workers and trump anti-Semitism. Instead, they hoped their small land, their virtuous people, would serve as exemplars to the world.

CULTURAL ZIONISM, the Zionism of Ahad Ha'am, offers perhaps the most relevant blueprint for contemporary Israel-Diaspora relations. With a literate Eastern European Jew's love of Jewish culture, Ahad Ha'am saw Israel as the spiritual, intellectual, cultural, and religious center of the Jewish people. Israel would be the center of the wheel, connected to each Diaspora community by spokes. The simple existence of the Jewish state would make the Diaspora Jew stronger, prouder, and freer.

RELIGIOUS ZIONISM saw no contradiction between "Orthodoxy" and Zionism. Religious Zionists understood that only in the land of the forefathers could all the *mitzvot*, commandments, be fulfilled. Religious Zionists viewed Zionism as an essential corrective to the violence done to Jewish coherence by Napoleon's Sanhedrin and all the fragmenting reformers in its wake.

Led by Rabbi Abraham Isaac Kook, Religious Zionists embraced the political state as the pathway to mystical salvation. "The state is not the supreme happiness of man," Kook taught. This denial applies to "an ordinary state that amounts to no more than a large insurance company, where the myriad ideas that are the crown of human vitality remain hovering above, not touching it." But Israel is no insurance company. This state "is ideal in its foundation…. This state is truly supreme in the scale of happiness, and this state is our state, the state of Israel, the foundation of God's throne in the world. Its entire aim is that 'God be one and His name one' (*Zechariah*, 14:9)."

REVISIONIST ZIONISM: The name adopted by maximalist critics of the post-Herzl Zionist establishment in the 1920s who wanted to revise Zionist policies not Zionism itself. While even more pragmatic and anti-Semitism-obsessed than political Zionists, the followers of Ze'ev Jabotinsky and other revisionists had a deep appreciation for the power of national symbols, which, in this case, are inherently and authentically Jewish. Revisionists were European romantics, Garibaldi-style nationalists, passionate about peoplehood, their common past, and their homeland. It is quite characteristic, therefore, that the first Revisionist elected Prime Minister, Menachem Begin, began his tenure by praying at the Western Wall. With this move, Begin began a now-venerable tradition that recognizes how deeply Jewish, how deeply religious, most Zionism is, and most Zionists are, often despite themselves.

It is easy to forget that, initially, Zionism was dwarfed by the mass migration to America. And the emigration to America triggered its own intellectual ferment. Still, on paper, Zionism offered a recipe for Jewish renewal that the American migration never did. In fact, most Americans bought into the Protestant notion that Judaism is "just" a religion and that each individual hews his own idiosyncratic path to God and goodness. This approach helped foster great individual successes in America while causing some of the communal failures that have triggered today's Jewish identity crisis.

CHAPTER 8

CONFLICT:
WAR AND PEACE IN MODERN ISRAEL

One hundred years ago, the notion of Jews reestablishing a state in their homeland was not just a dream, it was a delusion. Yet on May 14, 1948, David Ben-Gurion proclaimed the State of Israel a reality. It was not an easy birth. World War II had just ended, but the great Cold War standoff had already begun. In March 1948, the Communists seized power in Czechoslovakia; in June the Soviets would blockade Berlin. In Palestine, after months of skirmishing between Arabs and Jews following the United Nations' November 1947 partition plan, seven Arab armies prepared to invade as the British withdrew. The Jewish people were well versed in the problems of statelessness. Sadly, in finding redemption, the Jewish people would discover many of the problems that come with having a state.

Israel's great tragedy, of course, is the continuing conflict with her neighbors, an Arab world nearly half a billion strong. The clash of Arab and Jewish nationalisms – and the ironic jumpstart Zionism gave to Palestinian nationalism – has spilled rivers of blood. Millions have suffered along with the Arabs and Jews, especially since the 1970s when the scourge of terrorism exported Middle Eastern murder and fear throughout the world.

We historians know that where you begin a story often reveals what you think the ending should be. Consider the Bill Clinton-Monica Lewinsky sex scandal. Clinton's supporters, who saw a right-wing conspiracy afoot, began their tale with the Republican attacks on Clinton, hoping to end with a rejection of such partisan rumor-mongering. By contrast, Clinton's opponents began the tale with Clinton's oath of office, which they thought he violated, or with the Paula Jones sexual harassment case, which suggested a broader pattern of behavior that justified impeaching and convicting the President.

Palestinians who deny the legitimacy of the State of Israel, and the Jewish tie to the homeland, often begin the tale of what they call *"al Naqba,"* the "catastrophe" of 1948, in 1945, with the end of the Holocaust. This narrative implies that the Europeans colonized Palestine for the Jews to compensate for European guilt over German war crimes. Such a story ignores nearly a century of Zionist ideology, immigration and infrastructure that made Israel a viable state when it was founded in 1948. Such myth-making ignores centuries of continuous settlement and millennia of engagement with the land. Such tall tales treat every Palestinian as a "native" – even those who drifted in from Jordan, Egypt, Syria or Lebanon as a result of the Zionist-triggered economic boom – and dismisses every Israeli as an interloper, a colonizer, a Western imperialist, even if a family could trace its roots to the Second Temple times.

At the end of the day, peace will be elusive unless and until people on both sides can acknowledge two historical realities. First, both peoples have multi-dimensional and deep ties to this land. Second, just what this land constitutes has varied over time, making authoritative statements about just what is "occupied" or "liberated" absurd.

FLUID BORDERS: THE 1921 AND 1947 PARTITIONS

For starters, historically, Biblically, the land of Canaan, the land promised to the Jewish people in the Bible, is much larger than the land mass currently under discussion – it encompasses the EAST bank of the Jordan River, what is today the Hashemite Kingdom of Jordan. Saying this, acknowledging this historical reality, does not imply that Jordan should cease to exist or that Israel should expand east – it simply illustrates the fluidity of borders in that region, and the resulting confusion, and anger.

The modern map of the Middle East dates from the 1920s – when the British became the latest in a series of imperial powers to control this critical crossroads. Since Roman times, the land of Israel had been quite the historical way station – host to the Byzantines, the Persians, the Byzantines again, the Muslim Ummayad Dynasty, the Crusaders, the Muslims again, the Mamluks, the Ottoman Turks, and finally, after the first World War, the British. Note that Islam emerged as a religion only in the seventh century C.E., around the time Persians were fighting with

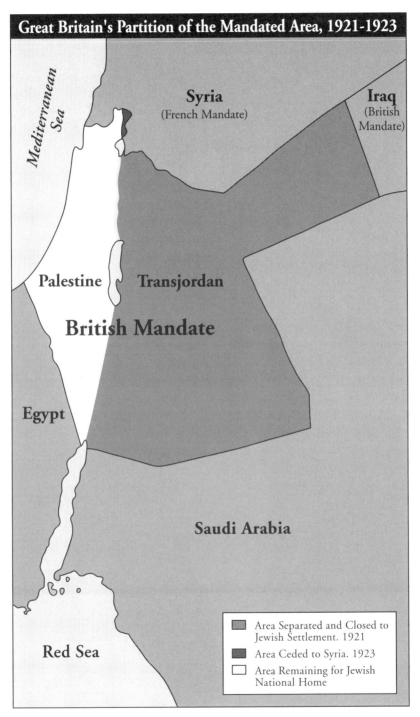

Great Britain's Partition of the Mandated Area, 1921-1923

Mediterranean Sea

Syria
(French Mandate)

Iraq
(British Mandate)

Palestine **Transjordan**

British Mandate

Egypt

Saudi Arabia

Red Sea

Area Separated and Closed to Jewish Settlement. 1921

Area Ceded to Syria. 1923

Area Remaining for Jewish National Home

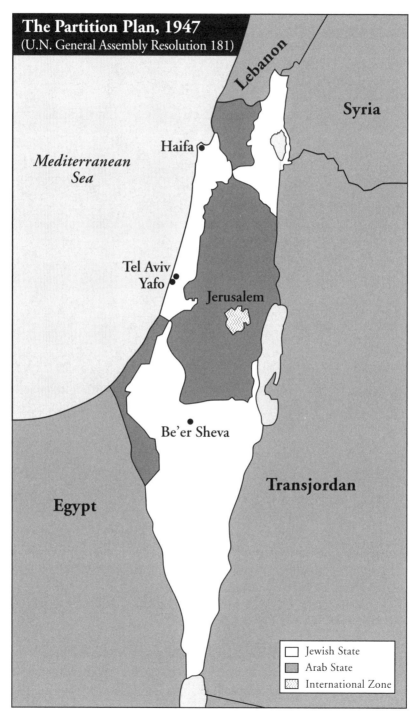

The Partition Plan, 1947
(U.N. General Assembly Resolution 181)

Lebanon

Syria

Mediterranean
Sea

Haifa

Tel Aviv
Yafo

Jerusalem

Be'er Sheva

Transjordan

Egypt

☐ Jewish State
▨ Arab State
▨ International Zone

Byzantines for control of Palestine. It was only in 660 that the Moslem Caliph Abd el Malik built the al-Aqsa Mosque, followed thirty-one years later by the Dome of the Rock, on the site of the *Bet HaMikdash*, the Holy Temple. This construction project followed standard Middle Eastern practice, which was to hijack conquered peoples' holy sites for your own use. Over a thousand years later, Moslems obviously feel a strong tie to that spot, which their tradition suggests was where the Prophet Mohammed began his ascent to heaven. However, in these days, when Arab leaders echoing Yasir Arafat negate any Jewish tie to these holy places, it behooves us to acknowledge that the Jewish tie not just predates the Moslem tie, but focused Moslem attention on the site in the first place.

The revolving door of empires that swept through the land highlights the miraculous nature of the current Israeli regime. The land of Israel is not Germany or Italy, China or Japan, whose peoples can speak of centuries of more or less continuous native autonomy. Palestine has long been orphaned, making it both ironic and predictable that two peoples are sure they have exclusive claim to the land. This history of instability also explains why Israelis are so unnerved by the many surrounding countries calling for the destruction of the Jewish state. The sensitivity to the vagaries of Middle Eastern history, combined with the awareness of the many tragedies of Jewish history, offers sobering lessons – and dire warnings.

When the British swept into Palestine after World War I, the map they drew divided the land into a Jewish area west of the Jordan river, and a Jewish-free zone, east of the river, which became Transjordan – Jordan today. A quarter of a century later, in 1947, the United Nations offered another partition in an attempt to mediate between the Jews and the Arabs – they did not call themselves Palestinians then. The Israeli leaders grudgingly accepted it, despite it being unworkable. The Arabs did not, and immediately launched guerilla attacks on Jewish targets up and down the country.

As a result, when David Ben-Gurion read Israel's Proclamation of Independence on May 14, 1948, he extended a hand of peace to the Arabs, even as the war clouds formed. Unfortunately, the young country would experience a major war in each decade from the 1940s through the 1980s. In 1948, it was the War for Independence, a war Israel had tried to avert by accepting the 1947 partition. The UN plan created a Swiss cheese country, where pockets of Jewish settlement went to Israel, neighboring Arabs carved out their state, and Jerusalem was supposed to be under

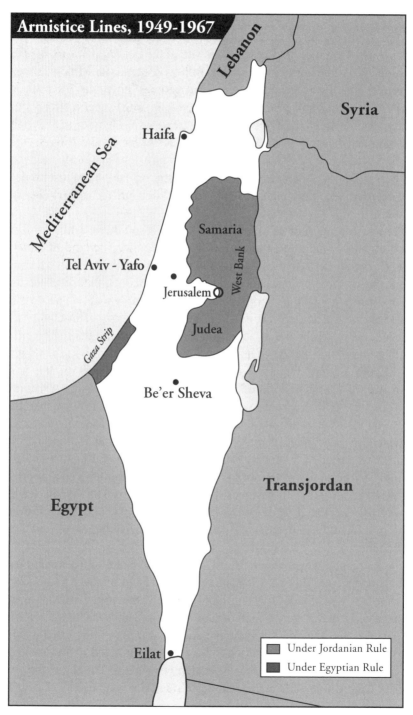

Armistice Lines, 1949-1967

Lebanon

Syria

Mediterranean Sea

Haifa

Samaria

West Bank

Tel Aviv - Yafo

Jerusalem

Judea

Gaza Strip

Be'er Sheva

Transjordan

Egypt

Eilat

Under Jordanian Rule
Under Egyptian Rule

international control. The 1948 war allowed Israel to forge a more viable land mass and to seize most of Jerusalem. But the victory came at great cost – six thousand Jews died, out of a total population of only six hundred thousand. Some Holocaust refugees went directly – and anonymously – from boats delivering them from Displaced Persons camps into battle, and then into a grave. And the Jewish Quarter of Jerusalem, including the Western Wall, fell into Arab hands.

Eight years later, in 1956, Israel seized the Sinai peninsula and the Suez Canal from Egypt. The lightning strike was coordinated with the British and the French. The Europeans disliked Egypt's seizure of the Suez Canal and the Israelis were fed up with persistent cross-border attacks by Arab Fedayeen guerillas. The United States, however, had not been informed of the plan, and forced Israel to withdraw.

THE SIX DAY MIRACLE, 1967

It is hard now to fathom just how fragile Israel seemed in those days, how close it always appeared to annihilation. In May 1967 Jews throughout the world feared a second Holocaust when the Egyptian leader Gamel Abdul Nasser blockaded the Straits of Tiran, Israel's southern waterway. Nasser had forged a pan-Arab alliance, and the airways sizzled with Arab promises that the Jews would be swept into the sea. The Israelis prepared for the worst – including having female soldiers begin preparations to turn public parks into mass grave sites. ("I still have nightmares about it," one of the soldiers recently told me.) In June, Israel launched a preemptive strike. In six miraculous days, Israel captured the Sinai peninsula from Egypt, the Golan Heights from Syria, and the rest of Jerusalem and the entire West Bank from Jordan.

The victory was emotionally and strategically monumental. Holding the Sinai offered Israelis a huge buffer zone between them and their largest and most powerful enemies, the Egyptians. Taking the Golan Heights freed Israeli farmers and city folk who lived in the valley below the Golan from the potshots Syrian soldiers enjoyed taking at them over the years. And conquering the West Bank gave Israel a more natural border, the Jordan River, which harked back to the 1921 British partition.

Of course, the West Bank also came with a huge unhappy population. Ironically, because this territory would become the great obstacle to peace thirty years later, we must remember that Israel never intended to attack Jordan in 1967. On the 5th of June, even as Jordanian shells rained down on Israeli West Jerusalem, Prime Minister Levi Eshkol sent a message to King Hussein via General Odd Bull, the Norwegian chief of staff of UNTSO, the United Nations Truce Supervisory Organization. Eshkol promised: "We shall not initiate any action whatsoever against Jordan. However, should Jordan open hostilities, we shall react with all our might, and the king will have to bear the full responsibility for the consequences." Hussein had already turned over his forces to the command of an Egyptian general. The Jordanian king would indeed mourn the consequences for the rest of his life – and did take full responsibility. Even Israel's historical revisionists do not doubt the sincerity of Prime Minister Eshkol's pledge.

The plucky Israelis' legendary victory delighted much of the world; the Arab world seethed. Two months later, on August 28, dejected Arab leaders began their first summit since the defeat, in Khartoum, the capital of Sudan. The Arab leaders vowed no recognition, no negotiation, and no peace with Israel. The infamous "three noes of Khartoum" would set the tone of Arab-Israeli relations for many years thereafter.

The Six Day War also resulted in the often-invoked, rarely-followed, UN Security Council Resolution 242. The UN identified two conditions as essential to a Middle East peace. One, "withdrawal of Israeli armed forces from territories occupied in the recent conflict," and, two, affirmation of the right of every state "to live in peace within secure and recognized boundaries free from threats or acts of force." Note that the carefully crafted document called for "withdrawal ... from territories," not "all" or "the" territories. Six years later, Resolution 338 would reaffirm the 242 framework.

Meanwhile, using the same rationale of creating facts on the ground that worked so effectively before 1948, Israel began populating the West

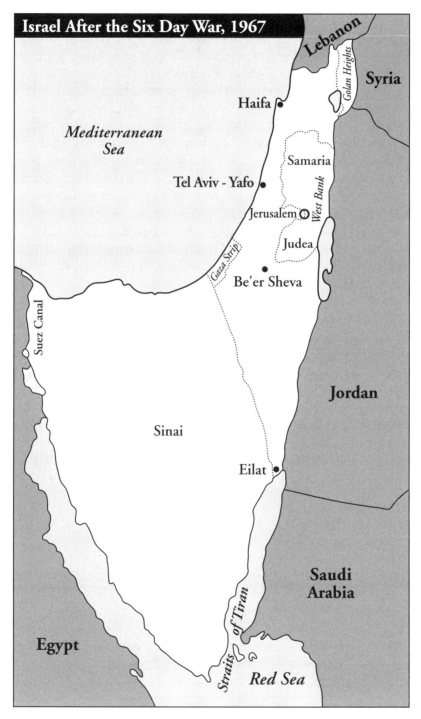

Israel After the Six Day War, 1967

Lebanon

Syria

Golan Heights

Haifa

Mediterranean
Sea

Samaria

Tel Aviv - Yafo

West Bank

Jerusalem

Judea

Gaza Strip

Be'er Sheva

Suez Canal

Jordan

Sinai

Eilat

Saudi
Arabia

Egypt

Straits of Tiran

Red Sea

Bank and Gaza with Jewish settlements. To some, this was the ultimate Zionist act, the fulfillment of God's promise and Jewish destiny; to others, this was the ultimate folly, the creation of obstacles to peace and a daily affront to the Palestinian population there.

Love them or hate them, four types of settlements developed:

– sentimental settlements, pre-'48 Jewish communities destroyed during the 1948 war – such as the Gush Etzion bloc – or earlier – such as Hebron – now restored, often by children of the original inhabitants.

– security settlements, following the Allon Plan and other strategies, to create outposts along the Jordanian border and at key military junctures.

– suburban settlements, within commuting distance of Tel Aviv and Jerusalem, to siphon off some demographic pressure choking the middle of the country, while moving Israelis to the disputed lands.

– salvation settlements, initiated by Gush Emunim and other diehards, to fulfill their understanding of God's decree to restore a Jewish presence in what they called Judea and Samaria.

By 2001, there would be over 200,000 Jews scattered in settlements ranging from small collections of housing trailers to booming and sophisticated cities.

Even as this Six Day War victory solidified the Israeli soldier's reputation as a secular superman, Israelis remained very conscious of their role in Jewish history. They saw the liberation of Jerusalem as a final righting of an ancient wrong. And after centuries of having Jews caricatured as weaklings, Israelis quite enjoyed their new reputation.

STUMBLING TOWARD PEACE, 1973 to 1993

Perhaps the Israelis enjoyed their reputation a bit too much. Seven years after the Six Day War, in October 1973, the Arabs surprised the Israelis. The war began on Yom Kippur, the Jews' holiest day, but it did seem that too many Israelis had grown too complacent.

Israel eventually repulsed the Syrian army in the North and the Egyptian army in the South. But it was a painful victory. Nearly three thousand young Israelis died, and nearly nine thousand were wounded. Moreover, the myth of Israeli invincibility suffered a deathblow.

The Yom Kippur War marked a major turning point in Israeli history. With that war, Israelis discovered complexity, ambiguity, ambivalence, and doubt. The Lebanon War of 1982 lacked the clarity and the *"ein breira,"* no choice, nature of the other wars. The Palestine Liberation

Organization, after launching a series of murderous raids in Israel and abroad in the 1970s, had established "a state within a state," north of Israel in Southern Lebanon. Most Israelis wanted to end the border incursions from the north – they disagreed, however, on the effectiveness of the military tactics, and many were disturbed by the ambiguous war aims. The Lebanon war proved triply traumatic, as Israeli tactics shifted from marching on Beirut to hunkering down in a security zone for the next eighteen years, as the casualty rate soared, and as Israel's reputation was soiled by their Christian Lebanese allies' massacre of Palestinian refugees at Sabra and Shatila.

By 1987, Israel was stuck fighting an Arab uprising in the West Bank and Gaza, the "Intifada." This prolonged non-war of riots, rocks, and rubber bullets, with high stakes and much confusion, demoralized soldiers trained to fight in conventional battles. More and more Israelis felt increasingly burdened by the continuing mess in the territories.

Ironically, the first possibilities of real peace emerged out of this miasma. The Egyptian president who surprised Israel in 1973, Anwar el-Sadat, visited Jerusalem in 1977 and signed the Camp David Treaty in 1979, winning back the entire Sinai through negotiation. Similarly, the 1993 Oslo Accords, heralding a major transformation in Palestinian and Israeli relations, were rooted in the Palestinians' pride after the "Intifada," and the Israeli exhaustion with managing hundreds of thousands of Palestinians who had their own nationalist aspirations.

OSLO DREAMS AND NIGHTMARES

The Oslo Accords created a complicated, gradual framework for peace negotiations. The hope for compromise seemed to lie in granting the Palestinians control over as many of their people as possible, while satisfying Israel's security concerns with control over strategic areas. The accords were supposed to be a confidence-building process, encouraging cooperation over the easy things – withdrawal from the largest cities and much of the Gaza Strip – while building good will for tackling the thornier issues – such as what to do with the settlements Israelis had established – or reestablished – since 1967, what to do with the Palestinian demand for all refugees to return to their original homes, and what to do about Jerusalem.

What the Palestinians called their "right of return" was indeed a complicated and volatile sticking point. One of the strange things about this call was that Palestinians were demanding the right to return to what, with a two-state solution, would be the Jewish state. And there was the rub. Even many Israeli peaceniks recognized this ploy as a Trojan horse which could change the demographic realities of Israel with a wave of Palestinians seeking citizenship in Israel in order to undermine Israel. It was hard not to conclude that the call for a right of return was in fact an expression of the Palestinians' maximalist demand to destroy Israel rather than compromise. The "right of return" upped the ante from a conflict of borders, which can be solved, to a mutually exclusive clash of national claims to the same piece of real estate, which cannot be solved.

Unfortunately, the beautiful headlines of Oslo, that by the year 2000 the Palestinian Authority would have control over ninety-five percent of the Palestinian population, and that leaders on both sides were interacting with each other regularly, were upstaged by the ugliness that festered – bloody bus bombings in Jerusalem and Tel Aviv, a right-wing Israeli militant's assassination of Prime Minister Yitzhak Rabin, the continuing indoctrination of hatred for the "Zionist enemy" in Palestinian schools and camps – often unknowingly bankrolled by Israel or other peace-seeking partners.

In July, 2000, Bill Clinton called Prime Minister Ehud Barak and Yasir Arafat together at Camp David, hoping to replicate the magic that had worked between Israel and Egypt. Barak offered sweeping concessions – going further than any Israeli leader had ever done, and probably further than the Israeli electorate would have accepted. Even so, Arafat rejected it, returned home a hero, and unleashed a second "Intifada" two months later – what Israelis uncomfortably call *"haMatzav,"* the situation.

And what an uncomfortable situation it is – terrorism has yet again unleashed its ugly head in the Middle East. The months after the Palestinians rejected Oslo were filled with one horrible moment after another – the lynching of two reservists who lost their way in Ramallah, the mutilation of two young boys skipping school in Tekoah, the sniper's bullets that killed a hematologist here, a peacenik there, and the bombings that murdered five in front of a shopping mall in Netanyah, fifteen eating pizza at Sbarro's in Jerusalem, or twenty-one young revellers outside a Tel Aviv night club. Every one of these people had a name, a story – Vadim,

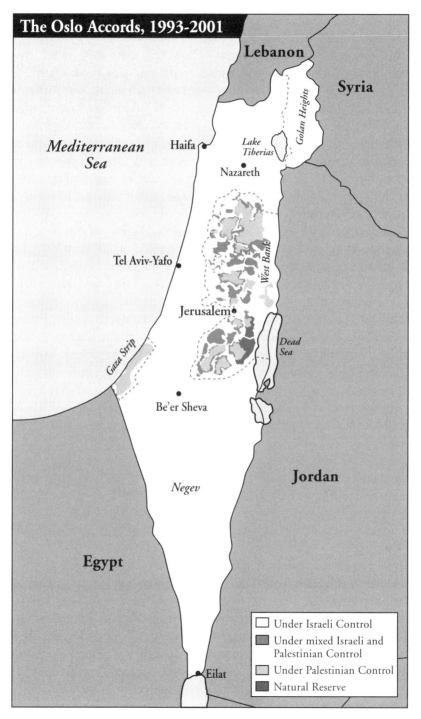

The Oslo Accords, 1993-2001

Lebanon

Syria

Mediterranean
Sea

Haifa

Golan Heights

Lake
Tiberias

Nazareth

Tel Aviv-Yafo

West Bank

Jerusalem

Gaza Strip

Dead
Sea

Be'er Sheva

Jordan

Negev

Egypt

Eilat

☐ Under Israeli Control
◼ Under mixed Israeli and
Palestinian Control
☐ Under Palestinian Control
◼ Natural Reserve

Koby, Shmuel, Shachar, Ayelet. Each victim represented a world destroyed, dozens of family and friends devastated.

Reflecting the power disparity within the territories, many more Palestinians than Israelis died, especially at first, generating great anger throughout the West Bank and Gaza, too. Israeli spokesmen noted accurately that many of the young Palestinians killed were functioning as human shields, throwing stones in front for the cameras, while grownups shot bullets from behind. These political and strategic arguments missed the human dimension, the multiple personal tragedies for mothers and fathers, wives and children, burying their kin. Each side ended up with its martyrs, young and old, and each incident, on either side, ratcheted up the tensions and the hatred, the doubts and the despair.

The death of Oslo destroyed many illusions. Yasir Arafat proved to be no Nelson Mandela. The Palestinian guerilla could not hang up his holster and become a statesman. Modernizers who presume that a little bit of progress, some education and some prosperity, will turn every society into a middle-class democracy, had to rethink their assumptions. Palestinian society has a small aristocratic elite controlling a huge impoverished mass. And studies showed that, contrary to the conventional wisdom, suicide bombers were often married, employed and well educated. Furthermore, Israelis from the left, right, and center discovered that this problem would not be solved so smoothly, or so peacefully.

By spring of 2002, many Israelis felt embittered, justifiably. They had traded land for peace under Oslo. They had brought Arafat back from exile. They had offered more land at Camp David, 2000. They, including Ariel Sharon, had endured eighteen months of murder with restraint. Finally, desperate, they felt compelled to invade the West Bank after the Passover Massacre. Even then, they tried to minimize Palestinian civilian casualties by fighting house to house instead of bombing block by block. Nevertheless, the world branded Israel provocative, aggressive, and guilty of war crimes.

It is easy to get depressed in the Middle East – but it is necessary to be hopeful. Twenty-five years ago, peace with Egypt and Jordan was unfathomable. Less than ten years ago, serious negotiations with the Palestinians and the Syrians seemed to be a pipe dream. Every day, each in their own sometimes cantankerous way, Israelis pray desperately for peace. Remarkable progress has indeed occurred – although much more remains to be done. Perhaps, some day soon, the entire world, friend and foe alike, will chime in after the Israelis' collective prayer for Shalom, Salaam, Peace, with the ancient affirmation "Amen."

CHAPTER 9

NORMALCY:
LIFE IN MODERN ISRAEL:
THE BLESSINGS – AND CURSE – OF POWER

An artist friend of mine painted a picture nearly a year after the Camp David negotiations failed, ten months into the Palestinian riots against Oslo. Good liberal Jew that he is, his picture had to be even-handed. A dove of peace hovered unsteadily above the canvas, which was divided into the blue and white representing the Israeli flag, and the black and white representing the Palestinian keffiyah. Bisecting the picture horizontally was a balance beam of sorts – evenly pitched, of course. On the blue and white side were more bullets and fewer dead doves; on the black and white site were fewer bullets and more dead doves. "The Palestinians have lost more people in the fighting," my friend explained, "and, of course, the Israelis have more guns."

I found my friend's accounting doubly fascinating. For starters, many Israelis I know do not perceive themselves to have the upper hand in the insane arms race of the Middle East. For, unlike my artist friend – and most Westerners – they count in the armies, and arms, of Syria, Lebanon, Hezbollah, Iran, Libya, and other countries that regularly call for Israel's destruction. Some would throw Egypt and Jordan into the equation as well. Just whom you count depends on whom – and how much – you trust.

Moreover, I could not help reflecting about how ambivalent we Jews are about the power we – and our Israeli cousins – wield. For years, I have prided myself on NOT being a Holocaust-obsessed Jew, on NOT seeing anti-Semites behind every corner, on NOT dividing the world into us (the good Jews), our self-hating Jewish critics, and the goyim who want to keep us weak and dependent. And yet, while I do not believe that most of the world believes that the only good kind of a Jew is a dead Jew, I am growing to fear that, to too many people, the best kind of a Jew is a weak Jew.

I remember the media coverage during the 1991 Gulf War, when Israelis acted with superhuman restraint as Saddam Hussein's SCUD rockets rained down on Tel Aviv and its suburbs. For the first time in a long time, coverage of Israel was positive again. Cameramen gleefully photographed the middle-class houses – which looked like those of the viewers' back home – reduced to rubble. One CBS News report ended with appropriately dramatic commentary, zeroing in on a destroyed bathroom, zooming in for a final shot of a broken toilet with a crumpled Israeli flag floating in the remaining water.

Unfortunately, the twentieth century demonstrated far too dramatically what happens to Jews without power. The Zionist revolution, which rebelled against the powerlessness of the European Jew, was too weak, too tardy, and too avant-garde to save the six million. Israel then emerged as a plucky survivor – committed to Jewish empowerment, but overshadowed by the Arab masses.

POWERFUL BUT NOT POPULAR

The sad truth is that Israel was most popular when it was most vulnerable, just as Jews were most popular after the ashes of Auschwitz exposed their great vulnerability. Philip Roth's Portnoy and others could be dazzled by the macho Israelis when they were outnumbered and outgunned – but the more powerful and prosperous Israel became over the years, the less popular it was, among Jews and non-Jews alike.

In fairness, this problem goes way beyond psychology and sociology. Israel, like every other country, is far from perfect – and Israel has bumbled with the best of them. The former Israeli foreign minister Abba Eban may have been correct that the Palestinians never "miss an opportunity to miss an opportunity," but the Israelis have missed chances as well. Israel, as a country, should have been dramatically more generous with its Arab population. Israeli leaders at various times could have done more to build bridges to their Arab neighbors. And, while there were good rationales for some settlements in the West Bank and Gaza, the dramatic investment of so much money into so many settlements over so many years was foolhardy and counterproductive.

Also, in fairness, it is not just "the world" or "Diaspora Jews" who have been ambivalent about power – Israelis themselves have their baggage as well. Not every problem can be solved with chutzpah; not every conventional system should be circumvented. The tragic collapse due to shoddy engineering of the Versailles wedding hall floor in Jerusalem, amid the terror of 2001, prompted a most necessary round of soul-searching wherein Israelis debated the dangers of being too clever by half and always disdaining conventional rules and methods.

ISRAELI SOCIETY: SEARCHING FOR A VISION

The truth is that Israel is a society that is both remarkably united – especially when attacked – and pathologically divided. Even as they continue searching for and arguing about peace, Israelis are also mourning their unfulfilled dreams, and their failure to unite behind one social vision. Western Ashkenazi Jews complain that the country is too Levantine, too unruly; Eastern Sephardi Jews bristle at many slights, real and imagined. Orthodox Jews wail that the state is not sufficiently religious, while Socialists lament that the collectivist impulse died as the land of kibbutzim and Jaffa oranges became the land of shopping malls and cellular phones.

Such conflicts are inevitable, not only because of the distractions of the Arab-Israeli conflict, but because of the country's complicated ideological and demographic legacies. Israel has a European head grafted on a Middle Eastern body. The ideology of the Sephardic majority of Jewish refugees from Arab lands – a passionate mix of traditionalism and survivalism – coexists uncomfortably with the more secular, theoretical Zionism of Israel's founders.

Zionism at once rejected and fulfilled Europe's great nineteenth-century ideologies. Many Zionists wanted to realize all the ideas they imbibed, regardless of the contradictions between, say, liberalism and Socialism, or rationalism and nationalism. Yet that other great "ism" – anti-Semitism – destroyed Jewish life in Europe. The result was an explosive brew of idealism and bitterness, especially after Germany harnessed the power of science and nationalism to create a Holocaust.

Amid the drumbeat of Arab-Israeli wars, a contrapuntal rhythm of economic, social, and political progress shaped the new Jewish state. In the 1940s and 1950s, Israelis endured the days of *tsenah*, of belt-tightening, as they absorbed thousands of immigrants, and defined their new state. In the 1960s, Israel was one of the world's great economic success stories, demonstrating how a young country could develop rapidly and relatively smoothly. By the late 1970s, the economy had faltered, and a devastating inflation began. When Americans were complaining about inflation rates of twelve and eighteen percent a year, Israelis were experiencing that per month. As they pulled out of this great inflation, Israelis became increasingly Americanized. Consumerism became the great theme of the 1980s, even as high tech became the great engine of prosperity – and a magic wand transforming the society – in the 1990s.

ISRAEL BEHIND THE HEADLINES

More than most people, Israelis recognize that, as the poet Natan Alterman and the statesman Chaim Weizmann taught, no state is given on a silver platter. Each year Israelis compartmentalize their feelings by observing *Yom HaZikaron*, their somber memorial day for some twenty thousand fallen comrades, before celebrating *Yom HaAtzmaut*, their festive independence day.

Just as the sirens marking the end of the mourning usher in twenty-four hours of joy, so, too, must we acknowledge that there is much more to celebrate than to mourn. Viewing all of Israeli history through the prism of the Arab-Israeli conflict is as distorting as reducing all of Canadian history to the French-English struggle or all of American history to the black-white struggle. The Israel behind the headlines is a country experienced at a high decibel and a hyperactive pace. It is also a stunning and tranquil land, a modern megalopolis where major pastimes include hikes in the barren yet vibrant desert, archaeological digs uncovering proof of Jews' deep roots in their homeland, and the quest for the most beautiful perch from which to see the sun set over Jerusalem.

Jerusalem best illustrates these odd linkages of the old and the new, the poetic and the prosaic. A city pulsing with love and hate, its skyline tells the story of the Jewish people's three-thousand-year-old romance with this land, and the land's pivotal role in world history. The brilliant golden Dome of the Rock – a Muslim shrine on the Jewish Temple Mount where Jesus preached – dominates the horizon. The ancient walled city with its narrow streets, exotic smells, and enduring enmities balances out the gleaming hotels, corporate towers, and government buildings to the west.

Perhaps the defining image of the New Jerusalem – and the new state – comes from the 1967 Six Day War, when young, mostly secular, warriors in full battle gear prayed, cried, and blew the ceremonial ram's horn, the *shofar*, at the site of their freshly liberated Western Wall, the living link through ancient stones to their Holy Temple. Although today Jerusalem most often appears on television as the site of riots and bombs, for twenty years, from its reunification in 1967 to the start of the Palestinian riots of

1987, it served as a model of Arab and Jewish cooperation, guided by one of Israel's most visionary leaders, Mayor Teddy Kollek.

In fact, in its short life, Israel has produced a colorful crop of leaders. The larger-than-life problems facing their small country have made the leaders seem larger than life – to their supporters, at home and in North America. The country's first president, the goateed scientist Chaim Weizmann, represented the European cosmopolitanism imported to the old-new land, just as the country's first prime minister, the gruff, rumpled, plebeian ideologue, David Ben-Gurion, embodied the pioneers' determination to reinvent themselves while making the desert bloom. In the 1960s and 1970s, the one-eyed hero Moshe Dayan symbolized the new Jewish supermen rejecting their historic role as victims, even as the urbane Abba Eban kept up the cosmopolitan tradition and the grandmotherly Golda Meir hid her toughness behind the false nostalgia for Eastern Europe's Fiddler on the Roof ghetto life. In the 1980s, the bespectacled Polish refugee Menachem Begin rejected the niceties of the world that had savagely betrayed his people, while injecting into the political mainstream an appreciation for the Sephardic community and for Jewish tradition. The farsighted Begin was bold enough to bomb Iraq's atomic plant without the world's permission and courageous enough to accept Anwar Sadat's challenge to risk trading land for peace. Most recently, the Yin and Yang of the Labor Party shaped Israel's destiny. The Polish-born statesman Shimon Peres dreamed about a peace treaty transforming Israel into the Switzerland of the Middle East, while Yitzhak Rabin, the first prime minister born on Israeli soil, the brusque soldier martyred as a peacemaker, rooted his dreams of peace in strategic realities.

Israel's larger-than-life problems have also produced a vicious and fragmented political culture, wherein political enemies branded these same leaders charlatans or fools. Their respective opponents blasted Ben-Gurion as a dictator, Dayan as a self-promoter, Golda as a provincial, Begin as a throwback, Rabin as a clod, Peres as a dreamer. In fact, both Peres and Eban proved consistently more popular in Europe and North America than at home, while the hard-drinking, chain-smoking, caustic Rabin became known as the warm, fuzzy, grandfatherly peacemaker only after his murder.

THE INGATHERING OF THE EXILES

These leaders suffered tremendous domestic headaches exacerbated by the constant international crises. Their country's greatest accomplishment has been its absorption of more than two-and-a-half million immigrants.

After two thousand years of wandering, the Jewish people's return home created a welcome refuge from oppression. A country founded on the ashes of Auschwitz has offered all Jews an invaluable life insurance policy – and many have felt compelled to cash in. Since the 1940s, from Yemen to Syria, from Iran to Morocco, the eight hundred thousand Jews expelled after hundreds of years of living in Arab and North African countries found a home in Israel. Today, sixty thousand Ethiopian Jews and one million Russians are rebuilding their lives, and revolutionizing their new home, as the "ingathering of the exiles" continues.

Israel's five million Jews and one million Arab citizens live in an odd mix of Athens and Sparta, a democratic oasis and a powerful fortress. This regional superpower is the only democracy in the Middle East. It leads the world in per-capita consumption of newspapers, books, and concert tickets while also being one of the world's leading weapons producers. The contradictions well up in the symphony of sounds that define the country – the ubiquitous ring-ring-ring of the cellular phones, the staccato rat-tat-tat of speech patterns on the street, the hypnotic whoosh… whoosh… of the Mediterranean's waves, the warbly awaa-awaa-awaa calls of the muezzin to prayer, the lyrical hey-hey-hey of robust Jewish children at play, the throbbing ba-dom, ba-dom, ba-dom of Tel Aviv's discos, the clanging bang-bang-bang of cranes, the heart-stopping pop-pop-pop sonic boom of maneuvering fighter jets, the aggravating honk-honk-honk of massive traffic jams, the furious *kama?–kama?–kama?* clamor of the pungent open-air markets, the shrill blah-blah-blah shouting in the *Knesset,* the paralyzing beep-beep-beep at the top of every hour heralding the latest radio news, and the ethereal hush that rolls over religious and secular homes every Friday night as the Sabbath descends.

This frustrating, inspiring, ancient, cutting-edge, old-fashioned, wide-open, bustling, spiritual, material, religious, secular mishmash of a place has dominated the Jewish imagination for the last half century. For all its faults, Israel remains the nerve center of the Jewish world, the heart, the soul of this people. Israel is the fountainhead, the source of pride, a model of electric Jewish living, a cause for exasperation, a cause celebre. It has given Jews a sense of normalcy, a country of their own replete with a flag, an army, and an unwieldy bureaucracy, as well as a sense of abnormality, a protectiveness, insecurity, and indignation that this little David has endured so much from its neighboring Goliaths. Some Jews who have never visited wonder what is so special; most who have visited gush about the ancient sites, the sense of community, the intimacy, the spirituality, the drama, then simply say, "experience it yourself."

THE WEST'S JUVENILE DELINQUENT OR
ITS GOLDEN BOY?

The compelling and tragic modern story rooted in the rocky soil that spawned Judaism, Christianity and Islam gives this tiny country a disproportionate role in the Western imagination – and among Western reporters. Zionism should be considered very PC, politically correct. This long-victimized people not only returned to its ancient homeland, but has been remarkably trendy over the past half-century. In 1948, the year Mahatma Gandhi was assassinated, the country symbolized the new post-colonial world order as new nation states formed in Asia, the Middle East, and, eventually, Africa. In the 1950s, although the country was never the big kibbutz mythmakers suggested, the Labor party establishment that ruled Israel until 1977 created a model social-welfare state, with minimal unemployment and maximum taxation. By the 1960s, despite its youth and poverty, this progressive country was sending foreign aid to struggling African nations – until Arab oil money had the Israelis banished from Africa after the 1973 war.

Today, the kibbutznik has become a programmer and Israel could be the poster child for the new information society: a high tech enclave with few natural resources that is rapidly shedding its statist economic yoke, for better and for worse. While the "Asian Tiger" economies whimpered, Israel's economic miracle continued to roar throughout the 1990s. And throughout the 1990s, more Israelis prospered as never before, but the gap between rich and poor mushroomed as well.

Of course, some of the ideals that made Israel so attractive in the 1950s and 1960s have faded. Nationalism, once seen as the vehicle of communal salvation, is now often associated with chauvinism, extremism, and violence, while Socialism has been flung on the dung heap of history. But more than anything else, it is the Middle East conflict that has cast Israel as the world's juvenile delinquent rather than its golden boy.

Israelis have fulfilled the Zionist dream, tasting of power, and discovering it tasted good. They have often used that power for good – to resettle the unwanted, including Vietnamese boat people; to send medical assistance to Rwanda during the tribal massacres, earthquake aid to Turkey, search and retrieval teams to bombed-out U.S. embassies in Africa. It is quite ironic – and heroic – that *Tsahal*, the Israel Defense Forces – the arm of society charged with fighting the ugliness in the Middle East – is also associated with these idealistic initiatives. It is one of the advantages of having a citizen's army. It is one of the payoffs from having a Jewish army. It also explains how during the bloody, painful, often door-to-door fighting in the West Bank in April 2002 many Israeli soldiers tried to be as humane as possible. In Tulkarm, some reservists raised 1500 shekels to help a Palestinian family repair a damaged wall; in Bethlehem, another group raised 2000 shekels to compensate a family whose house they used; in Jenin, Israeli doctors ministered to wounded Palestinians, even those who had Islamic Jihad tatoos on their bodies. Obviously, other moments were more brutal, and some soldiers behaved badly, but such acts of kindness testified to the kind of army *Tsahal* wants to be, the kind of country Israel tries to be – and so often is. The world had yet another opportunity to witness the Israeli Army at its absolute best during the difficult Gaza disengagement in mid-August, 2005. Wherever one stood on the complicated question of Ariel Sharon's decision to dismantle the Gaza settlements, move 8,500 people and redraw the Middle East map without any Palestinian concessions, most saluted the army's civility, efficiency, humanity and spiritual power. Just as, two weeks later, the American Army's field hospital at New Orleans' airport distinguished itself by saving lives during the Katrina hurricane disaster, treating approximately 50,000 patients within a few days, the Israeli Army's empathy and restraint during the Gaza evacuation illustrated how to avoid conflict peacefully rather than pursuing the expected military approach of resolving conflict violently.

That August, under Gaza's blazing desert sun, after journalists and extremists on both sides had predicted settler violence and massive military disobedience, Israel's soldiers enveloped Gush Katif's settlers in a warm, firm and very effective hug. Resurrecting the happy stereotypes of the 1960s, the sensitive soldiers illustrated the moral power of a citizens' army filled with Sabras revealing soft interiors behind their prickly shells. As Yisrael Meir Lau, the former Ashkenazi Chief Rabbi said, "They faced each other, evacuators and evacuees, but not one drop of blood fell to the ground - only the tears they shed together fell, blessing the land."

Alas, the tragic truth is that as the tensions festered in the West Bank and Gaza, as generation after generation of young Jews and Palestinians faced off, as Sharon's government had to deploy the IDF to implement its disengagement decision, Israelis also learned that the exercise of power can leave a bitter aftertaste. That lesson, like all the other lessons, is a lesson of real life – the blessing and curse of power is indeed one of the many mixed blessings the Jewish people experienced in returning to history, in escaping from the unreality and weakness of ghetto life, and exercising some control over their own destiny, and that of others.

PART 3

CRISIS ZIONISM:
MUGGED BY REALITY -
THE UNIVERSITY OF LIFE

The lessons of our history resonate today. Life is not a spectator sport. To protect ourselves, let alone to effectuate change, we must engage, we must act. If we do not shape history, history will nevertheless shape us.

But even if we act, even when we dream, reality sometimes proves sobering. The Zionist dream did not deliver all that it promised – and the Land of Israel proved to be a lot more complicated than most Zionists expected. Similarly today, the dream of peace, the Oslo venture, did not deliver all that it promised. We must, however, continue to pursue peace, even as we defend ourselves, our state, our common dreams. It is sad but true, we need to arm ourselves intellectually, ideologically, emotionally, for the difficult days ahead. Crisis Zionism may not be what we hoped for, but we cannot wish the challenges away – and must meet them directly.

CHAPTER 10

NATIONALISM 101:
WHY ZIONISM IS NOT RACISM

A joke that circulated on the internet in 2001:

The Israeli Prime Minister is sitting down with Yasir Arafat to try to work out an agreement. The Prime Minister asks if he might first tell a story. Arafat agrees.

The Prime Minister says: "When Moses was in the desert for forty years the Jews got very thirsty and Moses asked the Lord for water and there appeared a beautiful lake. The Jews first drank and then bathed themselves. Moses did the same but when he came out of the water his clothes were gone.

"Moses shouted, 'Where are my clothes? Who took them?' The Jews answered, 'The Palestinians took them.'"

Arafat quickly objected, "There were no Palestinians at that time!"

The Prime Minister looked at Arafat and said, "Now we can begin to negotiate."

This joke reflects fundamental tensions in the Middle East between each side's delusions, and the messy realities. At bottom, each of the warring peoples would love to click their heels collectively three times and make the other go away. As a result, each side is peculiarly susceptible to arguments that negate the legitimacy of the other side. If Israelis cannot eliminate the Palestinians, if the Arabs cannot eliminate the Jews, each can at least invalidate the other's claims.

It is at this point in arguments that I, the historian, will declare bombastically, "In the Middle East today history is irrelevant!" This statement means that, yes, Jews could engage in an academic exercise and prove again and again, in many different ways, that we got there first. But, at the end of the day, even a four-thousand-year-old claim can not completely negate a twelve-hundred-year-old claim, especially when there are millions of people who feel that second claim so intensely. And that is why some form of accommodation, some kind of peace agreement, is necessary.

Similarly, I understand emotionally why the Arab world is so deeply invested in negating Zionism, in ignoring the Jewish people's ancient and enduring claim to the land of Israel. Israel represents a remarkable failure on the part of the Arab world, after a century of futile but deadly opposition. Still, I cannot accept the negation or the many lies bolstering it, and I remained appalled by its intensity and its volume.

The story of the conflicting suitors, two peoples right now, today, in love with the same land, regardless of the past, is, alas, more tragic than romantic. Most of this book is devoted to affirming the Jewish people's romance with the land, despite the tragedy. But we cannot make the same mistake too many nineteenth-century Zionists did and pretend that history was frozen after the destruction of the Temple in 70 C.E., and that no other suitors subsequently appeared. Similarly, while we need to celebrate Identity Zionism and not always wallow in Crisis Zionism, we need to respond to our critics, we need to defend Israel and Zionism in the court of public opinion.

THE DEMONIZATION OF ZIONISM

Among the many casualties of the renewed Mideast violence is the term "Zionism." Whereas it once epitomized idealism, romanticism, and the best of nationalism to millions of Jews and non-Jews, Zionism today is politically incorrect. In a depressing retreat to the harshest days of the Arab-Israeli conflict, Zionism is again being demonized. Critics regularly twin the term with a grab-bag of reprehensible "isms": expansionism, colonialism, imperialism, racism, and, most perversely, Nazism.

The renewed attack on Zionism overshadowed the United Nations conference held in Durban, South Africa, at the end of August, 2001. The "World Conference against Racism, Racial Discrimination, Xenophobia, and Related Intolerance," wanted to condemn "the racist practices of Zionism," call Zionism a movement "based on racial superiority," and condemn Israel's treatment of Palestinians as "a new kind of apartheid." Some delegates distributed a booklet of vile and ancient anti-Semitic caricatures showing Jews with hook noses and fangs dripping blood. It was hard to take such overt racism at a supposed anti-racism conference seriously – but also hard to ignore it. The United States – and even the compulsively "evenhanded" Canadian government – mobilized against it.

To attack Zionism, rather than Israeli policies or the Israeli government, is to repudiate the State of Israel and the idea of a Jewish state. For Zionism at its simplest is Jewish nationalism, the understanding that Jews are a people, that Judaism is not just a religion, and that Israel is the Jewish homeland. At the same time, Zionism has never been simple. It is a diverse movement, with many competing conceptions about what Jewish nationalism means, and which vision should define the Jewish state, from religious to secular, from socialist to capitalist.

NATIONALISM AS KINSHIP WITH A COMMUNITY

Despite the globalization hype, we still live in a world of nation-states and nationalisms. Since the days of the American Revolution, hundreds of national, cultural, and ethnic expressions of collective identity have flourished. Some have been intimately linked to sovereign states, others have not. To feel kinship with a certain community is natural, not racist. Such kinship can inspire people to unite around noble concepts such as democracy and liberty – or it can rouse masses to wallow in ugly, xenophobic ideas.

Marxists – remember them? – negated nationalism. Karl Marx's vision of the workers of the world uniting, sought to unite – and divide – based on class distinctions. Marx himself was an individual of Jewish origin who negated his Judaism to become a citizen of the world. Even after the collapse of the most elaborate and sustained expression of Marxism – Soviet Communism – faint echoes of the old Marxist melody lingered on, especially in the universities. In the 1990s, many young Israeli intellectuals, beneficiaries of Zionism's triumphs, rebelled against their country and their parents, by negating nationalism in general and Zionism in particular. To do so, they needed to caricature all nationalism, and their own, as narrow and chauvinistic.

One young post-Zionist professor, Avi Shlaim, begins his history of the Arab-Israeli conflict by deeming all nationalist histories "one-sided and self-serving." On the first page of his book, *The Iron Wall: Israel and the Arab World* (2000, 2001), Shlaim embraces the French philosopher Ernest Renan's definition of a nation as "a group of people united by a mistaken view about the past and a hatred of their neighbors." Shlaim predictably proceeds to lambaste Israel, and despite writing a six-hundred-page "authoritative" history, has no room to mention events that were seared into the Israeli national consciousness, and affected prospects for peace, such as the Palestinian terrorist attacks on schoolchildren at Kiryat Shmona and Maalot, or the Palestinian murder of Israeli Olympians in Munich.

Coming as they do from the Middle East and Europe, respectively, perhaps Shlaim and Renan can be forgiven their harsh, all-or-nothing, with-me-or-against-me view of nationalism. Fortunately, we in North America, on both sides of the border, have experienced nationalism in more expansive and benign forms. In fact, it is not too much of a stretch to claim that many North Americans could define a nation as "a group of people united by a common romance with their past, and a love – or at least acceptance – of their neighbors" – meaning their fellow citizens, not their enemies across the border. (This definition, too, acknowledges current intellectual trends by talking about romance, acknowledging some element of fantasy, rather than insisting that all national histories are one hundred percent accurate).

Moreover, these romantic nationalists need not be monogamous. Here in North America we have learned that individuals can have multiple loyalties to different nationalisms. Those "unmeltable ethnics" who emerged in the 1960s and 1970s sporting "KISS ME I'M" Polish, Irish or Jewish buttons, were also patriotic Americans. Canadians have long balanced intense connections to their respective ethnic heritages with an ardent, if often understated, love for their land. The late historian Robert Wiebe, sifting through academic attempts to define what nationalism is – and is not – sighed, "We have created a jungle of definitions."

REFUGEES, THE RIGHT OF RETURN, AND THE LAW OF RETURN

The Palestinians scored many propaganda points by "simply" asking for a "right of return" to the homes they lost in 1948. Like many other aspects of Palestinian nationalism this call echoes a Zionist idea – Israel's "Law of Return" offers Jews automatic citizenship in the Jewish state. Wrapping their arguments, as usual, in liberal language, the Palestinians argue that it is "racist" for Israel to welcome back Jews who have been exiled for millennia while begrudging that same right to Palestinians who only have been exiled for decades.

This argument is clever but misleading. Many of the European nations quick to condemn Israeli "racism" make their own series of distinctions as to who can become a citizen. Every nation state has the right to make its own rules regarding citizenship. To demand that a hostile population loyal to one state be imposed on another state is absurd.

The argument also perpetuates the Palestinians' characterization of the Jews as "colonizers" and the Palestinians as indigenous refugees. It ignores the fluidity of borders and the volatility of population patterns in the area. In fact, many Palestinians who profess a tie to their supposedly ancestral homes in Jaffa or Jerusalem only arrived there after the 1880s – partially lured by the Zionist pioneers' economic boom. Moreover, the call ignored the unfortunate realities of the twentieth century wherein wars triggered many population transfers. World War II itself generated an estimated 79,200,000 refugees. When the Muslim state of Pakistan emerged from British India in 1947, as many as 15 million refugees abandoned their homes, with estimates that roughly half went from Hindu and Sikh areas to Muslim areas, and half in the other direction. Following that logic, the 800,000 Jews expelled from Muslim countries after 1948 balance out the Arabs who fled their homes during a war that began when the Arabs themselves rejected the 1947 UN partition.

In fairness, the origins of the Palestinian refugee conflict are murky. Zionist legend once had it that the Palestinians voluntarily abandoned their homes, eagerly awaiting a triumphal return after the Jews were "driven into the sea." Today, Palestinian legend has it that the evil Zionists ran all the Palestinians out of their homes. The truth lies in between. Israelis can point to generous invitations for Arabs to stay, along with incidents that drove out Arabs. Palestinians need to acknowledge their leaders' promise of a quick, easy, and bloody solution to the Zionist problem, which contributed to the refugee problem as well as the Arab leaders' refusal to integrate the Palestinian refugees into Egypt, Syria or Lebanon.

So, yes, Palestinians could construct an argument rooted in history demanding such a right of return, just as Jews could construct an argument rooted in even earlier history demanding that the borders of Israel stretch from the Mediterranean Sea to present-day Iraq. But compromise will only be achieved if both sides adapt to today's demographic and political realities. (In fact, in that spirit, the Palestinian moderate Professor Sarih Nusseibeh has proposed a "right of return" to a new Palestinian state not to the Jewish state).

DRUNK ON ANTI-ZIONIST VITRIOL

The complexity of the question, the dizzying diversity of nationalist forms, makes the attack on Zionism so offensive. In targeting Jewish nationalism in its broadest, murkiest, and most abstract incarnation, critics betray their true colors. Anti-Zionism goes way beyond the question of the settlements or Ariel Sharon or any particular Israeli actions. Anti-Zionism attacks the very rights of the Jews to their homeland. This sweeping assault then naturally metastasizes into the anti-Semitic rantings of Syria's President when greeting the Pope, and into the epidemic of attacks against Jews throughout the world that spun off from the Palestinian riots which began in the fall of 2000.

This anti-Zionist vitriol ratchets the conflict between Israel and the Palestinians from the realm of the negotiable up to an arena of mutually exclusive absolutes. Those who negate Zionism are declaring war on Israel and the Jewish people. This broad-based assault, combined with the vicious campaign of terror launched against all Israelis, explains why the Israeli left has all but collapsed, and why the region is so polarized.

It is tragic and ironic that this negation of Zionism persists despite a decade during which most Israelis, and most Jews, came to accept the reality of Palestinian nationalism. For all its flaws, the Oslo peace process acknowledged that neither Palestinians nor Israelis could wish the other away, and that only mutual acceptance and compromise would bring peace.

Oslo emerged from geopolitical realities. The collapse of the Soviet Union pulled the rug out from under many Arab rejectionists and helped Israel feel secure enough to compromise. Yet Oslo reflected the trendiest scholarly understandings of nationalism as a "process," and of nations as "imagined communities." While Professor Benedict Anderson's phrase ignores the fact that some nations are more rooted historically than others, the definition recognizes nationalism as a creative and fluid form of collective self-expression. Most Zionists have learned that you cannot negate your neighbor's nationalism – in many ways, if three million people think they are a nation, they are. It is time for Israel's enemies to learn the same lesson.

And that is why Jews need to take back the term Zionism from its opponents. In rejecting the libels, Jews will not simply be scoring points in a propaganda war. By redefining a new Zionism for the twenty-first century, Jews will learn how to express support for Israel, even if they occasionally disagree with some Israeli policies. A renewed Zionism could also help Jews in Israel and abroad stop focusing exclusively on political Zionism and think about how Israel and Jewish nationalism can help revive Jewish pride, Jewish culture, Judaism itself.

Of course, this conflict is about flesh and blood, about borders and armaments, not words. But hate can kill and the vicious rhetoric spewed forth in too many mosques, schools, and television stations has had fatal consequences. Those sadists who dip their hands in the blood of lynched reservists, who gouge out the eyes of two thirteen-year-old boys in a cave, who murder and mutilate an unarmed shepherd, who target a ten-month-old baby girl playing with her father, who fill their suicide bombs with flesh-tearing nails – or who cheer such abominations in the streets of Jenin, of Ramallah – are indeed egged on by words, and drunk on anti-Zionist venom.

Chapter 11

FAIRNESS 101:
WHY ISRAEL HAS EVERY RIGHT TO EXIST

"Traditionally, I had counted myself as a staunch pro-Israel supporter," a recent e-mail writer pronounced, but after delving "deeper into the history and nature of Zionism I find myself no longer able to articulate why a modern State of Israel should exist." Here is the latest post-modernist trend, delivered to my home computer. Four blood-soaked years ago, I would have deleted the letter. The very question offends, scrutinizing only Israel's origins and legitimacy. Unfortunately, today, many intellectuals are assailing Israel's legitimacy, making deletion no longer a viable option. Sticking to principles and refusing to engage the new breed of Israel-bashers risks losing the PR battle, especially when too many younger Jews don't feel motivated to defend the Jewish state and too many of their parents can only evoke Leon Uris's romantic, warm, and glowy "Exodus" feelings.

Over the last three decades, while the Jewish people slept, an unholy alliance of Islamicists and anti-colonialist intellectuals, supposedly devoted to upholding human rights, systematically libeled the Jewish national project. As a result, when we celebrate Zionism as an expression of Jewish nationalism, they yell "racism," as if the world is not divided into 190 tribalist enclaves. When we hail the waves of *chalutzim* (pioneers), the immigrant heroes delivering individual and national redemption, they yell "colonialism," as if the Jews lack a 3,000-year relationship with Israel. When we sing about making the desert bloom they yell "ethnic cleansing," as if Palestinians have always occupied every square inch of that once-desolate land and neither the populations nor the boundaries ever shifted. When we endorse a specifically Jewish state that synthesizes modern liberal democratic values with traditional Jewish ideals, they yell "apartheid," as if the Israeli Declaration of Independence does not consciously balance ethnic nationalism with civic nationalism, the yearning for a return to a Jewish homeland with the promise of rights for "all its inhabitants."

Israel's critics ignore Arab racism, sexism, homophobia, totalitarianism, medievalism, and barbarianism: that is an old story.

Meanwhile, they posit an idealized model of European nationalism. Post-modern anti-Zionists and many Israeli post-Zionists worship Europe as a multicultural paradise, a multilingual America with manners. They ignore how particularly French the French are, how German the Germans are, and how impermeable those nationalisms are to outsiders – a fact brought home by the riots in the Parisian suburbs that erupted in Fall, 2005.

Many Europeans disdain "multiculturalism" as a Yankee absurdity. A recent *International Herald Tribune* article noted that "many jobs in Europe are simply off-limits to foreigners." The xenophobic French republic bars non-European Union citizens from 50 professions, including "pharmacists, midwives, architects, airline pilots, funeral home directors, and anyone who wants to obtain a license to sell tobacco or alcohol. Similar laws exist in other EU countries, especially when it comes to government jobs," according to the story. "People don't really like foreigners here," one student in Germany told the *Tribune*.

With these considerations in mind, replying to the anti-Zionist e-mailer was easy. "I resent the question," I wrote, "unless we are willing to open the question to challenge the nature of nationalism itself and to explore other national myths and scars. Israel and the Jewish people are unfairly singled out. Israel is perpetually on probation and must behave nicely to be accepted. Shall we also examine Pakistan that enlightened center of patriarchal oppression and nuclear proliferation? Shall we consider America's two original sins regarding African-Americans and Native Americans, and question our own country's *right to exist*? Shall we talk about the artificial nature of Iraq, Syria, Jordan, Saudi Arabia, and Pakistan all shaped by Ottoman, British, or French imperial cartographers? And finally, shall we question the artificial, PLO-created nature of Palestinian nationalism? If so, given the Palestinians' consistent refusal to compromise, and given the cult of death they have spawned, perhaps they should not exist."

I don't usually negate Palestinian nationalism or anyone else's national expression. I prefer the high road, swatting off inquiries secure in the knowledge that from the 1947 U.N. Partition Plan through the Oslo years, Israel has compromised and pursued peace, albeit imperfectly, amid relentless Arab calls for its destruction. We have to rise to the new challenges and chide our critics for inconsistency, hypocrisy, and selectivity so intense and so obsessive that it undermines their credibility, integrity, and commitment to peace.

Chapter 12

POLITICS 101:
HOW THE ARABS CONVINCED THE WORLD THAT
ZIONISM IS RACISM

Here, then, is one of the great mysteries of the current conflict. Islam is a rich, multifaceted, complicated religion. The Arab world is similarly diverse, multidimensional, and downright confusing to insiders and outsiders alike. As with any religion, there are more progressive and less progressive pockets. Few would argue that the leading rejectionists, the leaders and clerics crying out "death to the Jews," the martyr wannabes strapping TNT to their chests, represent Islam at its most peaceful or progressive. In fact, a look at most of the Islamicists' rejectionist rhetoric reveals these folks to be hostile to Israel, Jews, Americans, Westerners, democracy, and a host of many of the most liberal ideals. These are Taliban Muslims who declare war on women; these are Khomeinists who issue fatwas promising money and glory for anyone who kills a harmless but outspoken novelist like Salman Rushdie. These are sadists who slaughter thousands at the World Trade Center – then celebrate their great "victory" over innocent secretaries and stewardesses. And yet, these are the very same people who have won the hearts of Europeans, academics, intellectuals, even some Jews. How can what we call "the world," meaning the liberal, democratic, progressive world, swallow this anti-Semitic, anti-Western poison hook, line and sinker?

For some Jews, the answer is simple: "the world hates us, and Jewish critics hate themselves." To these Jews, the bleaching of anti-Zionism into anti-Semitism, the Arab attack on Israel at an anti-racism conference with Goebbels-like anti-Semitic caricatures, all makes perfect sense. In an ironic parallelism, just as Palestinians mistakenly link the Holocaust with the founding of the State of Israel, these Jews view the Arab attacks on Israel as a continuation of Hitler's hatred – with the rest of the world once again acquiescing and even silently applauding.

THE GREAT INVERSION, BABY BOOMER STYLE

I actually believe the story is more complicated, though perhaps equally depressing. It begins, as do so many modern tales, in the 1960s.

In those days of ersatz revolutions, baby boomer elites in North America and Europe experienced what we might call the Great Inversion. Genuinely appalled by the sins of colonialism in Africa and Asia, by the sins of segregation in the United States, these leaders of tomorrow then and today now, rejected the status quo. Some of this rebellion was quite sincere, and salutary. Alas, many overcompensated, overly romanticizing Third Worlders, people of color, victims of racism and colonialism. As a result, they replaced one dogma with another. If the typical 1950s elites were blind to the excesses of whites in power, their children were blind to the excesses of the non-white and the powerless. The French philosopher Alain Finkielkraut sighs: "When an Arab torches a school, it's rebellion. When a white guy does it, it's fascism. I'm 'color blind.' Evil is evil, no matter what color it is...."

Throughout the decades, as many of these elites became part of the establishment, they often felt guilty about their own newfound power. The ensuing "bobo" sensibility that emerged, as the writer David Brooks calls it, balanced out the elites' new and plush bourgeois establishmentarian status with counter-cultural Bohemian trimmings. Overcompensating yet again, it became easy for Americans such as Bill Clinton, Germans such as Gerhard Schroeder, let alone academics, intellectuals, editors, and reporters, to leaven their guilt for succeeding with an instinctive sympathy for the little guy – which was often admirable but also easily exploited.

THE GREAT INVERSION, ISRAEL STYLE

At the same time, Israel experienced its own Great Inversion. The Camp David peace treaty of 1978-1979 removed Egypt, Israel's greatest threat, from most equations balancing Arab and Israeli power. Jordan eventually followed, and even Syria has been relatively quiet lately, especially since the Soviet Union fell. Israel also, finally, began to prosper, even as most of the Arabs in the territories remained poor and powerless. As a result, when the Palestinians rebelled in the late 1980s, and cast themselves as stone-throwing Davids against the Israeli Goliath, the world was ready to buy that line.

Moreover, from the 1960s to the 1990s, the "world's voice" had become rather monotonous. Wave after wave of media revolutions resulted in a world filled with an incredible cacophony of voices, yet with disproportionate power to set the world's agenda concentrated in very few hands. The media-meisters of CNN, the BBC, the *New York Times* – many of whom are the aforementioned baby boomers – work through their psychological contradictions, using their power to lash out at what they perceive to be power imbalances throughout the world.

But power imbalances are worth attacking only if they are easily photographed – and Israeli freedom of the press mixed with the ever-more-sophisticated Arab PR machine yields devastating coverage.

Examples of media bias far removed from the Arab-Israeli conflict abound daily. Reporters skew stories. They have their stereotypes to perpetuate, their shorthand to use, their presumptions to confirm, for example: the little guy is always right, the authority figure is always wrong. However, in North America as opposed to in Europe, most reporters are far less guilty of the sin of anti-Semitism, and far more likely to be guilty of one of the seven deadly sins, a generic sort of sloth, greed, pride, and, especially, sloppiness.

Those two inversions, along with the rise of the monolithic media, help explain what strikes many supporters of Israel as some of the absurd perversions of recent times, including the most dramatic fact that Palestinians rejected the Oslo peace process with violence, yet Israel's image has suffered. The round of finger-pointing on the first anniversary of the 2000 Camp David negotiations illustrated Israel's frustration. A spate of news articles chided the Israelis for not making more sweeping concessions in those negotiations, then declared that both sides were equally guilty for the troubles. This failure to distinguish between generosity at the bargaining table and murder on the streets dumbfounded and depressed Israelis.

Similarly, the Jenin Massacre Libel illustrated the clash between prevailing presumptions and inconvenient facts. Israel's entry into the West Bank in April, 2002 generated worldwide condemnation and a big lie – the claim that Israelis "massacred" up to 500 innocent Palestinians in the Jenin refugee camp. Pictures of Israeli tanks rumbling through Palestinian villages, and of piles of rubble left behind, seemingly proved the point. Here, once again, were the big bad Westerners oppressing the innocent indigenous people. Outraged that Israel dared to restrict their freedom of movement, reporters initially echoed the charges and broadcast them throughout the world.

Within days, even human rights workers often hostile to Israel had to acknowledge the "massacre" of Jenin was a figment of Palestinian imagination. Israeli tanks had entered the town after Palestinian terrorists murdered over 131 Israelis in March, 2002. The Jenin refugee camp was particularly notorious as the home of over twenty suicide bombers – and many more in preparation. Twenty-three Israeli soldiers died in difficult house-to-house fighting. And yes, a few dozen, not hundreds, of Palestinians died; mostly fighters not civilians. In short, Jenin was a battlefield not a killing field, and it was the Palestinians who chose to position themselves and their armaments in civilian neighborhoods. Nevertheless, Israel suffered the mass opprobrium.

WHY ARE DEMOCRATS SOFT ON DICTATORS?

Such twists are part of a larger pattern – in June 2000, when the Syrian dictator Hafez al-Assad died, the *New York Times* headlines cried that Assad's death "Cloud[ed] Mideast Prospects" and presented "A New Hurdle to Peace." These speculative headlines contradicted the evidence that Assad had been one of the major obstacles to peace, refusing to shake Israelis' hands, as the leaders of Egypt and Jordan signed treaties with Israel.

Four years later, many of the breathless eulogies for Yasir Arafat glossed over his methods. Ignoring terrorism when assessing Arafat was like evaluating Adolf Hitler without mentioning concentration camps. Arafat taught that terrorism could pay. He encouraged the world to rationalize his despicable trademark tactic. Arafat was the Typhoid Mary of modern diplomacy, spreading a virus of violence and relativism in the face of terror worldwide. A French President in 2004 who mourned a mass-murderer; elegant intellectuals who violated their beliefs in rationality, consistency and peaceful conflict resolution to toast killers; let alone a people seduced by a nihilistic nationalism worshipping a cult of death and venerating suicide bombers not nation builders: these are the bastard offspring of the Age of Arafat.

Both Assad and Arafat exploited the West's wishful thinking, double standards and softheartedness to get away with murder, literally. The absurd headlines proved that these wily autocrats helped shape the 21st century sensibility wherein Yasir Arafat's crimes of commission – planning murders – were forgotten, and Ariel Sharon's crimes of omission – not stopping massacres – were condemned; where when Israel bombarded a vehicle filled with armed gunmen en route to a terrorist action, the world was shocked, shocked, by the assassinations, and yet, had the terrorists succeeded, the world would also have been shocked, shocked, by the carnage; where when the United States targeted terrorists, Americans were being "brave," but when Israel targeted terrorists, Israel was being provocative; where it seemed the murder of innocents in Madrid, London, Amman, was incomprehensible terrorism, but the murder of innocent Jews was understandable politics.

Here, too, we see that words can kill. This new war against Israel is a post-modern media war. Palestinians follow world public opinion. The fact that the murder and mayhem stopped, albeit temporarily, after the Dolphinarium massacre in June, 2001, proves the point. When Arafat feared world opinion turning against him and his cause, he turned off the spigot of violence. One wonders how many Palestinian and Jewish lives would have been saved, had the world condemned Palestinian violence back in September, 2000, when Arafat and his people first turned away from talk and toward terror.

CHAPTER 13

LIBERALISM 101:
HOW ZIONISM AND LIBERALISM
WERE AND ARE COMPATIBLE

Amid this worldwide campaign to rob Israel of its good name, the long and proud association of Zionism with liberalism is also threatened. Too many progressives have turned on Israel and Zionism with a vengeance, especially in the university. Palestinians and their supporters have cleverly hijacked the rhetoric of human rights in service of that great human wrong, terrorism. In a classic case of intellectual irresponsibility, Israel-bashing has become great sport, with no thoughts to the lethal consequences, considering how much such hostility encourages Palestinian terrorists. The new, politically correct position of demonizing the Jewish state and Jewish nationalism, combined with the Palestinians' turn from negotiation toward terrorism, has confused Zionists and anti-Zionists. With most of Israel's peace camp reeling, with Israel fighting terror aggressively, with conservatives and evangelicals in the United States and elsewhere rallying to Israel's side, it is easy to see why campus radicals caricature Zionism as a conservative creation. Nevertheless, now, more than ever, it is essential – and surprisingly easy – to rise up and affirm the fact that not only can you be a liberal and a Zionist, but that liberalism and Zionism remain not just compatible but mutually reinforcing.

In so many ways, on so many levels, liberalism and Zionism spring from common sources. Both are modern movements, shaped by the

Enlightenment and other intellectual currents of the eighteenth and nineteenth centuries, with central tenets rooted in the Bible. Just as it is hard to tell the story of Zionism without going back to *"lech lecha,"* Abraham's charge in Genesis to "go forth" to a new land, the land of Israel, it is hard to tell the story of how Western notions of equality and social justice developed without going back to the ethical precepts of the Torah, let alone to the crusading passion of the Prophets. The contemporary stories of both Zionism and liberalism are intertwined with that great, defining, sometimes ennobling, and yes, sometimes cruel, but absolutely defining modern movement – nationalism.

In the founder of the modern Zionist movement, Theodor Herzl, these three intellectual currents harmonized. This enlightened Viennese progressive is best remembered for jumpstarting Zionism in reaction to the anti-Semitism of the Dreyfus trial. Yet in his visionary 1896 book *"der Judenstaat,"* Herzl dreamed of the Jewish state as a liberal model for the world. Herzl articulated the essential Zionist message that still holds true, and that echoes in the liberal nationalism of most Western nation states – that only through self–determination can utopian ideals be achieved, that a community first must unite and protect itself before it can become a force for good.

Nationalists believe that your own community provides the best framework for implementing high ideals – sometimes out of broad conviction, sometimes out of sad necessity. There is, of course, a rich, ongoing debate about how to balance universalism and particularism. But it is very odd that often the same Chomskyite forces that mindlessly celebrate Palestinian nationalism insist on negating Zionism. Sidestepping the entire debate about the historic origins of Jewish or Palestinian nationalism, many modern scholars accept Benedict Anderson's notion of nationalism as an "imagined community." Whether you accept that definition – or embrace Professor Irwin Cotler's notion of the Jews as the original aboriginal people, still speaking the same language, still developing the same culture, still tied to the same land after thousands of years, the legitimacy of Jewish nationalism is clear. And with another one of the great scholars of nationalism Professor Liah Greenfield identifying nationalism as the defining "constitutive" force of the modern world, singling out Jewish nationalism, meaning Zionism, as the only illegitimate form of nationalism is sheer bigotry.

Of course, Herzl was not the only Zionist in the nineteenth century. Zionism was a many-splendored thing, a broad, invigorating conversation attempting to create the perfect ideological mix of Judaism, nationalism, liberalism, idealism, rationalism, socialism and capitalism. Zionism was a bold experiment to realize these ideals, and often rejected the status quo. Nahum Syrkin in "The Jewish Problem and the Socialist-Jewish State" (1898) insisted: "For a Jewish state to come to be, it must, from the very beginning, avoid all the ills of modern life. To evoke the sympathetic interest of modern man, its guidelines must be justice, rational planning, and social solidarity. Once a Jewish state has been realized on such scientific social principles, the time will come for modern technology to flourish within it." These were bold, sometimes doctrinaire, intellectual pioneers, trying to fix all the evils of the world while making the desert bloom.

Israel's Proclamation of Independence from 1948 also illustrates the happy marriage between Zionism and liberalism, offering a model of how nationalism can be a force for good in the world. In reading these words, David Ben–Gurion ping-ponged from universalism to particularism, demonstrating just how intertwined the two concepts were, just how expansive, ambitious and progressive the Zionist dream could be. "*Eretz-Israel*, the Land of Israel, was the birthplace of the Jewish people," he began. "Here their spiritual, religious and political identity was shaped. Here they first attained to statehood, created cultural values of national and universal significance and gave to the world the eternal Book of Books."

Attempting to build a broad, appealing, ideological infrastructure based on what experts now call "civic nationalism" on its admittedly "ethnic" base, the Proclamation declared: "The State of Israel will be open for Jewish immigration and for the Ingathering of the Exiles; it will foster the development of the country for the benefit of all its inhabitants; it will be based on freedom, justice and peace as envisaged by the prophets of Israel; it will ensure complete equality of social and political rights to all its inhabitants irrespective of religion, race or sex; it will guarantee freedom of religion, conscience, language, education and culture; it will safeguard the Holy Places of all religions; and it will be faithful to the principles of the Charter of the United Nations."

It would demean Israel, and Zionist liberalism, to use the oppressive examples of Israel's self-righteous Arab neighbors as any kind of a behavior standard. And Israelis will be the first to detail all the ways their State has failed to fulfill its highest ideals. But it has been, overall, a gloriously successful experiment, carving out a little oasis of liberal democracy in a harsh, forbidding totalitarian desert.

Critics should be ashamed for singling out Israel for acting in the ways typical of the modern nation–state. Most critics are myopic, blind to

Jewish suffering, silent in the face of Palestinian violence, and able to see only Palestinian suffering and Israeli "aggression." Even many Israelis, especially far too many Israeli academics at home and abroad, lambaste Israeli "oppression" in a vacuum. They ignore Israel's risks for peace during the Oslo years. They forget Ehud Barak's generous Camp David concessions, which were not reciprocated by the Palestinians. Somehow, they fail to mention Yasir Arafat's rejectionism and the Palestinians' strategic decision to reject negotiations and rely on terror. There are even some who, after the elections in January 2006 overlooked the calls in the Hamas charter to wipe out Israel. In their zeal to demonize Israel and excuse Israel's foes, these so-called peaceniks missed the incompatibility between Hamas-style *jihadist* Islamicism and democratic liberalism, no matter how many votes these terrorists win, and even if some of these murderers put on a suit and tie.

These days, many critics also violate reasonable norms by indicting Israel for the "pre-crime" of transfer and expulsion – simply because there are a few marginalized voices in Israel calling for this immoral plan or because some outside analysts have decided that this is the right's only option or true intent. Such premature indictments may pass muster in the Hollywood of the Tom Cruise–Steven Spielberg collaboration "Minority Report," they are not acceptable in the real world, and should be especially rejected in academia. Similarly, it is fashionable to damn Israel as a mini-Bosnia or Serbia wallowing in its "ethno-religious criteria" when the rest of the democratic world has gone multiethnic and multicultural. In fact, the United States and Canada stand out as states based on an all-inclusive civic nationalism; most of Europe remains rooted in ethno-religious forms of nationalism.

It is suspicious that liberal critics spend much time demonizing the Jewish state but fail to mention the restrictions in most European countries for non-Europeans. In deeming Israel an "anachronism" in the *New York Review of Books*, NYU's Tony Judt claimed that the Western world had turned "pluralist… multiethnic and multicultural," making Israel "distinctive among democratic states in its resort to ethnoreligious criteria with which to denominate and rank its citizens. It is an oddity among modern nations… because it is a Jewish state in which one community – Jews – is set above others, in an age when that sort of state has no place." Here, as usual, hope triumphs over facts, selective perception distorts the truth. Noble liberty-, equality-, and fraternity-minded France endured serious riots in the fall of 2005, wherein immigrant youths – mostly Muslim – marked out the limits of French pluralism, multiculturalism and tolerance. Only twenty-one percent of Europeans polled in 2000 were considered "actively tolerant" of immigrants. Given such restrictions and prejudices, Israel can proudly compare its record of openness to immigrants, and openness to its Arab minority, despite difficult and often war-like conditions. And that is comparing Israel to Europe – let alone to its Arab neighbors.

Israel, then, is typical of modern nation-states, neither "anachronistic" nor uniquely oppressive as the Chomskyite relativists masquerading as moralists claim. Progressives can and should continue to delight in Israel, in the vigor of its press, the vitality of its democracy, the power of its courts, the creativity of its universities, the dynamism of its population, the latitude of its many internal dissidents, the rights afforded its minorities, the sophistication of its economy, the ease, freedom, and equality of so many of its citizens. Of course, Israel faces serious challenges and is far from perfect, like every nation-state, like all human creations. Shame on so many liberals, and so many academics, for jumping on the intifadist bandwagon, highlighting every Israeli imperfection – and doing it to delegtimize the Jewish state – while overlooking so many other countries' failures to fulfill many basic liberal ideals. Liberals who are Zionists can and should proudly celebrate Israel's many accomplishments, while prodding it persistently but constructively to do even better.

CHAPTER 14

DEMOCRACY 101:
HOW ISRAEL REMAINS THE ONLY DEMOCRACY
IN THE MIDDLE EAST

Thinking about Syria's dictatorship, Hamas Islamicism or what even Palestinian nationalists called Yasir Arafat's "kleptocracy," underscores the commonplace miracles that often occur in Israel. Despite a continuous half-century war over its very existence, Israel has maintained a robust democracy. If anything, Israeli democracy is infamous for its vehemence. The spectrum of opinion is rather wide in Israel, and most Israelis express themselves loudly and passionately. Judging by Natan Sharansky's now famous test for a robust democracy - can a citizen denounce the country's leaders publicly in the town square – Israel passes loudly and shrilly while Israel's neighbors and enemies fail.

The fights, the parliamentary maneuvers, the elections are, on one hand, commonplace. Yet these democratic expressions are miraculous, not only because they often occur amid great tensions, but because they occur at all in a democratic context. The chaos in Iraq in 2004-2005 amid free elections, the fact that so many Palestinians chose murderous Hamas terrorists in January 2006 proves that democracy entails more than voting – rule of law, civil liberties, civility itself are required. Even more remarkable, in contrast to Hamas's exterminationist ideology to destroy the Jewish State, and the constant attacks on "the Jews," is the fact that the Israeli electorate is 12.3 percent Arab with Arab Knesset members and civil servants. Back in 1948, amid a War of Independence with seven Arab nations, Israel nevertheless extended to its Arab inhabitants the most honorable title one can wear in a democracy, that of citizen.

Despite tremendous obstacles, Israel has remained committed to democratic values throughout its history. These values were integral to the Zionist founders of the state, even though democracy did not come that naturally to those of Eastern European origin. Sadly, reality has often placed democratic values in opposition to other goals and ideals, ranging from the country's security needs to the complicated attempt to keep this democratic Jewish state democratic and Jewish. Nevertheless, Israel's commitment to democracy runs so deep that many Israelis seek out the resonances, not the dissonances. One leading jurist, Haim Cohn, analyzing the country's core values, writes: "The Basic Law declares the values of the state of Israel to be *Jewish and democratic*. The conjunctive 'and' must be interpreted as combining Judaism and democracy into one supreme value – Judaism that is democratic and a democracy that is Jewish – as if Judaism and democracy were one."

In choosing to be a democracy, Israel is choosing to hold itself up to a higher standard. Simply noting that Hafez Assad murdered twenty thousand dissidents or that the Palestinian Authority shoots collaborators does not cut it. Adhering to this higher standard can often make Israel vulnerable to withering but justified criticism, from both outside and within. All democracies under threat struggle with this tension. After the horrific events of September 11, many American civil libertarians re-evaluated racial profiling. Even the great American democratic martyr Abraham Lincoln suspended basic liberties during the Civil War. The challenge for Israel is to strike the right balance, offering its citizens – and those affected by its actions – as much freedom as possible without threatening the stability of the state or the safety of its inhabitants.

These days, it is fashionable to complain, to focus on imperfections. I am often happy to do that. However, every now and then, and especially on Israeli election day, I risk being called a Pollyanna, and listen to the sweet sounds of democracy at work in Israel, the shuffle of shoes on the floor as people line up to vote, the rustle of paper as ballots are distributed, and the powerful silence when tanks do not roll down the street and the people wait patiently to hear what their collective voice has to say.

CHAPTER 15

PATRIOTISM 101:
HOW TO CRITICIZE AND NOT DE-LEGITIMIZE

Even as the Jewish community Juggernaut lurched further right after 2000, many Jewish voices on the left grew more shrill. After an Arab mob lynched two Israeli reservists in Ramallah, the editor of *Tikkun*, Rabbi Michael Lerner, proclaimed in the *Los Angeles Times* that "the preponderance of responsibility" for the troubles "lies with Israel." After Hamas's 2006 election win, Lerner obscenely claimed Hamas was merely as violent as "Ariel Sharon's government... George Bush's government," and "Israeli terrorists" such as Menachem Begin. Far too many on the left accepted the world's distinction between "innocent" victims who were killed within the Green Line, as opposed to soldiers and "settlers" whose deaths somehow seemed what – more justified? Such an invidious division ignored Arab rhetoric demanding Israel's extinction and death to all "the Jews," not just Israeli withdrawal from the territories seized in 1967. Such an invidious distinction fueled the Palestinian fire.

Among Israelis, the settlements remained controversial. Some noted that the settlements were doing what they were supposed to do, serving as the front lines, drawing firepower that would otherwise be directed within the 1967 boundaries. Others feared that the settlements caused the conflict itself, calling *"haMatzav,"* the situation, *"Milchemet Shlom HaMitnachlim,"* the war for the good of the settlers. Nevertheless, it was one thing to criticize the settlers, another to rationalize butchery, which reinforced the extremists and fed the violence. During the oft-violated cease fire after the Dolphinarium bombing in 2001, daily sniper attacks continued against "the settlers" beyond the Green Line, murdering dozens of motorists, with little world condemnation. Thus, two months later, after the Sbarro suicide bombing in downtown West Jerusalem, a Palestinian press release celebrated the death of the fifteen "settlers."

Furthermore, while some veteran peaceniks such as Amos Oz and Avraham Burg wrote eloquent essays in the *New York Times* warning Palestinians and the world not to confuse a longing for peace with disloyalty to the state, other activists were more hostile to the Jewish state itself. Playing on the media's thirst for man-bites-dog essays, many critics flaunted their Judaism as a credential to justify their Israel-bashing. All too often these dissenters not only criticized Israeli governmental actions, they delegitimized the state itself. In the Toronto *Globe and Mail* one self-described "Jewish physician" did not simply perpetuate the tired and inaccurate Goliath versus David stereotype of "one of the world's best-equipped military forces fac[ing] an army of stone throwers." He bashed the "Zionist dream," which "could never have been realized without visiting a nightmare on Palestinians." In the *New York Times*, Allegro Pacheco, "an Israeli lawyer who represents Palestinians," wrote a moving op-ed describing the very real pain and disruption Palestinians experienced under Israeli closures. She neglected, however, to explain why this "latest siege" had begun "[s]ince September" 2000, implying that Israelis woke up one morning and simply stumbled on yet another way to torture innocents.

Pacheco and many of her buddies also succumbed to a plague of promiscuous analogizing that further alienated these critics from the Jewish mainstream. She spoke of "the apartheid-like system" separating Jews and Palestinians. Others spoke of "Bantustans." Still other Jewish critics found the South Africa analogy too pallid, libelling Israeli troops as "Nazis." "I was disgusted," one young Jew told a reporter after hearing a presentation about Israeli demolitions. "I felt ashamed to be a Jew – fifty years after the Holocaust, the Jews are committing those sins."

Such attacks were so shrill, the analogies were so outrageous, that most supporters of Israel simply ignored them. The Nazis killed thousands daily; apartheid institutionalized racism unashamedly. Had the critics been more temperate in their language, more reasonable in their analysis, important alternative voices might have been better heard. Instead, the battle lines just became sharper.

THE EPIDEMIC OF EVENHANDEDNESS

Less offensive but also insidious was the epidemic of evenhandedness that repeatedly established false equivalences. Dismissing both sides as "barbaric" ignored who began the violence and who had the violence thrust upon them, who targeted children and who targeted buildings or terrorists in response, who mourned the World Trade Center-Pentagon massacre and who jumped for joy about it in the streets of Nablus and Arab East Jerusalem. Similarly, pointing to the one Jewish terrorist group that murdered a Palestinian family, including a three-month-old baby, as proof that both sides have their terrorists, profoundly distorted the truth.

The crusading liberal journalist Nat Hentoff, after acknowledging the Palestinians' "legitimate grievances," noted the "distinct difference in the reactions of many – not all – Palestinians to the loss of lives, as contrasted with the attitudes of most Israelis." The killings of the Palestinians "were roundly denounced by all elements of the Israeli public," while killings of Israelis were often loudly applauded. One Palestinian poll estimated that 76 percent of the Palestinians approved of suicide bombings after the Dolphinarium tragedy, and Hassan Hotari, the father of the twenty-two-year-old suicide bomber, told Reuters: "I was extremely happy when I heard that my son is the one who did this operation. I hope I have many sons to carry out the same act. And I wish myself I had done it." Sensitivity, even empathy, for the other, even your enemy, is admirable; but an ignorant echo of the Western "pox on both your houses" approach is not.

TWO OVERLAPPING WARS?

In an insightful essay in the *Nation* of April 22, 2002, Amos Oz attributed the confusion to the two Middle Eastern wars that were being fought simultaneously. One war was the Palestinian war of liberation, to end Israel's "occupation" of the West Bank and Gaza. The second war was the half-century Arab war to eradicate the state of Israel, currently waged most enthusiastically by radical Islamic groups. Most Israelis were fighting the second war – defending their lives and their state's right to exist – while the media often reported it as the first war – an attempt to perpetuate "occupation." And Yasir Arafat's diabolical genius was to shift between the two wars as it suited him, speaking *jihad* to the East while proposing compromise to the West. Unfortunately, too many Western reporters and politicians were hoodwinked.

HOW TO DISAGREE WITHOUT DENIGRATING

Underlying this issue is a deeper problem. We in the Jewish world, our brothers and sisters in Israel, need to reevaluate how we speak to each other and how we disagree with each other. Too many of us on too many issues denigrate those who disagree with us. Too many of us commit verbal violence against each other regularly. In June 2001, when the leader of the Reform movement cancelled all of his movement's summer trips to Israel, he did not simply say, "this was a difficult decision, honest people can differ." Rather, feeling defensive, he self-righteously pronounced that "we don't make political statements with other people's children." The comment implied that those who continued with the summer programs were indeed exploiting "other people's children." That comment provoked an equally unacceptable response from an Israeli politician, dismissing Reform Jews as only interested in "bagels and lox."

There is an Arabic expression, *"sikin b'sikin,"* knife to knife, that each blade sharpens the other. Verbal violence begets verbal violence. The combatants in that case deserved each other.

Let us be honest, these are difficult and quite literally life-and-death issues. And if we cannot even figure out how to disagree with each other respectfully, how can we ever hope to make peace with our enemies?

I confess. I am guilty of a pro-Israel bias. Even as I harbor moral qualms over Israeli soldiers controlling millions of unhappy Palestinians, I remember that it was an unintended occupation – and that security concerns make it impossible for Israel to waltz out everywhere. Even as I question some of the settlement policies, I note that both Israelis and Palestinians have ties to the West Bank, and that made it difficult for Israeli governments to stop the settlers. Even as I disapprove of violations of Palestinians' civil rights, I understand that Israeli soldiers are often scared and often boxed into acting harshly in their harsh neighborhood.

Still, as the opening clauses of each sentence suggest, I have my criticisms, I see faults. In fact, the only ones who cannot see any flaws in an existing government are fools or fanatics. And I am willing to concede that Israel might have more flaws than the average democracy (and more challenges, too). Nevertheless, self-criticism is necessary to grow, for individuals and for societies. Good democrats understand that criticism is often an expression of love. In fact, true love – and not Hollywood love – includes loving someone who is not perfect, for who can attain that standard?

I do not, therefore, condemn Israel for being imperfect. However, I do condemn many of my fellow Jews for loving Israel only when they think Israel is perfect. Such love is immature and inconstant. And I do find many Israelis far too harsh on their society and on each other. The challenge, here, is to keep perspective, to recognize the legitimacy of Israel's right to exist – as any other state – and Israel's right to make mistakes without constantly putting its legitimacy into question – as any other state. That is the "normality" the Zionist revolution sought to achieve, and that is the normal standard we apply to our home countries, loving them despite their flaws.

CHAPTER 16

HISTORY 101:

J'ACCUSE! ISRAEL IS NOT TO BLAME
FOR THE WORLD TRADE CENTER CATASTROPHE –
BUT MANY OTHERS ARE

The nightmarish attacks on the Pentagon and on the World Trade Center were a vast, unfathomable human tragedy. The four hijackings and resulting mayhem shattered thousands of lives, bruised millions of souls, and traumatized the civilized world. The multilingual chorus of torment in New York City hospitals, in English and Russian, in Hebrew and Arabic, in Spanish and Swedish, in French and Farsi, in Yiddish and Yoruban, made that clear.

That Black Tuesday, September 11, 2001, was also an American tragedy. That is why the entire United States Congress assembled and burst out in a spontaneous chorus of "God Bless America" on the Capitol steps as the fires still smoldered. That is why the Queen's band at Buckingham Palace played "The Star Spangled Banner." That is why good people throughout the world waved red, white, and blue flags.

Yet in the horrific aftermath, as we lit Yahrzeit candles and waved American flags, Jews in Israel and the Diaspora wondered where Jews fit into this terrible story. This concern was more than the proverbial "the elephant and the Jewish question," the uncanny ability of Jewish provincials to relate anything to the Jewish agenda. The hijackings came after nearly a year of Arafat's War – and nearly a year of increasingly vehement denunciations of the United States and Israel throughout the Arab world. Moreover, the tragedy occurred two days before the eighth anniversary of the signing in Washington of the Oslo Accords. And while almost everyone throughout the world condemned these bombings, thousands of anti-Zionist Palestinians on the West Bank and in Gaza celebrated this slaughter of innocents.

Many observers, Jews and non-Jews alike, noted that "finally," Americans understood what Israelis were "going through." Even as the civilized world rushed to say: "We are all New York, we are all Washington," many in New York and Washington said, "We are all Jerusalem." All of a sudden, but alas, only in the initial aftermath of the massacre, Israel's policy of assassinating known terrorists did not seem so "provocative." All of a sudden, Israel's refusal to negotiate in the face of terrorism did not seem so "intransigent," that is, until America's need to ally with the Arab world kicked in.

Many of the same Jews who felt relief that the West finally "got it," also feared a potential backlash. "What if middle America blames Israel for this mess?" many Jews asked. How much did America's support for Israel contribute to the Islamic terrorists' lethal hatred of the United States?

All the talk of "a second Pearl Harbor" and of a new world war once again provoked the historian's question "Where do I begin?" It is worth contemplating what the first chapter of a future history of the war on terror might look like. The roots of Islamic fundamentalism go back to the founding of Islam thirteen hundred years ago as well as to the first encounters between Islam and the modernizing West from the 1800s. But to understand how America rather than imperial Europe became "the Great Satan," and how Islamic extremists developed the temerity to attack America the once-invulnerable, requires a less daunting but deeply depressing trip back in time to the 1970s.

Three unhappy forces coincided in the 1970s. In the Middle East, Ayatollah Khomeini's successful overthrow of the Shah of Iran unleashed a new politicized strain of anti-American Islamic fundamentalism. Supporting Zionism certainly was an American "sin," but it was only one of many. At the same time, Yasir Arafat unleashed terrorism throughout the world in embassies, the Olympics, airports, and schools in his campaign to legitimize Palestinian nationalism. Back in the good ol' USA, the social revolution of the 1960s, combined with the Vietnam debacle, undermined American confidence abroad. All this came together from November 1979 through January 1981, when Iranian "students" supported by Khomeini held American diplomats hostage for 444 humiliating days. The theological zeal coursing through Khomeini anti-Americanism, the bloody pornography of Palestinian terrorism, and the wishy-washy

American response, made for a novel and dangerous brew.

By contrast, the Arab oil embargo imposed on the West after the 1973 Yom Kippur War, a mere half a decade earlier, had a very different flavor. In that case American and Western support for Israel caused the embargo. But the Arab oil states used the boycott for economic and geopolitical gains in a very secular way. They wanted to flex their muscles and pad their bank accounts. There were no calls for *Jihad*. And in the early 1970s, the West, and especially America, did not flinch.

Sadly, from 1979 on, even as the United States enjoyed an economic and patriotic renewal, it failed to recapture its footing in the Middle East. And tragically, Khomeinism metastasized throughout the Islamic world, even as Arafat, with the world's assistance, transformed himself from "Public Enemy Number One" into a Nobel Peace Prize winner. The more America and the West dithered, the more the Islamic extremists despised the West, and especially America. As the new millennium dawned, Benjamin Netanyahu and others made a convincing case that Islamic extremists did not hate the West because of Israel. Rather, the fanatics hated Israel and Zionism as an extension of the West. Moreover, you did not have to be an Islamic fundamentalist to hate Israel. Many secular Arabs hated Israel as well.

It is funny. People cling to their perceptions – often regardless of the evidence. Over the years, the Palestinian cause has been low on Osama bin Laden's priority list. Bin Laden has repeatedly emphasized that his fight is with the West, with Judaism and with Christendom, with modernity and with democracy, and, most especially, with the American military presence in Saudi Arabia, which he believes desecrates Islam's holiest land. "It is well known that the policies of these two countries [the United States and Great Britain] bear the greatest enmity toward the Islamic world," bin Laden declared in 1996, when he declared war "against the American regime which is against every Muslim." Bin Laden emphasized: "Our trusted leaders, the ulema, have given us a fatwa that we must drive out the Americans. The solution to this crisis is the withdrawal of American troops…. Their military presence is an insult for the Saudi people."

Moreover, like so many Arab leaders, bin Laden does not seem to care that much about the Palestinians, except as propaganda tools. Nevertheless, Westerners were eager to explain his irrational and evil deeds by linking them to the Palestinian conflict, and Muslim anger toward Israel made him and his terrorism popular on the proverbial Arab street. As a result, a month AFTER the bombings, bin Laden made sure to champion the Palestinian cause. He is evil, but he is not stupid. (Ironically, as bin Laden rushed toward the Palestinian cause, Yasir Arafat, trying to charm George W. Bush, tried to distance himself and his people from bin Laden. "Islam as a religion forbids anyone to harm any civilians, any innocent people around the world," the father of modern terrorism belatedly and piously proclaimed.)

Clearly, blame for the mass murders resides with the mass murderers. The hijackers and their direct supporters, their handlers, their money-men, their strategists, their bosses, are truly responsible for this sophisticated and well-planned crime – a crime, by the way, which was hatched long before the "troubles" in Israel began in September, 2000. Some hijackers entered flight school long before that date. Still, Western weakness made the job of these direct criminals eminently easier. Recriminations are not productive but the bipartisan march of folly demands examination. Politicians, diplomats, strategists, and ordinary citizens all functioned as "enablers," failing to stop milder forms of this ugly behavior, and thus helping to foster its escalation – or at least failing to prevent it.

And so, in the name of the nearly three thousand dead and the eight thousand wounded, in the name of thousands of children who lost a parent that awful day, in the name of the hundreds of thousands whose lives will never be the same, I stand up and say, as Emile Zola did a century ago, *"J'accuse!"*

– *J'accuse*, I accuse President Jimmy Carter of flinching in the face of the first serious threat to America in the Middle East, and thus letting the Iranian hostage crisis spawn two decades of Islamic fundamentalist terrorism against the United States of America.

– *J'accuse*, I accuse President Ronald Reagan of building on Carter's bad example by cutting and running after two hundred and forty-one Marines were murdered by a suicide bomber in Lebanon in 1983, and by negotiating with terrorists and humiliating the United States in the Iran-Contra debacle.

– *J'accuse,* I accuse President George Bush of stopping short during the Gulf War, thus missing an opportunity to rid the world of an arch-terrorist, Saddam Hussein, and putting the United States in the uncomfortable position of sustaining an embargo against Iraq, which fomented Muslim anti-Americanism for supposedly starving the Iraqi people.

– *J'accuse,* I accuse Colin Powell, as soldier and statesman, of perpetuating the post-Vietnam American delusion that wars can be fought cleanly, neatly, and cost-free, telegraphing a message to terrorists of American decadence and dithering.

–*J'accuse*, I accuse President Bill Clinton, the good-time-Charlie who administered band-aids rather than solving problems, of lobbing rhetorical bombs at Osama bin Laden and a few cruise missiles at a pharmaceutical factory, but not bringing bin Laden and his followers to justice no matter what they did, be it bomb American embassies or kill American soldiers and sailors.

– *J'accuse*, I accuse most conservatives who preferred occasional saber rattling and terminally tough talk to the hard work of rooting out terrorists from our midst.

– *J'accuse*, I accuse most liberals, who foolishly and dangerously legitimized horribly illegitimate tactics in their zeal to hear what sometimes were legitimate grievances.

– *J'accuse*, I accuse military bureaucrats and their congressional supporters, who too often preferred vast public works projects in favored districts to relevant weaponry.

– *J'accuse*, I accuse defense skeptics and their woolly-headed supporters, who deluded themselves that everyone makes nice in the world and shackled Western intelligence agencies.

– *J'accuse*, I accuse Canadian and European diplomats, whose commitment to talking to everyone, and validating everyone, perpetuated a delusion of moral equivalence and obscured important distinctions between right and wrong, between acceptable and unacceptable conduct.

– *J'accuse*, I accuse those Muslims who rushed to proclaim that Islam rejects suicide only after September 11, but before that either were silent or actually glorified suicide bombers in pizzerias, malls, and discos as "martyrs."

– *J'accuse*, I accuse reporters who called Palestinian radicals who kill Jews "guerillas," or "activists" or even "freedom fighters," but consider Osama Bin Laden and his henchmen "terrorists."

– *J'accuse*, I accuse America and its allies of failing to draw clear lines, and allowing the formal entities that sponsored terrorism such as Syria, Sadam Hussein's Iraq, Iran, the Taliban and the Palestinian Authority to enjoy a legitimacy and a latitude they did not deserve.

– *J'accuse*, I accuse decadent and corrupt Arab dictatorships, even supposedly moderate ones such as Saudi Arabia and Egypt, which happily accepted American military or monetary support, while allowing hatred of America to fester, even among their elites.

And finally, *J'accuse*, I accuse, most of us, for failing to demand serious leadership and hard choices from our representatives, until it was too late, for caring only when terror hit close to home, wherever that may be, and for failing to remember the warning "that if you are not part of the solution, you are part of the problem." We owe it to the vast community of grief created on September 11 not to repeat such colossal errors, and not to suffer from a failure of nerve.

PART 4

IDENTITY ZIONISM

The Bible tells how Moses sent twelve spies to scout out the land of Israel. Ten came back with tales of horror and woe, while two told of the beauty of the land. It is a natural human tendency, and a well known Jewish pathology, to focus on the negative. Especially these days, it is easy to wallow in Crisis Zionism, doing all the right things for all the wrong reasons. Our challenge is to be like the two, not the ten, and as Caleb and Joshua did, see the beauty despite our fear, articulate a positive vision that can uplift even while engaging the realities that don't just tether us to the ground, but deeply depress us. Identity Zionism need not be delusionary, but it must be visionary.

CHAPTER 17

MULTICULTURALISM 101:
WHY I NEED TO BE A ZIONIST

On the hit television show from the 1980s about the 1960s, "The Wonder Years," when the young protagonist Kevin Arnold envies his best friend's Bar Mitzvah, he does not lust after the goodies Paul's relatives bestowed, he yearns for the sense of belonging Paul's heritage provided. "What are we anyway, Mom?" Kevin asks. "Nothing?" Zionism can help us avoid feeling like "nothings" as we dash around madly trying to buy everything we can possibly afford but don't really need.

THE ZIONIST CURE FOR AFFLUENZA

Remarkably, even in the dawn of the twenty-first century, much of the world remains hungry, sick and poor. The modern Jewish world, however, is largely freed from those scourges. Yes, there is Jewish poverty. Yes, there are Jews living in depressing conditions. Yes, there is an unconscionably large gap growing between the superrich and the very poor in Israel. But in the two centers of Jewish life, North America and Israel, Jews are living in prosperous and progressive societies, where most citizens have food on the table, clothing on their backs, roofs over their heads, and access to an array of magical medicines that have doubled the average life span over the past two centuries.

And yet, amid all these riches, North Americans are unduly worried, jumpy, lost. It has been a most anxiety-provoking prosperity, one characterized by fancy creature comforts and great individual discomfort. Surprisingly, the higher up the class ladder you climb, anxiety increases – one poll found that poor and middle class children were more likely than the children of richer parents to believe that their lives were better than their parents', while wealthier children believe that the older generation had it easier.

It is a mind-boggling world, where twenty-somethings vie to be the next dotcom zillionaires, where BMWs crash into SUVs in high school parking lots, where sixth graders sport diamond studs and cell phones, where babies are decked out in $50 bibs and $90 booties. Many construct a meaningful life with these golden building blocks. And yet, many others of these lucky, coddled, children of widespread middle-class wealth feel neglected. In response, the *New York Times* diagnosed a new malady: "affluenza," a spiritual influenza of the affluent.

Affluenza is about "having it all" and feeling strangely empty inside. Affluenza comes from "arriving," then feeling "there is no there there." Affluenza is the malady of the huge house echoing from emptiness because both parents are working crazy hours, where teenagers ache for more time with mom and dad, even as they recoil from their embarrassingly unhip progenitors.

Affluenza is also only the latest psychic ailment to afflict the prosperous Westerner. In the nineteenth century, aristocratic women suffered from neurasthenia and other diseases of the nerves. In the twentieth century, a whole library of sociology and psychology treatises diagnosed the problems of alienation and of anomie. In post-World War II America, we went from struggling with the problems of the "Lonely Crowd," fearing becoming yet another anonymous "Man in a Gray Flannel Suit," to a world in which we are "Bowling Alone" and "Amusing Ourselves to Death."

In truth, we are lucky. We can have it all. We do not have to choose between a comfortable life and a meaningful life. But it is a challenge, and it goes beyond money.

At the end of the day, the problem is not the accumulation of fancy toys per se or an overdose of leisure. The problem is the loss of human contact, the gradual attenuation of ties to the community that often comes with growing wealth, zippier technology, and greater leisure. Moving from a village to a city, from an inner-city apartment house to a suburban split level, from a house on a block to a manor on an estate, increasingly insulates and isolates an individual, just as does the retreat from movie houses to television sets to computers and Game Boys.

At the same time, an ideology of the self has emerged. In the last thousand years, particularly in the last hundred years, the West went from being God-centered to being self-centered. In the last twenty years, the most powerful and progressive ideologies have been about empowering one's self and liberating one's self from authority, tradition, community.

Even the Jewish world talks about "identity" – an individualist notion – rather than "community" – a collectivist one.

BOWLING ALONE, AND REVIVING COMMUNITY

Increasingly, scholars are calling for a revival of community to cure America's social problems. In *Bowling Alone* (2001), Harvard sociologist Robert Putnam notes that, unlike in the 1950s, more Americans bowl on their own today than in leagues. This represents to him Americans' shrinking access to "social capital," a mass withdrawal from the public sphere. Yet, Putnam argues, the stronger your social bonds, the happier you are. Harvard philosopher Michael Sandel argues that a broader sense of community engagement fosters communal success as well as individual happiness. America began as a civic republic that posited national success on communal virtue; the modern procedural republic, where nothing is more sacrosanct than individual rights, threatens the very fabric of society which has been so essential in granting those rights.

In my own history classes at McGill University, I always tell my students: "I don't worry about your economic futures. Some of you will be richer, some of you will be less so, but all of you have proved that you can jump through the necessary social hoops to survive, and, for most of you, to thrive. I do worry," I say, "about your souls. Find a community, find a framework, find a way to bring meaning to your lives."

When wearing my professorial mortarboard, I stop there. I pose the challenge but do not dictate the solution. We Jews, however, are blessed. We don't have to construct or create a community. We have one. We don't have to develop a framework. We have many. We have philosophies of life and ways of bringing meaning into our lives, ways that are rooted in our common past, and in our commitment to a common future.

One hundred years ago, many Zionist thinkers recognized the challenge individualism posed to our Judaism and to our humanity. Collective economic arrangements such as the kibbutz, the communitarian nature of even the most capitalist of Zionists, all sanctified and sought to preserve the power of community. You don't have to be a socialist to realize that humans are social beings. You don't have to insist on turning off the computers in Israel's Silicon Valley and once again tilling the soil to find salvation in the twenty-first century. "Modern life is being blighted by the vapor of idealism and science, by the dust of atomism," Moses Hess mourned in 1862; "these are resting like mildew on red corn and stifling the germinating life in the bud. It is against these encroachments on the most sacred principles of creative life that the national tendencies of our time are reacting, and it is only against these destructive forces that I appeal to the primal power of Jewish nationalism."

ZIONISM AS A UNIVERSE OF ALTERNATIVE VALUES

Zionism can offer a universe of alternative values. A renewed appreciation of Zionism as a critique of modernity, as a call for community, as an appreciation of the essential glue that binds people together, can help cure what ails us. A newfound Zionism can help us realize that we often don't have to choose between our human identity and our Jewish identity, between what Moses Hess one hundred and fifty years ago called "Rome and Jerusalem." A renewed community, an alternative to the more-more-more, rush-rush-rush, me-me-me, money-money-money modern world can square the circle, making both one's human and one's Jewish soul sing.

Alas, while burdened by Israel's failures, Zionism has also repeatedly been victimized by its own successes. Zionism's greatest achievement – the establishment of the state in 1948 – substituted survivalism and statism for utopianism and universalism. Nineteen years later, the Six Day War miracle lulled Israelis into a false sense of security, saddled them with a hostile population, and triggered the messianic crusading of Gush Emunim, a movement whose zealous settlement policy upped the emotional stakes in the volatile territories.

Even the peace and prosperity of the 1990s damaged the movement. Israelis' understandable craving for normalcy triggered a mad dash for the goodies denied them for so long. With Israelis modeling themselves on Americans, and with secular Israelis fighting religious Jews, Israel seems to offer a less appealing model to most Diaspora Jews. It often seems a fountain of problems rather than the wellspring of any solutions.

EXILE, NORTH AMERICAN STYLE

And yet, for all our comfort, for all our wealth, North American Jews are still uncomfortable, still in exile. We express our discomfort in many ways, large and small. Even in an increasingly multicultural America, many of us still want to pass as "real" Americans – we'll say we are vegetarians when we keep kosher; as more Americans turn to offbeat names, we name our children Tiffany and Amber, Jason and Steven, so they won't seem different.

At the same time, our experience as outsiders affects even many of our secular pursuits. Steven Spielberg, one of the most famous American Jews today, has built his career on an oeuvre of exile. His best works are about displacement, interplanetary and otherwise, from "Close Encounters of the Third Kind" to "ET," from his underappreciated "Empire of the Sun," the story of a young British boy in a World War II Japanese prison camp, to his heartwrenching "Amistad," the story of kidnapped Africans trying to avoid the scourge of slavery. Many of Spielberg's blockbusters tell the story of a fish out of water. Many of his movies yearn for the comfort, the security, of the familiar. It is no coincidence that his great gift to the American idiom comes from one of his extraterrestrial movies: "ET Phone home!" Couldn't that be the modern Zionist's motto?

This fascination with exile, this search for home, is most intense in Spielberg's explicitly Jewish movies. "An American Tail," which he produced, features the plucky cartoon character Fievel Mousekewitz, and is about the Jewish migration from Europe to America. "Schindler's List" is about two levels of exile, the trauma of the exiled and oppressed Jews during the Holocaust, as well as the double life Oskar Schindler must lead. Even the first animation blockbuster Spielberg's Dreamworks Studio produced, "Prince of Egypt," was about the Jews' bondage and Moses's search for his identity.

Even worse, in Spielberg's big budget Middle East movie, "Munich," his Jewish characters are strong, but they are either soulless or neurotic. Leon Wieseltier of *The New Republic* charged that in attempting to give both Palestinians and Israelis a voice and in equating terrorists and counter-terrorists, "Munich" is "soaked in the sweat of its idea of evenhandedness." To be fair, Spielberg's caricature is tougher on the Palestinians than the Israelis – most of the Palestinians come across as violence-addled goons, while the Israelis come across as violence-addicted goons with occasional pangs of conscience. The familiar obsession with "home" comes through – but as an albatross ruining both Israelis and Palestinians.

While many criticized Spielberg's softheadedness regarding terrorism, "Munich" performed a broader disservice to the Jewish people. Spielberg and his screenwriter Tony Kushner only see Jewish death not Jewish life. "Munich" and "Schindler's List" together define Judaism and Zionism by violence and victimization without splendor or serenity. Reducing our magnificent, multi-dimensional, life-affirming civilization and homeland to surviving the Holocaust and fighting terrorism lets Nazis and Palestinians not Jews, define Judaism. In adding yet more neurotic Jews to his pile of cinematic stereotypes, Spielberg missed the humanistic values, noble dreams, land-based romanticism, faith in the future, day-to-day beauty, and the impressive nation-building and world-transforming accomplishments of the modern Zionist movement and traditional Judaism.

It is usually not a pretty picture. Spielberg's Jews are weak, not strong, cerebral not physical, more Woody Allen than Kirk Douglas. In "Schindler's List," Ben Kingsley's main Jewish character is a hook-nosed accountant who is more clever than virtuous. The non-Jewish hero, played by Liam Neeson, is a typical blonde-haired, blue-eyed Hollywood star.

It is time for Steven Spielberg to come home. He has arrived. Israel has arrived. Why not celebrate both? Why not offer an ode to principled Jewish power, not powerlessness, to the pleasure and pain of being rooted in one's world not opposed to it. This generation needs an updated "Exodus," a new, technicolor Zionist dream to inspire Jews and charm non-Jews. How about a big, vivid, bloody epic about liberating Jerusalem during the Six Day War in 1967? Call it "Six Days!" Show us the Israelis' ingenuity, drive, confidence, in defending their homeland, in freeing the Old City, and in building a beautiful country. Use the story to explain why Jews are in Israel, how they sought peace, how they unhappily learned to master the art of war. Give us some romance, some tragedy, some comedy, some grandeur – but make it less bloody than "Private Ryan." Yes, show some complexity and demonstrate compassion for the Arabs caught in the crossfire. Tug at the heartstrings. Endure the inevitable slings and arrows that will come in the media – for Jews as victims get Academy Awards, Jews are only acceptable as heroes if they are rumpled like Walter Matthau, neurotic like Woody Allen, or deJudaized like Michael Douglas.

Or, perhaps as *tshuva* penance, Steven Spielberg should be really bold and create a sweeping, inspiring, epoch-defining epic that lacks blood, tragedy, trauma. Let him confront the real Israel of day-to-day modern life rooted in ancient soil. Let's see a three-hankie romance about a love affair between an American Jewish woman torn between her comfy life in suburbia and her new, hot Israeli bloke, or a thriller about a crack team of Israeli geniuses inventing an alternative energy source pursued by greedy oil barons and car-makers trying to sabotage them. Show us what Spielberg so far fails to see, a thriving, exceedingly normal Western country prospering and developing in an historic and exotic locale with stunning scenery. It is time for Steven Spielberg – and the rest of us – to bring the joy back to Judaism and Zionism, not just the "oy."

THE ZIONIST SOLUTION

Modern Zionism needs to be radical, subversive, visionary, inspiring, provocative, evocative and relevant. Zionism needs to be more than writing checks and letters-to-the-editor; it even needs to be more than making *aliyah* (emigrating to Israel). Zionism, the national liberation movement of the Jewish people, was not just an attempt to find a solution to the "Jewish problem," it was a far-reaching crusade to fix the problems brought on by trying to adapt traditional Judaism to the challenges of the modern world.

Certainly Zionism sought to establish a Jewish homeland. But this was the first step in a more ambitious program. Once having their own land saved the Jewish people from anti-Semitism, most Zionists hoped to save the Jews' souls. And most of these visionaries believed that the new Jew recreated in a old-new homeland could serve as a model to a Western world that was struggling to find its moorings in a newly Enlightened but alienating world.

Zionism repudiated both the ancient Judaism that had fossilized over two thousand years in the *Galut*, exile, and the more modern mutations created by the initial nineteenth-century clash between Judaism and modernity. Early Zionists rejected the Faustian bargain their fathers had made to get accepted into European society. When Enlightenment and Emancipation first became widespread in the late 1700s and early 1800s, many Jews gave up their Judaism to be accepted as Frenchmen or Germans or Austrians. Zionists refused to do that and they refused to define Judaism solely as a religion, so it could be easily compared to Protestantism and thus rendered less foreign. This understanding of Judaism as uniquely integrating religious and national components distinguished Zionism then and now. To the Zionist, Judaism is not just a religion. Thus, despite the good intentions behind it, the much-vaunted Judeo-Christian ethic is anathema to the Zionist. It creates a false parallelism, it demotes Judaism from a complex, many-splendored thing wherein peoplehood, faith, and ethics interact, into a unidimensional religion which makes the church (the synagogue) the center of Jewish gravity, rather than the home or the homeland.

It is unfortunate that Zionism is not politically correct – it does not grab young Jews in the same way that feminism grabs many young Jewish women, gay liberationism grabs many young Jewish men, or Afrocentrism grabs many young African-Americans. Unfortunate but not surprising, for Zionism today grabs few people by the *kishkas*, the innards, as do these other movements. Battered by decades of the Arab-Israeli conflict, flummoxed by the complexities of modern Israel, Zionism is no longer the alluring rallying point it was a few decades ago.

ZIONISM AND THE "CONTINUITY" QUESTION

Sadly, just as Zionism seems to have lost its shine, North American Jewry is starting to ask the kinds of questions a reinvigorated Zionism could answer. The current obsession with "continuity" and with Israel experiences as a magic bullet to guarantee Jewish survival points to an interesting shift that occurred in the last decade. In the 1990s, as Israel became more stable, as the Arab-Israeli conflict seemed to subside, North American Jews turned to their own problems. What they saw in their own community terrified many: rampant assimilation, soaring rates of intermarriage, plummeting indices of Jewish involvement, from keeping kosher to studying Hebrew, from attending a seder to supporting any of the alphabet soup of Jewish organizations.

If a previous generation suffered from dyspeptic Judaism, a Judaism constantly in turmoil, agitated by this anti-Semitic slight and that perceived abuse, this generation suffers from narcoleptic Judaism, a Judaism that is too placid, too complacent, too non-threatening, too habitual. We don't need our Judaism to give us ulcers, but a little more excitement, a little more electricity, would be welcome.

Here is a recipe for a Jewish group volcano. Take a random group of North American Jewish students. Throw them on a bus, unleash them in Israel, and BOOM, a burst of energy erupts. Be they birthright israel strangers or movement friends, most young Israel tour participants transform from a "normal," subdued, laconic collection of North American individuals into a wonderfully raucous group of Jewish singers and dancers, *ayi-yi-yi-ing* from Jerusalem to Tel Aviv. This miracle of self-identification occurs so frequently, the energy is released so easily, because so many young Jews yearn for authentic, inspiring, energizing Jewish experiences.

Sadly, as Disapora Jews crowd synagogues for their annual three-times-a-year-High-Holiday pilgrimage, a different phenomenon usually occurs. It often seems as if a huge vacuum is sucking the energy out of too many of our vast cathedrals. A staleness settles in. Competent individuals are cowed by their unfamiliarity with the rituals. Exuberant people wear an air of awkward formality, as if their new shoes pinch them. Most endure the lengthy, disconnected service in dignified but strained silence. No wonder it will take most Jews nearly a year to muster the courage to return.

The missing ingredient here is passion. Passion releases the Israel trip's volcanic energy. Israeli tour guides and bus drivers, medics and passersby, exude an "*echpatiyut*," a sense of caring and responsibility for visitors that contrasts with the typically distancing American Jewish experience. Israelis – and most visitors – care about the land, the people, the nation, the state; they engage intensely with the rich past, the demanding present, the boundless future. The alluring thing about Israel, especially to the American Jew, is that it is, with all its problems, a living, breathing Jewish entity, striving to go forward. If you ignore it, it may not thrive - and thus it invites engagement.

Unfortunately, most American Jews just don't care that much about Judaism, Jewish life, even their own Jewish identities. As a whole, we are more passionate about our careers, our diversions and our possessions than we are about Jewish community, traditions and ideas. Few see Judaism as a compelling force in our lives and even fewer see Judaism as an active force for good, a change agent, rather than simply a passive vessel. Few non-Orthodox Jews approach Judaism as a necessity, as the answer to deep needs, rather than as a pleasant luxury, which better not inconvenience us too much. Moreover, many of us fear passion, leaving that to the fundamentalists, rather than embracing it as essential even to us moderates.

We have organizations galore and more denominations than we need. Together they have created a modern Judaism that is frequently more alienating than inviting, more materialistic than altruistic, more strident than upbeat, more inert than energizing, more interested in taking attendance or raising funds than in changing the world, more a pale imitation of the latest cultural trends than a tradition-rich alternative to modern vapidity. We need a new synthesis that combines the joy of Hasidism, the rigor of Orthodoxy, the erudition of Conservatism, the prophetic ethics of Reform, the intimacy of Reconstructionism, the humanitarianism of secularism, all leavened with the people-oriented passion and visionary activism of Zionism.

The institutional "hardware" of the Jewish world needs work. Synagogues need to become known as spiritual centers regularly filled with Jewishly-literate and ethically-motivated seekers rather than architectural wonders occasionally hosting prosperous and well-dressed burghers. Jewish schools need to prize *menschlichkeit* over materialism, community over careerism. Jewish organizations need to stop functioning as self-perpetuating bureaucracies and start acting as ethical and ideological sparkplugs. But institutional reform also requires a "software" revolution, if you will, a change in modern Jewish ideology and praxis. Modern Jews must act like owners not customers; rather than always talking about what "they" do wrong, we have to talk about what we can do right. We need to look at Judaism and Zionism as answers to some of our own problems, as ways of finding meaning in a confusing world, rather than simply as the source of problems we need to be guilted into trying to solve.

The half-century obsession "Will Israel survive?" is now vying with the older question "Will Judaism survive?" Zionism needs to address some needs, it must be a solution to some kind of Jewish problem. And it is. But rather than being the answer to Jewish misery in the *Galut*, it must respond to Jewish success. The North American teenager who has never experienced anti-Semitism, whose parents assimilated for him, who has an alphabet soup of creature comforts with his iPod, his TV, his DVD and his PC, still feels deprived. The modern technological world offers a smorgasbord of individual delights which dissolve the ties that traditionally have kept human beings together. Insulated from one another by our toys, we need a meaningful community.

THE ZIONIST COMMUNITY

Zionism offers Jews that community. Zionism, the national liberation movement of the Jewish people, helps us understand our Judaism better and like it more. Zionists teach that Judaism is not simply a faith, nor is it merely an ethnic affiliation. Zionism invigorates the theology and the vague sense of brotherhood. It gives us a land, a people, a history, as essential structures and bonds. It gives us a sense of belonging.

Israel, even if we have not fought for it, or even visited it, belongs to us. Serbians and Croatians and Bosnians feel a primal claim to their territory, to their people, as do we to ours. If such instincts do not exist, if we are all so sophisticated and cosmopolitan, why do Canadian Jews take pride in the Bronfmans' successes? Why do American Jews rejoice in the accomplishments of a Joe Lieberman, a Barbra Streisand, a Henry Kissinger? Why would many of us be pleased to find out that Columbus was Jewish? Why did my grandmother always count how many Jews passed the bar when the newspaper published the exam results?

Of course, if the sense of belonging were limited to an ethnic chauvinism, such ties would not be worth preserving. Zionism, however, is transcendent as well as tribal. As a movement of individual and national self-determination, Zionism is a call for Jewish dignity, cooperation and self-sacrifice. Zionism pushes the individual beyond the self, thereby rejecting the modern world's prevailing ethos. For over a century, Zionism has been making a "*mensch*" out of the Jewish people. In the 1880s, Zionism transformed pale scholars into strapping *chalutzim.* In the 1940s, Zionism turned European victims into Middle Eastern soldiers. Today, Zionism needs to help disaffected and self-indulgent suburbanites throughout the world (including Israel) inject meaning in their lives, find community, and find worth in themselves.

Over seventy years ago, the American Supreme Court Justice Louis D. Brandeis said it well: "Jewish life cannot be preserved and developed, assimilation cannot be averted, unless there be reestablished in the fatherland a center from which the Jewish spirit may radiate." Louis Brandeis had it all – wealth, power, a fancy title, friendship with the President of the United States, Woodrow Wilson. Yet he understood that he and his fellow Jews needed to look to their ancient homeland for spiritual satisfaction, communal inspiration, and, in essence, the very justification for continuing to exist as Jews.

Seen in this way, Zionism is an antidote to contemporary alienation. It repudiates today's aimlessness, materialism, and nihilism. Just as rappers articulate a critique of the white world while calling for black self-determination, Zionism offers the Jewish response to modernity. Rather than escaping into drugs or searching for intensity by crisscrossing the continent with the Grateful Dead or getting excited about the latest sale at the Gap, young Jews can turn to Zionist values and a Jewish community.

Even something as trendy as concern for the environment achieves greater depth if linked with Biblical concerns and the Jewish people's ancient love for the land.

It would be nicer and easier if more heroes like Golda Meir and Moshe Dayan would come around, if the romance of Israel from the 1950s and 1960s would revive, but that would also be false. Zionism can stand without its props. Zionism can also thrive without necessarily negating all of North American Jewish life – it can be a complement, not just a substitute. Even without *Aliyah* – moving there – ties to Israel, ties to the community, can redirect an aimless life.

MY ZIONIST ROOTS IN HISTORY AND COMMUNITY

While I leave it to others to judge whether my life is aimless, I feel blessed to be rooted as a Zionist in a people with a proud 4,000-year history, who venerate tradition and deify memory. Having reenacted the Exodus every Passover, the receiving of the Ten Commandments every Shavuot, the wandering in the desert every Sukkot, I wonder how you can grow up Jewish and not become an historian.

My grandfather, Leon Gerson, taught that Jews invented the idea of history, for without a sense of moral purpose and progress, history is merely chronology. My father, Bernard Dov Troy, further shaped my historical consciousness, mixing memoirs of his exploits smuggling gun parts to Palestine in large sweet potato cans before 1948 with inspiring tales about Jewish heroes and sages.

Growing up in New York, and thanks again to my father, who taught American history in public school by day and Jewish history in Hebrew school by night, the proud national narratives of both the American and the Jewish people resonated together. While it is fashionable to contrast our Jewish and secular identities, I learned there can also be harmonic convergences – being a good Jew makes me a better American, just as being a good American makes me a better Jew – even in Canada!

Being a Jew heightens my appreciation for American liberty; being an American increases my respect for Judaism's moorings. From this invigorating pool of ethics and ideals, stories and sentiments, I learned to juggle identities and ideas, to delight in nationalism's positive potential, democracy's duties and freedom's fruits. I learned about the power of the written word, critical thought and the well-chosen rhetorical flourish. I learned to balance faith and skepticism, optimism and realism, individuality and community, memory and vision, traditionalism and modernity.

I know that being an Israel-loving, *tzedakah*-giving Jew sensitized me to the challenges of modern terrorism and inspired our family decision to donate our book royalties to help terror victims. I know that being a people-oriented, freedom-worshiping Jew made me fear Soviet oppression in the 1970s and 1980s, priming me to applaud Ronald Reagan's condemnation of the "Evil Empire," even when the professoriate shuddered. I know that being a community-minded, tradition-venerating Jew honed my ethical sensibilities, heightening my discomfort with the shop-till-you-drop, MTV ethos.

I know that being an action-oriented, democracy-loving Zionist sharpened my respect for American nationalism, even as remembering the Holocaust illustrated the dangers of demonization and demagoguery. And I know that being an American, a Zionist and a Jew living in Canada these past few years has intensified my disdain for neutral postures that often foster immorality.

ISRAEL AS THE TOUCHSTONE

Focusing on Zionism as a movement of Jewish nationalism will also save Judaism from the false choices offered by North American culture. For all the talk about Judeo-Christian ideas, ours is not just another faith. We are connected to a land, a sense of peoplehood, a common history. But we are not merely another ethnic group like the Greeks and the Italians, because there is a value system, there is a theology, that comes with our history, with our peoplehood.

Individual Jews will place different values on the peoplehood and the faith. But they cannot separate the two. For years the Reform movement tried to sustain the faith without the nation and finally gave up –the Reform movement is now Zionist. Many secular Jewish parents tried to convey a sense of peoplehood without a respect for the religion and ended up brokenhearted as their children married "out of the faith."

Just as early Zionists like Ze'ev Jabotinsky and Theodor Herzl struggled to prove that Jews could be proud and strong once again, their successors must struggle to rebuild the modern Jews' sense of community. Israel offers the essential building block in all this – it is the touchstone. Rather than boasting of achievements in others' societies, Jews can now focus on creating a society of our own. The vision of rebuilding a land on Biblical soil, continuing a four-thousand-year adventure, should be enough to inspire anyone. We should not need enemies or heroes to spur us on. This kind of Zionism is motivated not by outsiders or insiders, but by one's soul. Zionism without heroes and without villains reminds us of who we are – and what we can become.

CHAPTER 18

POST-MODERNISM 101:
ZIONIST DREAMS AS NORTH AMERICAN DREAMS

For too long, what we have feared has dictated our Jewish agenda, and our Zionist agenda. Jean-Paul Sartre overstated it in 1946 when he claimed that "it is the anti-Semite who makes the Jew." But it certainly seems that it is the anti-Semites who make most Jews Zionists. Even during this crisis, we have to look for what we love, what we can love, and what we can learn from, both from Judaism and from Israel.

FRIENDSHIP 101 – TOWARD A REAL RELATIONSHIP

For starters, we need a more sophisticated support model, one that acknowledges complexity, one that gets beyond the simplistic black and white, all or nothing, you're either with us or against us, approach. We must acknowledge that supporting the state and its people does not entail supporting every governmental policy or agreeing with every Israeli individual. Even as we fight the propaganda war on the outside, we need to spur a rich debate about the rights and wrongs of the conflict from within.

We must also demand that the Israeli government and its representatives stop treating Diaspora Jews like idiots. At the November, 2000 General Assembly in Chicago for six thousand five hundred Jewish leaders, the Israeli Foreign Ministry had a booth running two videos simultaneously. One offered a bloody parade of images from the violence. The second was a cliché-ridden series of *Hava Nagila* images of happy Israelis at work and at play. A handout – in broken English – asked what people were "interestING" in receiving: "Beautiful Israel" or "Palestinian Violence In Israel." Such laughably false choices insulted the intelligence of all North Americans, let alone the cream of the Jewish leadership crop. One Israeli *shaliach* there grumbled, "The person responsible for this should not just be reprimanded – but should be shipped home, tomorrow!"

While acknowledging complexity, we also need to stop interacting with Israel solely through CNN. Calling an Israeli periodically, let alone visiting; occasionally reading *The Jerusalem Post* on-line, let alone doing it habitually, deepens ties and injects notes of normalcy amid the chorus of crisis. This friendship model is what Israel truly needs.

Once we have depoliticized our relationship with Israel somewhat, we can begin to reconceptualize it. Here, we must acknowledge a growing fissure in the Jewish community, and an historical inversion. A century ago, the religious community was overwhelming non- or anti-Zionist, and Zionism was the special province of some secular Jews. Today, the religious community – except for the most extreme fundamentalists – is overwhelmingly Zionist, and secular Jews are increasingly non- or anti-Zionist.

For religious Jews, a positive connection to Zionism, to the land of Israel and the state of Israel, is easy. Love of the Holy Land is reaffirmed thrice daily in prayer, thrice weekly in almost every Torah reading, and regularly with so many of the Holy Days, which mark historical moments and celebrate theological breakthroughs to the rhythms of the Israeli agricultural calendar. Moreover, ties to Israel, love of the land, are no more or less questioned than other key *mitzvot,* such as observing *Shabbat* or *kashrut.*

By contrast, in the rest of the community, the Jewish link to Israel is as open to debate as any other area of Jewish praxis. Non-religious American Jews of the last third of the twentieth century worshiped the trinity of Holocaust, Israel, and Tradition, meaning family habits, ethnic traditions, and Jewish rituals. Overall, in North America today, distance from Judaism correlates with distance from Israel. And in the twenty-first century, for many secular and now highly-Americanized Jews, the Israel connection is the weakest of the three modern pillars.

Beyond the political tensions we experience through the media, broader ideological obstacles are blocking a healthier, more positive role for Israel and Zionism in building modern Jewish identity. For starters, the narratives clash. The American Jewish narrative, like the narratives of many immigrant-driven Diaspora communities, is triumphal, emphasizing America's centrality as redeemer. Arrival there is the great leap forward, guaranteeing all ensuing progress. Israel's narrative weaves triumph with tragedy – "*dvash v' oketz,*" "honey and sting," – striking a more sober tone. Zionism also posits a different center – Israel.

Intensifying the obvious ensuing clash of loyalties, competing cultural impulses collide too. Western consumer cultures offer the weightless lure of freedom transcending the gravitational force of tradition. We live in a world of radical selfishness, of dizzying pluralism, of contingencies not commitments. "Bowling alone" discourages working or singing or praying or building together. In our throwaway society being rooted in history or community or morality or faith is tragically unhip.

Belonging and committing are passé in today's Western culture of doubt. It is a clash of epistemologies, of ways of thinking. Jews teach *na'aseh v'nishmah*, we will do and obey; the Zionist imperative is *livnot u'lhibanot*, to build and be rebuilt; to which the lazy, dismissive, stereotypical American slacker responds, "whatever." If a previous age tended to oversell, idealizing Moshe Dayan and Golda Meir, today we undersell, demonizing promiscuously. Our cynical world, with Jon Stewart and Jay Leno feeding us news, mocks leaps of faith fostering communities, common mythologies, shared identities. In a post-mythological age of exposé, it is hard to build faith in Zionism, Israel or God. This "whateverism" encourages holding back rather than plunging ahead; prizing individuality and disdaining community. We seek custom-fit idiosyncratic notions rather than collective "isms" and enduring ideals. How do we learn complexity and maintain love, how do we acknowledge imperfection, while still supporting Israel, America, our parents?

To make matters worse, during the Oslo interregnum, battling Orthodox, Conservative and Reform Rabbis imported Israel's religious wars to North American shores, at once polarizing the Diaspora community and alienating many Diaspora Jews from Israel. North American Jews took to the ramparts, with little understanding of the peculiar secular-religious dynamics in Israel, with little awareness that in Israel tensions were growing over funding and politics even as many religious restrictions eased. Such a turn of events is particularly disturbing because Israel could and should unite religious and non-religious Jews rather than dividing them. Israel, in peace and in war, should be something both religious Jews and ethnic Jews can cherish, even if for different reasons. Zionism, after all, explains one of the great conundrums of Judaism, the perennial question of asking, are we a religion or a nation, are we defined by a common theology or by a peoplehood – by answering yes to both questions.

Whether for reasons of theological commitment and-or ethnic identity, all Jews should seek a real friendship with Israel. For the modern Diaspora Jew, this friendship is rooted in the past, mutually beneficial in the present, and oriented toward the future. At its best, it combines the reverence a Catholic has for his church, the pride an immigrant Italian has in the old country's culture, and the faith an American has in his country's ideals.

COMMON ROOTS

The first essential bond between the Diaspora and Israel comes from our shared and rich history. North American Jews have to embrace the past, to nurture our roots, to celebrate our heritage. Such an appreciation is easier said than done in a pop culture which worships the new and the here and now, which reduces "Roots" to a brand name on sweatshirts and celebrates rootlessness. Moreover, we need to recognize that having been disgorged from Europe and the Arab lands, the places where our immigrant ancestors were born were merely way stations in a long and meandering historical saga. The nostalgia the children of immigrants had for Morocco or Moldavia, for Prague or Pinsk, should be transferred to Israel. Our true roots are in our homeland, Israel. There we can see and feel a modern Jewish civilization growing and thriving on the foundations built over thousands of years by our people.

One of the most magical things about being in Israel is that your perspective shifts – you begin counting in centuries and millennia rather than in years and decades as we North Americans usually do. Coming from a society where eighty-year-old buildings get "landmark" status, you find yourself walking past ruins that are nine hundred, thirteen hundred, eighteen hundred years old – in favor of the ruins that are twenty-one hundred, three thousand, or four thousand years old. The Bible becomes a guidebook, not just a storybook. Abraham, David, Joshua, Deborah become real, three-dimensional people, not abstract two-dimensional characters.

In embracing the past we reject the Palestinian lie that Israeli history begins in 1948. We do not just go back a century ago to the rise of Zionism but we hark back four millennia ago to God's first commandment to Abram – *"lech lecha meartzecha,"* Leave the land of your birth, and go to a new homeland, what we now call Israel.

In celebrating that history we have to feel it deeply. Moreover, in a big leap for all American patriots, we need to view living in Diaspora as an accident of birth rather than as some special fulfillment of destiny. The American national project, borrowing Biblical imagery, views the immigrant's passage to America as a rebirth, as a deliverance *"meavdoot lecheroot,"* from slavery to freedom. American ideology considers life today, in the here and now, as the climax of world history, a progressive story culminating in the freedoms, luxuries and leisures of this moment.

It is unrealistic and unnecessary to negate American exceptionalism. Rather, in our post-modern world of multiple identities we have to cultivate another dimension, a parallel Jewish narrative. It is the story of the wandering

Jew, a story which accepts America as a most glorious, comfortable and welcoming way station for Jews, while offering us an added bonus. We are fortunate not only to be tied to and shaped by our homes, but to be tied to and shaped by our homeland. The historically-unique openness of America, the deep friendship between the United States and Israel, saves us from having to make false choices. Rather, it allows us to be doubly blessed by a host nation that embraces us and empowers us, and by a Jewish nation, an ancient and eternal address, that anchors us and sustains us.

FEELING PROUD OF OUR HOMELAND

Note, however, to the extent that we live in a host nation, no matter how hospitable, it may not be home in all senses of the word. Israel today, in the present, still serves an essential grounding function for the Jewish people, even for those of us who have never been there. Having traveled to Israel since February 2000 with over one thousand birthright israel participants, most of whom are first-time visitors there, I have been struck by how often they talk about "coming home," "feeling at home," when speaking about this exotic Middle Eastern outpost. Clearly, they do not mean home in the most literal sense. A few enthusiasts may consider it as "the place in which one's domestic affections are centered." But most mean it in the sense of "a person's native place or country." Instinctively, many Jews recognize and feel the link: Israel is our source, it is the opening act and main stage of Jewish history.

The students have also used another word repeatedly, which at first I did not know how to take. Many talked of their "pride," how "proud" they were to be Jews in Israel. Initially I heard this as "proud" of Israel's accomplishments, the miracle of renewing this ancient homeland in the second half of the twentieth century – but that is not what they meant. I then cynically dismissed it as self-esteem talk, the touchy-feely tendency encouraged by overly psychological high school teachers to turn every experience into a me-building, feel-good moment. I learned that that is not what they meant either. When students spoke of "pride," they spoke of a feeling of belonging, of connectedness, of community, of self-respect that comes from a sense of ownership. Many felt Israel was theirs, that they belonged to Israel and Israel belonged to them.

The events of 2000-2004 demonstrated that linkage through tragedy. We saw that the Jewish people's nerve endings are connected in an elaborate web – when an Israeli Jew is cut, we bleed. We are FA-MI-LY, as the song says. Four thousand years of history, two thousand years of exile, have fostered our family feeling. We believe that *"kol Yisrael areiveem zeh lazeh,"* all Jewish people are connected to one another, we are all brothers and sisters. Moreover, our destinies are linked – the surge of anti-Semitism in North America that began in 2000, the heightened security arrangements, the slurs on campuses, the occasional beatings on the streets, are faint but unpleasant echoes of the uglier conflict taking place in the Middle East. The flip side of that shared sense of trauma is the pride, the love, we do feel and should build with our brothers and sisters in Israel, whether or not they are embattled.

WE WON! IT'S TIME FOR A ZIONIST RENEWAL

This, then, should be a moment of Zionist renewal, not only to defy our immoral enemies, but because in confronting Palestinian terror, Zionism – and Israel – again triumphed. The Palestinians' futile war forced us to relearn some essential Zionist lessons. We relearned the prime Zionist directive of *ein breira*, "we have no choice." Over the decades, hundreds of thousands of Jews from Europe, Arab countries, the Soviet Union and Ethiopia left their homes and came to live in the Jewish state because *"ein breira,"* they had no choice. Similarly, these last few years, Israelis had to fight, reluctantly, this wave of terrorism because they, and we, had no choice.

Thanks to Yasir Arafat's evil, we also rediscovered the central Zionist experience of unity in peoplehood. Even in this post-ethnic, hyper-individualistic age, the Jewish people's nerve endings are intertwined. When one of us is cut, we all bleed. Too many Christians yawned as Christian aid workers were slaughtered in Pakistan, Christian children were enslaved in Sudan, Christian girls were raped in the Palestinian territories. But most Jews empathized with Israel's terror victims, and many mobilized to help. Arafat offered negative proof that the Jewish people remain interconnected; we must rally around positive symbols, ideas, actions and initiatives, too.

Watching the Israeli center re-emerge, seeing how the separation fence buried the right's maximalist territorial illusions that Palestinians would fade away and the left's naive millennialist delusions that the Middle Eastern Age of Aquarius would come, we also remembered the pragmatism and big tent centrism that traditionally characterized Zionism. The early Zionists were quarrelsome and fragmented. Still, for most, when faced with historic choices such as the painful 1947 United Nations Partition plan, hardheaded, realistic problem-solving trumped ideological purity. Israel grew from the center, and it survived this latest round of violence by staying levelheaded, losing neither democracy nor dignity, balancing civil liberties and civil survival, seeking protection from Palestinian terror, not vengeance, and improvising as the situation demanded.

Hidden within these mostly reactive Zionist lessons, two more affirmative values can shape a positive Zionist renewal. Zionism at its best always sought particularism, meaning Jewish nationalism, as a path into universal values, not an escape from broader ideals. We can best advance humanistic values by concentrating communal energies in service of those ideals.

Tikkun olam, repairing the world, is hot these days, but do-gooding should be more than merely Christian charity with a Jewish inflection. Zionism defined effectively can provide a Jewish national or communal framework for responding to modern challenges, be it the values crisis in our material world, the alienation and individuation of consumer society or the worldwide epidemic of terror. Fighting poverty in Israel or alleviating misery in the Darfur region of The Sudan through an Israeli framework focuses and anchors actions that otherwise might dissipate as individual initiatives.

By having a "we" not a "me," and a Jewish "us" at that, by taking responsibility for individual, communal and world problems together, *ani v'atah neshaneh et haolam*, you and I *can* change the world, as the Zionist hymn goes, or at least have a better shot at succeeding.

In doing that, we will also uphold the Zionist value of returning to history. In 1990s America there was much cheap talk about ending history. That ended with 9-11. We cannot escape history. We might as well be the best actors and activists we can be, broad in our vision, deep in our idealism, united in our purpose. Let us use our lucky accident of birth – membership in the Jewish people (or our choice to join) as a way to enrich our lives, save our souls, work together, multiply our impact, build a country that we need and improve a world that needs us and our values.

Suitably anchored in the past, and proud in the present, Israel can have a vital role in shaping our Jewish future. Rather than just preaching to Israel, and bailing out Israel, we need to recognize Israel as the answer to some of our communal challenges. Yes, Israel, along with the Zionist enterprise, has failed to bring the sense of normalcy and security the early Zionists hoped. But Israel is more than an albatross around the Jewish communal neck. When we shift our focus back to our own internal challenges, Israel can help fight the three horsemen of modern Jewish apocalypse – assimilation, anomie and intra-communal infighting.

Israel, offering fifty-seven varieties of Jewish life, presents various models of Jewish living that often seem more dynamic, more authentic, more integrated, than our schizophrenic existence as hyphenated Americans. Israel is the world headquarters of what Rabbi Yitz Greenberg calls "24/7 Judaism." To the extent that Jewish renewal pivots on a shift from synagogues, afternoon schools and federations to camps, day schools, and youth movements, Israel becomes the natural focal point of that round-the-clock Judaism, a Judaism which is normal, electric, inspiring, and all-encompassing.

Israel, seething cauldron that it is of passionate Jews combating each other over how to shape the Jewish future, makes it hard to be indifferent. It can push Diaspora Jews to care, to get involved and to rethink fundamental assumptions about Judaism, spirituality, the meaning of life. And Israel, appealing as it does to the God-fearing while also offering a model of ethnic identification for the secular, can serve as a uniter, not a divider, a rallying point and a plane of agreement recognizing the unique national and religious character of Judaism, rather than a flashpoint and a bone of contention.

In the United States, African-Americans have begun celebrating Kwanza, seeking to consecrate, ritualize, and concretize ties to Africa during the Christmas season. In Israel, every day is a Jewish Kwanza, a living, breathing, corporal expression of concepts that sometimes feel weird or fuzzy in the Diaspora. It is no coincidence that people talk of "roots" – roots are natural, roots are physical, roots are real. Roots are also long, meandering, malleable, enduring, and, most important of all, life-sustaining.

TOWARD A NEW ZIONIST DREAM

We need as a Jewish community to posit a Zionist dream to sit astride the North American dream – in our have-your-cake-and-eat-it-too world it is unrealistic to expect an either-or choice. If the North American dream is about individual self-fulfillment and prosperity, can the Zionist dream be about communal fulfillment and individual meaning? If the North American dream is about making it despite being a Jew, can the Zionist dream be about making a better world? If the North American dream is about individual ambition, can the Zionist dream be about Jewish communal ambitions?

Granted, this kind of Zionism may sound pie in the sky, and does not always comport with Israeli realities. But such is the power and tragedy of all symbols. The starry-eyed secular North American Jew who kisses the Western Wall reverently and sees it as a sacred link with the past is no more or less accurate than the hard-nosed secular Israeli Jew who pooh-poohs the Wall disdainfully and sees it as a contemporary symbol of religious corruption. Both are seeing selectively and responding to abstractions. And it may not hurt Israelis and Israeli Zionism to see Israel every now and then from the sometimes rose-tinted glasses of the passionate Diaspora Zionist. Here, too, the friendship needs rebalancing – Israelis have much to learn about Zionism and Judaism, as well as liberalism and democracy, from North American Jews.

No matter how intense the battle gets, we must not see ourselves and our co-religionists just as soldiers in Israel's propaganda wars. Rather, we should try to unite the entire Jewish world by focusing on Israel as fellow seekers, partners, pilgrims, friends. We need to end the missionary mentality, we need to stop treating Israelis as our poor beleaguered cousins and embrace them as friends, as equals, at best as both teachers and as students, sometimes learning from them, sometimes teaching them. Zionism can rescue Judaism – on both sides of the Atlantic – from the false dichotomies that have boxed it in and sapped its energies. We need not choose between religion and nationalism, between ethnicity and spirituality, we can have it all. Zionism, with its promiscuous embrace of values, history, national pride, spiritual quests, and, most of all, community, can offer an alternative to the hollow lives too many of us lead. Zionism, in a revitalized and edgy form, can bring passion back to a Judaism that is all too often lifeless. The great turn-of-the-century Zionist A.D. Gordon in his forties threw away his bourgeois Russian life, rolled up his sleeves, and began draining the swamps of the Holy Land. He said "What we need is zealots of Labor – zealots in the finest sense of the word." We too need our zealots – and not only on the West Bank.

Zionism can help us find spiritual, social, and ideological traction in a world of vast choices and deep loneliness. To provide such footing, Zionism needs to go beyond today's unidimensional pro-Israelism. We must return to an ideological universe that is Protestant not Catholic, with many different denominations united under a broad rubric. A Liberal Zionism could try to reconcile American-style individual liberties with the collective ethos so central to Jewish thought and the Israeli experience. An Ethical Zionism could deploy prophetic Judaism as a compass in navigating dilemmas the nation and individuals face in our complicated modern world. A Green or Environmental Zionism could build on the historic love of the land and the turn-of-the-century infatuation with socialism as a way of coping with the materialism so many of us enjoy and crave. A Spiritual Zionism could seek transcendence through more secular Israeli and Jewish symbols, while a Traditional Zionism could seek to find a balance between modern life and our ancient lifestyle rooted in the past, yet comfortable with the future.

Many of these visions attempt to fix the world, not just Israel or the Jewish people. This kind of broad-based humanistic idealism pulsed through the writings of most Zionist thinkers. This is the kind of wide-ranging visionary thinking that can resurrect Zionism as both an effective and a subversive force in people's lives.

Such a newfound Zionist denominationalism should address deep yearnings and serious problems on both sides of the Atlantic. It would integrate individuals' mainstream passions into their Jewish lives. The various ideological impulses would be anchored in the touchstones that unite Jews and could confront the puzzles that vex so many of us as secular human beings beginning a new millennium. All these approaches recognize Jewish nationalism as an essential component of Jewish identity, and locate Israel at the center of the Jewish universe.

In short, Israel – and a dynamic, challenging Zionist identity – should be the answer to the modern Jew's secular, ethnic, individualistic, nondenominational prayer. Israel should be the premier Jewish identity-builder, inspiring Jews worldwide, be they religious or secular, leftist or rightist, Israeli or Diaspora-based. Israel should be a living laboratory allowing modern Jews to experiment in the Jewish people's fertile, energetic, pluralistic, old-new land with the different elements shaping their identities. Jews in Israel should be generating exciting formulas synthesizing tradition and modernity, liberalism and Judaism, tribalism and humanitarianism, ethnicity and cosmopolitanism, nationalism and idealism, democracy and spirituality, East and West, the "I" and the "we." The country's intimacy, the land's grandeur, history's echoes, the society's vitality, the state's idealism, should provide that sense of community, pride in heritage, framework for meaning, vessel of values, vehicle for self-fulfillment and forum for self-expression many modern Jews lack in the leisure-oriented, material-filled world we live in – and love.

It is easy to blame the obvious suspects for the gap between this idealistic vision and reality. Arab exterminationists, Palestinian terrorists, hysterical journalists and hostile leftists have battered Israel's self-image and clouded the Jewish people's collective vision of the Jewish homeland. In Israel, scheming politicians, unreasonable zealots, greedy rabbis and carping academics have done damage, aided unconsciously throughout the Diaspora by heavy-handed educators, guilt-generating community leaders, and lazy parents. An unhappy mélange of good and bad intentions has unduly politicized Zionism, making Israel advocacy the primary vehicle for Israel expression – and often Jewish identity building.

TO LIVE IS TO CHOOSE:
PERFECTING THE ZIONIST JUJITSU

Considering the sobering headlines, failed leaders and clashing narratives, loyalties, epistemologies and sensibilities, the continuing vitality of Israel-Diaspora ties appears downright miraculous. Decoding that continuing miracle provides the potential genomes for redemption. And acknowledging that many of these cultural challenges have been exported to Israel, and embraced by young Israelis, suggests that a renewed Zionism could help Jews in Israel as well.

Modernity not only offers "freedom from" age-old constraints and contemporary truisms. We also have "freedom to," freedom to commit, to take stands, to be bold. My mother warned me, "Don't be so open minded your brain falls out." To live is to choose, to stand for something, to be one thing not something else. Better to choose with integrity, for you can choose consciously or unconsciously; not choosing is also choosing.

Thank you Yasir Arafat – may his name and memory be expunged. Arafat's war, waged in Jerusalem and Mombasa, not just Hebron and Gush Katif, launched against women and children, and assailing Israel's very legitimacy, imposed a moral clarity lacking during the

easy living 1990s. Arafat returned us
to the fundamental building block of
Jewish and Zionist identity - our shared
destiny as a people. The Jewish people's
nerve endings remain uniquely
entangled: together we mourn the loss of
astronaut Ilan Ramon on the space
shuttle or of the latest victim of
Palestinian terror, and together we
celebrate an Israeli Gold Medal in the
Olympics or Israelis winning Nobel
Prizes in Chemistry and Economics. Our
tribalism often mystifies our Christian
friends, just as we are mystified by their
silence when fellow Christians suffer.

Even many of the most supposedly "assimilated" among us take this
peoplehood thing so for granted that we ignore its uniqueness and its grip on
our imaginations, emotions, and identities.

While these last bloody years evoked comparisons to the horrific 1930s
and 1940s, it may be more instructive to consider the 1960s and 1970s.
Both the 1967 and 1973 wars galvanized Diaspora Jews, solidifying Israel
as a central pillar of a modern, upbeat, secularized Jewish identity. Even as
the stereotypical "sixties kids" fled to Ashrams or rebelled against their
parents and upbringings, the baby-boomers triggered a Jewish ideological
and institutional renaissance and redirection.

We are now poised for a similar communal jujitsu, transforming the
negative force of Palestinian terror into a positive force for Zionist and
Jewish renewal. A generation that "feels Jewish" – often without an
accompanying theology or even much education – can embrace the Zionist
trinity of peoplehood, history, homeland. If we think "What's Israel got that
America ain't got?" we see that Israel's got ancient history and
contemporary mystery, which fosters fascination; it's got intimacy and
intensity, which invites engagement. Isaiah Berlin said Winston Churchill
in 1940 lifted "a large number of inhabitants of the British Isles out of their
normal selves, and, by dramatizing their lives and making them seem to
themselves and to each other clad in the fabulous garments appropriate to
a great historic moment, transformed cowards into brave men, and so
fulfilled the purpose of shining armor." Plunging into Israel's story, both the
honey and the sting, can similarly transform modern North American Jews.

THE ZIONIST Rx FOR WHAT AILS US

Invigorated, expanded, historically-based, updated Zionism or Zionisms could address many of the diseases currently afflicting the Jewish community, including:

Paranoia: This all-consuming fear that anti-Semitism poses the same threat to American Jews that it did in Europe makes Judaism defensive and reactionary. Zionism can emphasize positive motivations for being Jewish.

Dyspepsia: This angry insistence that we must remain Jewish so as not to let Hitler win distorts the Jewish past and present. It raises Jews who are long on aggressiveness and short on substance, who have more edge than commitment. A Zionist reading of history focuses on the Jew as actor, not simply as victim.

Amnesia: This deep ignorance of the most basic Jewish concepts and values reduces us to mimics who simply ape what our grandparents did in a diluted form. Those who distort our history into one woeful tale of oppression at least remember our history. Discounting the many Jews who do not even acknowledge their Judaism, many Jews who actually went through the Hebrew school system are functionally illiterate. Many lawyers, doctors, and professors who flaunt their secular educational achievements spent many more hours watching Sesame Street than learning about their heritage. Zionist education, with its emphasis on culture, on history, is more exciting, and could be more successful, than the failing Hebrew schools.

Schizophrenia: This overstated and growing chasm between "religious" and "secular" Jews threatens Jewish unity and alienates far too many on both sides. Rooted in traditional and secular concepts, Zionism can bridge the gap, can transcend the false choice between 100 percent, take-it-or-leave-it Orthodox Judaism defined by our most fundamentalist sects and total assimilation.

Narcissism: This epidemic of materialism and self-involvement, wherein the malls have become our temples and Neiman and Marcus our high priests, demeans us all. Given the widespread and relatively recent affluence many Jews have been lucky to enjoy, given many Jews' great skill at assimilating, it is not surprising that so many have internalized modern America's me-me-me, mine-mine-mine, now-now-now ethos. Zionism can be and must be a forum for social criticism, and an instrument for liberating Jews from the values and habits they take for granted. We need to return to the days when young Jews were known for distributing blue boxes that collected charity rather than for purchasing – and keeping – blue dresses from the Gap.

Anomie: This isolation we endure from one another, this social disconnect so many experience as we hole up in our suburban palazzos, is inhuman as well as unJewish. With its emphasis on community, Zionism rejects the individuation of our world – and could help us learn how to rebuild social networks that are vital not virtual.

Depression: This low-grade fever that afflicts our community manifests itself in a chronic worry about "continuity," and a lethargic approach to Judaism whereby too many of those who bother to remain Jewish go through the motions without real joy or passion. In North America, we have gone from being an oppressed people to being a depressed people; a revitalized Zionism can restore our communal energy.

In short, a revitalized Zionism can help "anti-religious" Israelis see how religious they are, and can help the Protestant Jews of North America appreciate that their identity is richer than they thought. Even if not everyone signs on, a loud and passionate debate can only improve our too-pale, too-placid Jewish communal lives.

This revitalized Zionism can teach constructive lessons to the rest of American society as well. A revitalized Zionism will bring substance to an identity that is currently more of an external posture – a label – than a source of internal meaning, a way of life. Many modern American Zionists have unknowingly inverted Y.L. Gordon's formula for Enlightenment success, proudly affirming their Judaism on the street, but acting like "regular" men and women at home. This approach, emphasizing sub-group identity publicly without mining it for deeper significance in one's personal and family life, is growing more common in an America riven with identity politics. Too many young Americans today aggressively embrace their ethnic or racial identity in the political arena, while watching the same banalities on television at home, rocking to the same music, dressing according to the same code. America works best with Jews, Poles, Italians, African-Americans celebrating and drawing meaning from their differences at home, but working together as citizens on the street. Similarly, an America-based Zionism will work best with a revitalized Jewish identity at home, and some of those positive Jewish values shaping our behavior on the street as well.

Nearly three-quarters of a century ago, at the Hebrew University dedication, Chaim Nahman Bialik praised the purifying passion of the young Zionists. "Ladies and gentlemen," he exclaimed,

Thousands of our youth, obeying the call of their hearts, are streaming from the four corners of the earth to this land for the purpose of redeeming it from desolation and ruin. They are prepared to pour all their aspirations and longings and to empty all the strength of their youth into the bosom of this wasteland in order to revive it. They are plowing rocks, draining swamps, and building roads, amid singing and rejoicing. These young people know how to raise simple and pure labor – physical labor – to the level of highest sanctity, to the level of religion. It is our task to kindle such a holy fire within the walls of the house which has just been opened upon Mount Scopus.

Let us hope and pray that such fires can be kindled without the sparks of anti-Semitism, that for positive rather than negative reasons we can harness the same kind of energy that so inspired – and healed – Chaim Nahman Bialik and his generation.

A NEW LADDER OF ZIONIST ACHIEVEMENT

In fact, since 2000, at every stage of a young Jew's educational journey, new initiatives and infrastructures have sought to rekindle Bialik's "holy fire," building a positive contemporary Jewish and Zionist identity.

◆ Jewish day schools and camps - enjoying their own 1990s-fed resurgence – have pioneered new curricula for teaching Israel and twinned with Israeli schools. These initiatives acknowledge the complexities of Israeli politics while still celebrating Israel's thriving society and delighting in Israeli culture's sights, sounds, tastes, and smells.

◆ Resurrecting an idea the 1970s Soviet-Jewry movement popularized, many Bar and Bat Mitzvah celebrants have begun twinning with Israeli children victimized by terror. The best of the twinning projects use the Israel link to push the Bar Mitzvah beyond materialism, shifting the questions of celebrants from "what did you get" to "what did you give?"

◆ And speaking of rites of passage, the group trip to Israel has begun embedding itself in the American Jewish mind as a new "rite of passage," thanks especially to birthright israel's magic carpet ride for young adults between the ages of 18 and 26 – with a follow-up program of growing effectiveness building Jewish identity through a positive group Israel experience.

◆ For the same age group, a new generation of Israel advocates who are hipper, savvier, more individualistic, more careerist, more media-fluent have emerged – with armies of blue-blazered undergraduates convening across the country to develop a new pro-Israel language tailored to today's ambivalences and complexities.

◆ Academically, students are not just challenging the anti-Zionist orthodoxies of so many Middle East Studies departments, but are developing a new branch of Israel Studies. This model builds on the proliferation of Holocaust Studies, while delivering a message of pride and empowerment not just pity.

◆ And the latest Jewish Agency undertaking, MASA, seeking to increase the number of young Jews studying or living for six months to a year in Israel from 5,000 to 20,000, offers an exciting culminating step in this emerging ladder of Zionist achievement and Jewish identity building.

Each of these initiatives reflects a key idea essential to building a positive Israel-Diaspora friendship. The curricular revolution – and a positive, proactive, yet authentic Israel-oriented curriculum which would be transformative – focuses on education. The twinning programs, transcending the traditional model of Diaspora Jews as social workers or philanthropists to emphasize Diaspora Jews and Israeli Jews as friends – cultivate empathy. Birthright israel and other programs, emphasize experiencing Israel, not just reading about it, or even defending it. The new brand of Israel advocacy provides young Jews with an opportunity to engage Israel, honing important skills, cementing emotional, social, political and ideological ties among fellow Zionists in Israel and at home. A wave of Israel Studies will enlighten American Jews, going beyond the depressing facts of Holocaust victimology. And MASA will promote entanglements, those messy, complex, often-emotionally draining and confusing yet enriching and inspiring ties to a home six thousand miles away from home, as friendships bud, professional associations sprout, serious connections to Israel take root.

These new stops on the Jewish journey should become as ubiquitous as Hebrew schools and Bar Mitzvahs were in the 1960s and 1970s – but hopefully far more inspiring and constructive. If that happens, Diaspora Jews will enjoy a richer relationship with Israel and their own communities – as demonstrated by the birthright bounce, the epidemic of enthusiasm that birthright returnees have been spreading these last few years.

With birthright as the model, a renewed Israel-Diaspora relationship will benefit Israelis too. One unexpected consequence of birthright has been the birthright bounce among Israelis, the positive impact the *"Mifgash"* meetings between Israeli and Diaspora peers have had on the Israeli hosts. Even brief, two-day *mifgashim* have taught Israeli soldiers about their role on the world stage, shining their proverbial "armor" to participate in the Jewish historical epic. Many IDF education officers have become quite enthusiastic about giving soldiers some days off to get turned on to a new appreciation for Israel's role in Jewish history and the modern Jewish world. Other so-called secular Israelis have described – with tears in their eyes – their excitement at discovering from North American Jews different forms of Jewish expression that have nothing to do with the either-or "rabbi's way or the highway" stereotype nurtured in too many non-traditional Israeli households (and fed by a hamhanded rabbinate).

Savvy Israel advocates have discovered that pro-Israel students, both Jewish and non-Jewish, respond to retail not wholesale approaches. Customized messages work better than mass sloganeering, and the most effective Israel advocacy is the result of a positive relationship with Israel rather than the only dimension of an Israel connection. Similiarly, this Zionist rebirth cannot be mass-produced on either side of the Atlantic, nor can it be too politicized. We need a big tent Zionism, broad, inclusive, using Zionism as a response to the challenges of the modern world and the lure of assimilation, not as a social work project, a political initiative or a guilt trip. The ingredients are there, the need is growing, the timing is ripe, for a similar, step-by-step Zionist resurgence. Perhaps we can start by taking back the term "Zionism" from its enemies and its more cynical friends, making it a term of pride, openness and this kind of one-on-one, culturally savvy creativity.

Our sages taught about a *Yerushalayim shel maleh* and a *Yerushalayim shel matah,* a Heavenly Jerusalem of above and a Corporeal Jerusalem of below. Scholars teach about a civic nationalism that unites people around ideas and an ethnic nationalism that unites people around common origins. Precisely now, after a decade in which many of us recoiled from Israel because of its growing materialism and its intensifying religious tensions, after a time in which many of us rushed toward Israel in its pain and terror, precisely now, when we are bogged down in the mud, we have to seek the romantic, the transcendent, the enduring. We cannot ignore the messy realities, the disappointments, the immediate challenges, but we also cannot allow our relationship to be defined only by them. Let us take the return of Israel to our communal agenda as a wake up call, a spur for a reevaluation and a renewal of our ties with our Jewish state, with our homeland. And in that spirit, with apologies to John F. Kennedy and his 1961 inaugural address, ask not only what you can do for Israel, ask also what Israel can do for you. That mutuality is the basis of true friendship, that is what Israel – and the Jewish people – need today.

PART 5

BUMPING INTO HISTORY: ZIONISM IN ACTION

"I was an honest writer who was walking down the street one day when he bumped into history," the Oscar-winning screenwriter Ben Hecht would recall about his Jewish awakening in the 1930s. Until then, Hecht had indulged himself, worshipping art and entertainment. But the Nazi threat to Jews and democracy transformed him. Unlike his peers, he did not wallow. Angered, he became an activist.

Although the situation of the early twenty-first century was less dire than the 1930s, some of us also responded rationally with anger and activism. But anger can curdle and activism for its own sake can become tiresome, reactive, reductionist. The best response to the nihilism of today's terrorists and their cheerleaders is to turn the negatives into positives, to turn the anger into constructive advocacy, to celebrate positive, traditional Jewish, Zionist, Western values of decency, democracy, civility, community, and rationality rather than simply reacting to the hatred.

CHAPTER 19

PROGRESSIVISM 101: THE NEW ANTI-SEMITISM – AND HOW TO FIGHT IT ON CAMPUS AND OFF

THE NEW ANTI-SEMITISM AND THE BROKEN COVENANT

I hate talking about anti-Semitism. Despite the stereotype that Jews are hypersensitive, my generation was raised to consider Jew-hatred an outdated, European disease. Born into North America's post-Auschwitz meritocracy, we believed that anti-Semitism had been cured along with whooping cough and polio. We were Daniel Pearl Jews, raised, as the murdered *Wall Street Journal* reporter was, to be citizens of the world.

Growing up in the 1970s, we believed our identities were malleable – and infinitely elastic. We believed Marlo Thomas that we were Free to Be You and Me. We learned that if we jumped through the right hoops, we could go as far as anyone else in society. We felt protected by our American or Canadian passports.

Climbing the ladder of achievement, we internalized varying amounts of good liberal guilt about our good fortune. Our relationship to oppression was as fellow crusaders fighting for justice, not potential victims.

We were empathetic, not paranoid, guarding against injuring others rather than worrying about protecting ourselves. We had zero-tolerance for racism, sexism, homophobia and any kind of religious intolerance. We learned to avoid creating hostile working environments, even unintentionally, and saw that the burden of proof is always on the potential oppressors to establish their innocence, not on their victims.

Many of us pooh-poohed older relatives and Jewish leaders who seemed obsessed with anti-Semitism. They were stuck on yesterday's news – and history's burdens – rather than liberated by the miracle of North America.

Yasir Arafat's war of terrorism and propaganda against the Oslo Peace Process changed the equation – especially when the world applauded him and his tactics. Soft, spoiled, naive and terrible soothsayers, we never imagined that we would be living in a world of ever-coarsening anti-Semitism and despicable rationalizations for suicide bombings, in a society where, as occurred in Montreal in the spring of 2003, a children's elementary school library would be firebombed, and the crime could trigger debate in the letters to the editor section of *La Presse* about its underlying rationale. (One letter dismissed the big reaction to the burning of "a little library" and the second sneered: "If our friends in the Jewish community were... not so almost unanimously supportive of the hateful and intransigent policies of Israel, we would obviously be more scandalized by these unfortunate acts.")

Moreover, how do we understand the intellectual dishonesty festering at Concordia University, where a Swastika scribbled on an Israeli flag was justified by the lie that the hated Nazi symbol functioned as a neutral Hindu emblem? Why would someone write, even in the "personals" section of a supposed humor magazine at Rutgers University: "Die Jew. Die, die, die, die, die, die. Stop living, die, die, DIE! Do us all a favor and build yourself [an]... oven"? What do we make of the insanity at my home institution, McGill University, where an idealistic student in my History of Presidential Campaigning conference was publicly libeled as a racist because she dared to raise the moral issue of deploying children as suicide bombers? And who could possibly fathom what Professor Laurie Zoloth witnessed on the campus of San Francisco State University: "posters of cans of soup with labels on them of drops of blood and dead babies, labeled 'CANNED PALESTINIAN CHILDREN MEAT, SLAUGHTERED ACCORDING TO JEWISH RITES UNDER AMERICAN LICENSE'" and, for good measure, "MADE IN ISRAEL"?

In fighting modern anti-Semitism, the moral neutrality of the politically correct – which often masks moral sloppiness or even outright bias – is a particularly insidious problem. We need Winston Churchills, not Neville Chamberlains; lions, not lambs; leaders, not appeasers. We need to hunt down hatred aggressively, creatively, systematically.

Again and again I note the noxious nexus, the way criticisms of Israel and anti-Zionism camouflage the new anti-Semitism, how little hurts grow into big traumas. There is a link, and the firebombers of Montreal's United Talmud Torah school library made it in their anonymous note, between the violence against Jews in Israel, Istanbul, Montreal and Mombasa, the ugly Jew-baiting rhetoric festering in so many mosques and madrassas, and the genteel but unfair, obsessive and disproportionate expressions of exasperation or indifference toward Jews and the Jewish state in so many seminar rooms and parlors.

When Jews note the obvious connection these days between anti-Zionism and anti-Semitism, they are accused of being thin-skinned, intolerant, even McCarthyite; yet when anti-Semites justify attacks against Jews by pointing to Israeli actions as the United Talmud Torah vandals did, there are supposedly reputable people around who deem the connection reasonable, "contextualized," as academics like to say, and thus, implicitly justified. Harold Evans, former editor of the *London Sunday Times*, says while it is not anti-Semitic to criticize Israel, "It is anti-Semitic to vilify the state of Israel as a diabolical abstraction, reserving tolerance for the individual Jew but not the collective Jew; it is anti-Semitic to invent malignant outrages; it is anti-Semitic to consistently condemn in Israel what you ignore or condone elsewhere."

Once again, we insist that Jews deserve equal treatment, not special treatment. If vandals firebombed an Italian church, would any respectable newspaper publish letters minimizing the "little fire" or suggesting any community behaviors that justified the crime? Are there any campus geniuses ready to rationalize cross burnings on African-Americans' lawns, given the cross's many positive meanings? Would Mary Robinson and the other organizers of the Durban Conference in late summer 2001, have declared their UN anti-racism conference a success had it degenerated into Muslim-bashing?

Jews should not be burdened with proving that anti-Zionists are merely critics of Israel and not anti-Semites. Given the thousands of incidents targeting Jews in the last few years, the burden of proof is on the anti-Zionists. Harsh critics of Israel and of Zionism must work harder to disconnect themselves from the noxious nexus, from the rivers of ugly rhetoric feeding and blurring together hatred of the Jew, Jewish nationalism and the Jewish state. And intellectual, moral, religious and political leaders should be extra alert to weed out this hatred, rather than standing silently by and watching it grow.

Anti-Semitic acts, be they "minor" or "major," rhetorical or physical, violate the fundamental covenant we all share as citizens of a democracy. Democracy is more than one person, one vote; it begins with values of equality, mutuality and civility, rooted in our common humanity. "Zero-tolerance" means we all must combat all forms of bigotry, be it in bathroom stalls or on editorial pages, in the halls of the UN or in the context of difficult political strife.

DEFINING THE NEW ANTI-SEMITISM AND FINDING IT, ALAS, ON THE LEFT

There is a new anti-Semitism festering in North America – more subtle, genteel, elusive and seemingly more defensible than the pre-Auschwitz variety or even the modern European manifestations. It will not bar Jews from country clubs or Ivy League schools, nor will it directly insult your Jewish friend, neighbor, co-worker or son-in-law. Although there have been some campus riots and some ugly anti-Jewish slurs, overall it lacks the violence of today's Islamic anti-Semitism whose handiwork one sees in the burning embers of a Turkish synagogue, the carnage of an Israeli seder, the scars left on a beaten French Jew.

After the Holocaust, experts deemed anti-Semitism the social disease of the right, rooted in lower class thuggery. Sixty years later, many critics detect this new anti-Semitism among professed liberals, metastasizing in the university seminar room and the writer's salon, masquerading as "merely" anti-Zionism, then coexisting with, and justifying, the cruder anti-Semitism of the Arab and occasionally European street.

This new anti-Semitism is heard in talk of "the Jews," rather than Jews and, as other observers have noted, of the Jewish "lobby," but the Asian, black or Chicano "community." It has been felt in university campaigns to disinvest from Israel – but no other country – and in charges that "the Jews" triggered the 2003 invasion of Iraq – when some Jewish Democrats opposed the war as passionately as some Jewish neoconservatives endorsed it. It has been felt in broad condemnations of terrorism that somehow overlook Israeli victims or Jewish victims.

Admittedly, this new anti-Semitism begins with Israel, and the searing, decades-long Arab-Israeli conflict. But the evil marriage of Islamic fundamentalist hatred for Western civilization with traditional European Jew-hatred has produced shrill, ugly, obvious rhetoric that transcends the conflict's realities. Princeton historian Bernard Lewis, offering some perspective, notes: "There have indeed been many... occupations and conflicts... on a vastly greater scale than in the Middle East. None of them... has produced this kind of vicious racist campaign." Moreover, unlike most criticism of Israel – or of the United States, Saudi Arabia, the

Sudan or the Palestinian Authority – it goes from the incidental to the essential, from condemning specific acts to repudiating the country and its supporters. As discussed in the earlier chapter, "Politics 101," often using the rhetoric of anti-colonialism, and, ironically, anti-racism, to conceal their anti-Judaism, many of these critics reveal their bias through their one-sided actions and venom. The tics of the new anti-Semites include:

• their obsessive and disproportionate focus on Israel;

• their zeal to demonize with the most painful of symbols by "Nazifying" the Jewish state;

• their double-standards, not just holding up Israel to uniquely high standards, but also judging Jewish nationalism as if the world were not divided into at least 190 other tribes;

• and their insensitivity to Jewish suffering.

Given the centuries-long scourge of anti-Semitism, talk of "the Jews" comes laden with historical baggage. Given the current cultural climate – where the burden is on critics of traditionally oppressed groups such as blacks and women to prove they are not racist or sexist – vehement detractors of Israel must demonstrate that their denunciations are justified and not hate-filled.

EXPLAINING THE NEW ANTI-SEMITISM: CONVERTS, FUNDAMENTALISTS AND SKEPTICS

The new anti-Semitism, which partially stems from the so-called intelligentsia, has triggered a vigorous debate among authors reflecting various attitudes and approaches toward this ancient scourge. Experts arguing about the new anti-Semitism divide roughly into three camps: converts, fundamentalists and skeptics. The converts are Daniel Pearl's spiritual brothers and sisters, patriotic and successful masters of the meritocracy who report how betrayed they feel when encountering "the longest hatred." The feminist Phyllis Chesler in her sobering and angry book, *The New Anti-Semitism*, Harvard's President Lawrence Summers at his now famous Memorial Church sermon, Jonathan Rosen in the *New York Times Magazine*, David Brooks in the conservative *Weekly Standard*, repeat the same mantra: I grew up without anti-Semitism; I thought it was eradicated; I am reluctantly, surprisingly, angrily, denouncing it, even when it masquerades as "only" criticizing Israel. These converts demonstrate that if once a conservative was a liberal who has been mugged by reality, many modern conservatives are liberals who have been bombed.

The fundamentalists offer deeper, more enduring, sometimes too far-reaching explanations. These prophets have long warned about anti-Semitism – and are dismayed that they were right. These vindicated Chicken Littles who warned that the sky was falling place this longstanding social disease into global and historical context. Rabbi Abraham Foxman of the Anti-Defamation League notes that anti-Semitism unites strange bedfellows, with Muslim jihadists, neo-Nazi skinheads and radical black intellectuals all rallying irrationally against "the Jew." Echoing that ancient and now-renewed cry "Why Do They Hate Us?" Dennis Prager and Rabbi Joseph Telushkin identify Judaism as "the root cause of anti-Semitism." Their theory pushes the depressing debate about hatred into a wonderful, rollicking argument about the rich Jewish narrative, the story of an extraordinary combination of both a religion and a nation, a people with a theology who sometimes annoyed the rest of the world. Even if not convincing, the argument is intellectually more inviting than Foxman's conversation-stopping conclusion that just as "the origins of good and evil… are mysterious," so "it is with anti-Semitism."

Foxman's answer echoes our grandparents' knee-jerk traditional response: "they" have always hated us. Accepting this notion repudiates years of conditioning in America's welcoming embrace. It resurrects the idea of the "*goy*" as foreign, threatening.

Yet the world, and even the modern Jews' relationship to the world, is too complex for such atavistic sloganeering. We need to analyze this renewed anti-Semitism carefully. Even as we remember the long tragic history of anti-Semitism, even as we seethe at the revival of the "Protocols of the Elders of Zion," we need to assess this ancient plague's modern dimensions.

Harvard's Ruth Wisse explains Liberal anti-Semitism as a deflection, better to blame Israel and rationalize Islamist fanaticism than confront the Arab world or the failure of reason. University of Waterloo Professor Robert Jan Van Pelt blames academic "relativism" for rejecting Western notions of objective truth and validating any narrative, and many lies. Columbia's Simon Schama faults European ghosts festering on unmediated modern Web sites.

Still, Israel's adversaries are correct – today's tensions are rooted in criticism of Israel's policy toward the Palestinians. The spike in anti-Semitism began with the Palestinian war against the Oslo Accords. Anti-Semitism soared in Europe in April 2002 when Israel reentered the West Bank after the Passover massacre.

In a world of black-and-white media coverage where images rule, sound-bites triumph and attention spans are fleeting, Palestinian cries of "occupation" trump lectures explaining Israel's justified actions in the Six Day War, let alone history lessons about the deep Jewish ties to Israel. Palestinian charges of "oppression" trump recitations of all that Israel conceded under the Oslo Accords, let alone the fact that no other country ever willingly surrendered disputed territory it seized in a war of self-defense, until Israel gave Egypt the Sinai in 1979, and then, again, offered the Palestinians territory in 1993.

There is a broader obsession with Israel that needs explaining. Even in peaceful times the *New York Times* published more stories about Israel than about Canada. The unique epic of the Jewish renaissance in the Holy Land, of building a modern Western-style nation in the ancient Middle East, has made Israel newsworthy since its founding.

Israel is not only complicated and conspicuous, it is also out of step with contemporary progressive fads, especially on campus. It is no secret that most academics lean left. As discussed, many have blindspots which block out violence emanating from the left's darlings, especially when the attacker is a person of color, and the victim is Western, white or somehow tainted as conservative. The slaughter of 800,000 innocents in Rwanda during the 1990s barely registered on academic mattering maps because such black-on-black tribal violence did not fit the post-colonialist paradigm of noble Third Worlders rebelling against oppressive Westerners.

Vicious and vulgar anti-Zionists, who regularly call for "death to the Jews" and support anti-Semitic and anti-American terrorism when they are not wooing gullible students, have exploited the instinctive skepticism toward the West on so many campuses to make Israel a modern-day bogeyman. Israel's enemies have hijacked the language of liberalism to cast democratic Israel as a "colonialist" and "imperialist" power.

Like the United States, Israel is victimized by a peculiar form of modernist democratic decadence, an anti-chauvinism, if you will. Just as many American progressives are particularly harsh on their own country – even as they enjoy its bounty – so too are they, along with many Israelis and Jews, harsh on Israel. Dictatorships, especially Third World dictatorships, seem to invite understanding from sophisticates; excuses for bad behavior abound. Nevertheless, imperfect democracies such as Israel and the United States merit little understanding and stinging criticisms.

Underlying it all is a multiplier, an "x-factor" driving and intensifying the current campaign against Israel. Just as many Jews respond in a way shaped by centuries of hostility, so too, alas, do too many of our neighbors. Today's systematic assault against Israel, this Zionophobia, follows a historically anti-Semitic template. Jews have long been controversial, conspicuous and cast as contrary to the mainstream. In the bad old days, Jews often functioned as scapegoats. Jews were saddled with the sins of the capitalist and the communist, just as Israel today is saddled with the West's alleged sins.

The civil rights fights against racism, sexism and homophobia demonstrated that in fighting bigotry subtleties count. Language, tone, context and pitch often betray true intentions. The obsessive, disproportionate hysteria, the demonization, the delegitimization, the odious comparisons, all reflect anti-Semitic tropes in too many critics' anti-Zionism.

These anti-Zionists find comfort from a third school of thought in the debate. Many progressives insist there is no great anti-Semitic evil in the modern world. These skeptics could also be called anti-anti-Semitism anti-Zionists. Overwhelmingly from the left, the skeptics dismiss complaints about modern anti-Semitism as a modern blood libel directed by "apologists for Israel." One Canadian professor, Michael Neumann acknowledges the "genuine anti-Semitism in the Arab world" and deems it "utterly inexcusable." Then he adds: "So was your failure to answer Aunt Bee's last letter." To Professor Neumann – and his comrades – "the scandal today is not anti-Semitism but the importance it is given."

Many of the skeptics would never write about women or blacks or homosexuals the way they write about Jews. Would progressives ever trivialize racism, mock sexism, compare homophobia to being rude to "Aunt Bee"? In the introduction to a collection of such skeptical essays called *The Politics of Anti-Semitism*, the first line of the editor's introduction reflects the problem. Claiming that "there's no more explosive topic in American public life today than the issue of Israel... and its influence on

American politics" raises suspicions in a world of terrorism, economic transition, environmental depredation, and continuing racism and poverty. In fact, it reeks of the anti-Semite's historic tendency to place the Jew at the center of all social evils. Looking over the sorry record of reporters, academics and other supposed sophisticates these last few years, the journalist Tom Gross recalls George Orwell's reply to a Communist: "You must be an intellectual," Orwell said. "Only an intellectual could say something so stupid."

Anybody who reads the Jewish press, talks to North American Jews, or even reads many of the most influential essays condemning the new anti-Semitism, would discover that mainstream Jews – let alone Israelis – have no difficulty criticizing specific Israeli policies and most Israeli politicians. The torrent of Jewish and Israeli self-criticism proves that it is possible to distinguish anti-Semitism from honest criticism of Israel. Too many of Israel's critics make the distinction clear by plunging into crude Jew hatred, rationalizing it or soft-pedaling it. The vitriol and the masquerades must end. As with any disease, proper diagnosis is the first step toward finding a cure. The next step is to mobilize people of conscience throughout the world to eradicate both the milder and more virulent strains, for all our sakes.

If the fight against anti-Semitism is seen only as a Jewish issue, we all lose. The new anti-Semitism festers in the same cesspools of modern thought which have spawned Islamicist terrorism. Fed by this pathological combination of modern Islamicist throwbacks and cutting-edge post-modernists, the new anti-Semitism needs to be defeated along with a broader anti-Western bigotry. Fighting against anti-Semitism is fighting for democracy, liberty, tolerance and civility. The German sociologist Ralf Dahrendorf teaches that you can judge how civilized a society is by how it treats its minority members; now, as in the past, one of the ways to judge the world's civility is by seeing how most people treat the Jewish people.

Israel's Arab opponents have scored a great victory. Not only have they turned many people against Israel, they have also reduced all conversations about Israel to this one obsessive discussion about the Arab-Israeli conflict. There is so much more to this marvelous country. The challenge is not only to defend Israel and eradicate Zionophobia and anti-Semitism, it is also to reconfigure the balance so that Israel can be seen in all its multidimensional complexity and democratic glory.

CHAPTER 20

ACTIVISM 101:

WE NEED EFFECTIVE STRATEGIES
AND CREATIVE EXTREMISTS

BADGES OF HONOR:
WAKING UP TO OUR DUTIES AND OUR BLESSINGS

These challenging times demand creative, effective, affirmative responses. Reacting is not enough. We must respond strategically, intelligently, constructively. There have been many wake-up calls – from the Palestinians' turn away from negotiation and toward violence in September 2000 to the Islamicists' mass-murders of Sept. 11, 2001; from Hezbollah's lethal attempt to kidnap three Israeli soldiers near Lebanon to the kidnapping - and beheading - of journalist Daniel Pearl; from the UN's orgy of anti-Semitism masquerading as anti-racism in Durban, South Africa, to the anti-Semitism exposed behind "mere" anti-Zionism when rioters who squelched former Israeli prime minister Benjamin Netanyahu's right to speak at Concordia University threw pennies at Jews; from the world's unfair denunciation of Israel when it responded aggressively to Palestinian terrorism to the bigotry underlying the Iraq war debate in 2003, when critics acted as if the biggest hawks were Jewish, as opposed to Donald Rumsfeld, Dick Cheney and George W. Bush.

Those of us who responded often found our positions caricatured and condemned. Since 2000, and especially since I publicly proclaimed that I am a Zionist – I have been called a racist, a Nazi, a propagandist, a hypocrite, a fanatic, a false prophet, out of the mainstream, and a right winger. I get bombarded with illiterate e-mails from fake addresses, such as nauseatedwithzionistlies@aol.com, fedupwithzionists@yahoo.com and damtheusrulers@hotmail.com. Even more depressing are the well-written rants that degenerate into crude anti-Semitism and anti-Americanism and are signed by people who lack the shame to hide their names.

These attacks are badges of honor – proof that my feeble attempts to defend the right ideals are annoying the "right" people. The perverse charges of Nazism and racism, damning Jews and Americans with their enemies' sins by inverting reality, do not merit consideration (although I wonder why when Jews condemn suicide bombings, we are "racists," but when Saudi Arabians and Jordanians finally do when they are attacked, they're heroes).

Still, I plead "guilty" to many charges:

If appreciating American democracy, though imperfect, makes me a "propagandist," I plead guilty to viewing worthy ideals in proper perspective.

If contrasting Israeli culture's yearning for peace with Palestinian political culture's deification of death – which lionizes the late PA President Yasir Arafat, the tyrants of Hamas, and other mass-murderers – and if distinguishing innocent victims from suicide bombers makes me a "hypocrite," I plead guilty to rooting my judgments in reality, proportionality and morality.

If having zero-tolerance for anti-Semitism and refusing to judge Israel by unrealistic standards makes me a "fanatic," so be it. Moderation and democracy need more passionate advocates.

If testifying to terrorism's evils, wherever practiced and regardless of rationale, makes me a "false prophet," I hope I am also a soothsayer, foreseeing the eradication of this evil and a return to sanity, with no thanks to a complacent world.

terror /'terə(r)/ *n* **1** [U ~·ism /-izəm/ *n* use of viole[nce for] political purposes. ~·ist /-ist/ or acts of violence.

If disagreeing with the conventional wisdom among reporters, academics and Canadian and European elites boots me "out of the mainstream," there is nowhere else I would rather be.

And if championing fundamental liberal ideals of free speech, religious tolerance, democracy, rule of law, fair play, and the right of civil disagreement, let alone the right of Israelis to enter pizzerias in peace, makes me "a right winger," then show me how to join the "vast right-wing conspiracy."

I particularly resent the charge that I am a right-winger, which is often academic shorthand for being evil AND stupid. I say, "You don't know anything about me – other than the fact that I am anti-terror and pro-Israel. You don't know where I stand on true liberal principles, on Thomas Jefferson's ever-expanding salute to equality, on John Stuart Mill's commitment to a free marketplace of ideas, on Franklin D. Roosevelt's embrace of the Four Freedoms, on John Kennedy's vision of muscular idealism, on Mario Cuomo's lyrical warnings to remember the poor, on

Betty Friedan's demand for gender equity, and on Martin Luther King's creative extremism." I am an American historian, so I can go on for a long time about liberal heroes and liberal ideas that enriched our world – and that reinforce my commitment to fighting terrorism and championing Zionism.

Atlanta's mayor in the 1960s, Ivan Allen Jr., said, "If there wasn't a race issue, I could play golf every afternoon." If there weren't so many unreasonable attacks on Israel, the United States, and western civilization, I could stay hidden in my archives. But in mobilizing, we must not simply fight our enemies. We must celebrate the joys of Judaism, the blessings of Zionism, the magic of Israel and the importance of the West's democratic and liberal ideals, even while acknowledging shortcomings, criticizing imperfections and pushing harder to fulfill our ideals. And we need more people, more galvanized moderates, more creative extremists, more infuriated liberals, to stop playing golf, to bump into history, to risk criticism and to fight in today's multi-front war against terrorism and for democracy.

BEWARE THE CASUAL BIGOTRY OF THE POLITICALLY CORRECT

Unfortunately, universities have been on the front lines of this intellectual Clash of Civilizations. But we need to view things in perspective. The modern campus should not be caricatured as a hostile, anti-Israel environment where Zionists fear to tread. Headlines from universities tell of banned Israeli speakers and anti-Zionist hate-fests, of anti-Israel professors harassing Columbia University students and British academics boycotting Israeli universities and not their Chinese, Saudi Arabian or Sudanese colleagues. But these brouhahas tell only part of the story. To champion Israel on campus effectively, hysterical overreactions are no better than apathy or complacency.

Overall, this is actually a golden age for Jews in universities. Jewish Ivy League presidents, Nobel Prize winners, honor students, even Jewish athletes, abound. Columbia University, long mocked as "the Ivy League's Yeshiva University," is teeming with kipah-wearing young men and modestly dressed Orthodox Jewish women, not to mention their bare-headed secular brothers and bare-midriffed secular sisters. The counterattack against pro-Palestinian educational malpractice in Columbia's classrooms during the 2004-2005 academic year succeeded because so many politically savvy students there feel comfortable expressing themselves as Jews.

Still, anomalies abound. While individual Jews excel and thrive, as Jewish life sometimes flourishes and sometimes wilts, "the Jews" and certainly "the Jewish state" are all too often mistreated. In spring 2004, celebrating Israel with a light, even sugary touch, students at Washington University in St. Louis distributed a "piece for peace." Cleverly appealing to collegians' hearts through their stomachs, the activists gave out pieces of cake with palm cards describing Israel's quest for peace. While many students took both gifts in the spirit in which they were intended, some Jews and non-Jews chided the activists for distributing a "one-sided" pamphlet.

In these days of combustible campus politics, this incident should be viewed in perspective. The student activists were not bullied. There was no anti-Semitic name-calling. And yet this criticism was disturbing.

Days later some of the students remained miffed. Trained as good American Jews to be conformist, careerist and non-controversial, to get along with others to get ahead, the students internalized the criticism and feared they had behaved badly.

This incident represents an insidious undercurrent in the current assault against Israel and Zionism on campus and elsewhere. It reflects a phenomenon that Natan Sharansky identified in his powerful jeremiad of October 24, 2003 in *The Forward* against academic anti-Zionism. The most disturbing issue Sharansky raised, the problem far more representative than violence at Concordia University and San Francisco State, was the poisonous atmosphere polluting many discussions about Israel, the one-sided, unique expectations Israel activists endure. One Israel activist told Sharansky "he could no longer stand the peer pressure of those around him who viewed him as a pro-Israel obsessive. He now pours his idealistic energies into an organic farm he started," Sharansky reported sadly. "Now that he is involved in environmental activism everyone is happy with him."

Jews don't want or need special treatment, they merely demand and deserve equal treatment. Let us judge Jews and Zionists by the standards of other campus activists. Has anyone ever chided feminists for not carving out room in their literature to defend patriarchy? Do gays explain the downside of homosexual marriage during Gay Liberation Awareness Day? Are Palestinian and Muslim activists asked to divert some of their resources toward explaining the Zionist idea?

The casual bigotry of the politically correct imposes unfair burdens on pro-Jewish politics and on Israel itself. It demands that Israel and its supporters act unnaturally nobly. It forces Jewish students to apologize for doing what their non-Jewish peers do naturally; it inhibits many pro-Israel professors from standing up, especially if they are untenured.

Many academics have abandoned what should be their intellectual calling cards - nuance, subtlety, an appreciation of complexity. Instead, a simplistic, black-and-white rigidity treats anything pro-Israel as automatically suspect – while demonstrating tremendous flexibility in rationalizing the most heinous Palestinian crimes.

Thus suicide bombers become "resisters" and Israeli self-defense inevitably becomes "oppression." Amid such pressure, too many of Israel's allies hide, apologize or – equally problematic – lurch rightward, creating a false blue-and-white Hava Nagila universe imprudently setting up Israel as the one perfect country in the world.

In the ensuing dialogue of the deaf, political posturing eclipses political thought.

SELF-DEFENSE WITH SELF-CONTROL: FOR OUR SAKE

The debate about the security barrier reflects the problem. In a toxic variation of the Fiddler on the Roof horse-mule routine, Palestinians yell "Apartheid Wall," Israel's supporters yell "security fence." Pro-Israel activists are justifiably furious that effete intellectuals who live in gated communities or Americans who accept the electrified fence with Mexico object to blocking, say, the death valley between Jerusalem and Bethlehem-Bet Jalla, which ten suicide bombers casually crossed to commit mass murder.

Indeed, the fence – the brainchild of the Left now being implemented by the Right and thus denounced now by the Left – is complicated. It raises important questions worth debating about Israel's approach to land, to Palestinians, to the future. It poses conundrums that Abraham Lincoln and other wartime leaders faced regarding what a democracy can do to defend itself.

Tragically, Israel gets little credit on campus, at the UN or elsewhere, for the added expense and risk it incurs worrying about Palestinian quality of life, just as Israel gets no credit for procedures demonstrating respect for women – which a mother of two exploited to murder four Israelis at a Gaza crossing and another woman tried to exploit in a failed attempt to blow up Soroka Hospital in Beersheva, which was treating her, as it treats all patients, humanely, efficiently, properly, equitably.

Some Israelis, naturally, wonder why they should bother and consider jettisoning morality amid the world's unfairness. Most Israelis, know, however, that engaging in self-defense with self-control is not only for their opponents' sake but for their own.

Pro-Israel activists have to learn from Israel. The hostility of the outside world, the casual bigotry of the politically correct, should not stifle debate or short-circuit our consciences. Israel's supporters need to celebrate Israel flamboyantly, creatively, occasionally calorically, while also finding time for more balanced, nuanced, even painful, contemplations.

The prejudices of others should not imprison us in our own prejudices. We need a vigorous discussion assessing the complexity of living in Yasir Arafat's and Osama Bin Laden's world of terror. We need to make it clear on campus and elsewhere that we don't fear honest debates and real learning, that trusting democracy and free inquiry demonstrates strength, not weakness.

At the same time, we must also transcend the debate. All conversational roads about Israel, Judaism and Zionism must not lead back to the Palestinians. We have to stop making the late Yasir Arafat and the Palestinian terrorists who keep alive his immoral legacy the most effective on-campus recruiters for Jewish identity.

When we make "doing Jewish" being political only, we give the Palestinians a victory they do not deserve. We need our pieces of cake for peace. We need our dollops of wisdom. And we need a richer, more multi-dimensional vision of Jewish student life that puts all these troubles in perspective.

ADVOCACY IN THE AGE OF THE IPOD

Let's be honest. For too long too much Israel advocacy was simplistic, rigid and infamously heavy-handed in its all-or-nothing,   my-country-right-or-wrong approach. But a hipper, more fluid, extraordinarily open-minded and often self-critical approach has emerged. From venerable powerhouses such as AIPAC (the American Israel Public Affairs Committee) to revolutionary initiatives such as birthright israel, pioneers are developing a new pro-Israel argot, reconciling the dizzying diversity of modern life with a passion for celebrating Israel and Zionism, not just refuting libels (although many instinctively shy away from the Z-word, at a time when the only "ism" students admit to is cynicism).

Advocates understand the challenge of embracing Israel in the age of Ipod. These Starbucks-sipping, web-blog surfing, body-piercing, savvy, energetic, creative and critical Israel lovers, boogying to the multi-cultural sounds of the Israeli-Ethiopian Idan Reichel Project or rapping with edgy HaDag Nahash hip-hoppers have moved beyond yesterday's blue-box-toting, kova-tembel-wearing, hora-dancing cheerleaders. This conceptual, linguistic, tactical and strategic revolution was rooted in the 1990s' peace and prosperity, when Jews feared being loved to death – facing elimination by intermarriage – rather than being targeted by terrorists. The continuity crisis demonstrated that modern, Americanized Jews were, like their peers, afflicted with "affluenza," living in an era of intense individualism, "bowling alone" rather than building identity together. Many also realized that the materialistic, controversial Israel of the 1990s lost some allure, more defined by "fanatic" settlers and the Lebanon War than romantic kibbutznikim and the Six Day War. Simultaneously, traditional American Jewish institutions, especially synagogues and afternoon schools, often failed to energize and engage young, increasingly secular Jews.

Visionaries responded with the Israel Experience, epitomized by birthright israel. A fun-filled but challenging, nonjudgmental, pan-ideological group trip to Israel offered "24/7 Judaism." This acknowledged American Jewish diversity and openness while repositioning Israel, Judaism and the Jewish people as responses to modern youths' values, confusion and identity crisis. When Palestinian terrorism, followed by 9/11 and the campus assault on Israel's legitimacy, traumatized this new generation, the elements of a new strategy already existed.

Birthright israel – which has brought more than 100,000 Jews aged 18 to 26 to Israel since 2000 – proves that Israel advocacy works best as a result of a positive Jewish identity and a love for Israel, a theme echoed by Hillel's "Big Tent" commitment to "doing Jewish" on campus. In a political vein, AIPAC's leadership development team developed a strategy of "Ubiquitous Customization" befitting an age of radical individualism, empowering thousands of students to find their own voices, develop their own initiatives and contribute their own talents.

These students do not fear dissent while celebrating Israel, with all its imperfections, as a pluralistic democracy which deserves the right to exist and the opportunity to make peace in peace. They stand proudly by Israel as Americans, be they right, left or center, religious, secular or muddled. As a result, Jewish students have taken back the night on many campuses, as reflected by Columbia University students' campaign against pro-Palestinian professorial bullying, after years of passivity.

Recognizing that love for Israel, like charity, begins at home, "Write on for Israel," which instructs young journalists, and other initiatives at the elementary and high school level began educating about Zionism, in all its complexity and glory. Trusting knowledge and balance to maintain passion long term, many of these programs distinguish between criticizing any country's specific policies and demonizing or delegitimizing that country.

Building on all this positive energy, the Jewish Agency has launched project MASA – jointly funded with the Israeli government – to increase the number of college and post-college youths studying in Israel from 5,000 to 20,000 annually. This project will succeed only if it culminates a process, serving as the final act in a multi-part drama, whereby Diaspora Jews, individually and collectively, engage Israel, educate themselves and others about Israel, experience Israel, embrace Israel and ultimately agree to entangle their lives with Israel and Israelis.

These initiatives are not a simplistic propaganda process engineered by master puppeteers. Today's independent, critically-minded students would reject such manipulation. Rather, they reflect a happy synergy, an exciting explosion of ideas, triggered by trauma but demonstrating the traditional Jewish genius for transforming bitter herbs into sweet *haroset*.

WANTED: CREATIVE EXTREMISTS

Whether or not you spend serious time in Israel, whether or not you call yourself a Zionist, whether or not you even develop a positive Jewish identity, the broad challenge remains: to find meaning in life amid all the distractions of modern life. I once spoke to some suburban Montreal high school students about Martin Luther King, Jr. I began by asking the students to name their heroes. Of 27 students, two said their fathers, three mentioned friends, three others picked random leaders, two identified superheroes – Batman and Spiderman – nine specified particular sports stars or rock stars, and nine said they had no hero at all.

Although in our current educational climate guests are supposed to mollify rather than confront, I challenged this shocking conclusion. "Don't you think it is disturbing that a collection of intelligent and energetic students cannot find heroes who matter?" I asked. "It seems either you worship useless celebrities, or nobody." The students bristled. After feebly attempting to praise Michael Jordan's generosity and glorify the value of building your body through sports, one student, in that exasperated tone modern teenagers reserve for their elders, sighed: "You don't understand the world we live in. This is our world, celebrities and sports stars." I responded that this was precisely what I understood, and abhorred.

"Well, of course it's different now," another student added. "Heroes from the past like King, Mahatma Gandhi and Winston Churchill faced all these serious problems and solved them. We don't face such serious problems." As I reeled off a litany of problems from terrorism to poverty, the student acknowledged, "I guess there are problems, but we don't really feel them where we live."

The student was right. Even after Sept. 11 and the Iraq War, most Americans, let alone Canadians, remain happily insulated. Most of us, thankfully, live in cozy cocoons where our great challenges revolve around how to spend our leisure time and fritter away our disposable income. Most of the coddled students of the middle- and upper-middle-class, represented by the students I met, may struggle with the stresses of careerism and the strains of modern relationships. Nevertheless, few have experienced the direct dread of terror, the crushing limitations of poverty, the stinging humiliation of injustice.

North America's bounty, as channelled through today's culture of creature comforts, consumerism and celebrity worship, risks depriving our youth of the moral ambition necessary to achieve personal and national greatness. Their social imaginations are cramped and impoverished, hemmed in by the debris of our leisure culture, seduced by the celebrity promise of great fame and endless riches. Consumerism addicts them to convention, just as it has handcuffed us, their elders, to the world that is, for we can achieve, advance, prosper, only if we harness ourselves to the status quo.

Forty years ago in his "I Have A Dream" Speech, Martin Luther King, Jr. challenged us all to do better. King urged his followers not to fear crises. "I must confess that I am not afraid of the word 'tension.' I have earnestly opposed violent tension, but there is a type of constructive, nonviolent tension which is necessary for growth," King had written that spring in his "Letter from a Birmingham Jail." Invoking Socrates' creation of "tension" to free individuals "from the bondage of myths and half-truths" and spur "creative analysis," King called for "nonviolent gadflies to create the kind of tension in society that will help men rise from the dark depths of prejudice and racism to the majestic heights of understanding and brotherhood."

Dr. King even embraced the mantle of "extremist." "Was not Jesus an extremist for love?" he asked. "Was not Amos an extremist for justice?" The question, King taught, "is not whether we will be extremists, but what kind of extremists we will be? Will we be extremists for hate or for love? Will we be extremists for the preservation of injustice or for the extension of justice?" In the 1960s, surrounded by racial prejudice and too much poverty in the land of plenty, King suggested: "Perhaps the South, the nation and the world are in dire need of creative extremists."

Only such creative extremists could have the faith that fuelled the dream King articulated so beautifully in Washington four months later. Only they could "hew out of the mountain of despair a stone of hope," only they could dream of a world where "we will be able to work together, to pray together, to struggle together, to go to jail together, to stand up for freedom together," without trying to gain "our rightful place" through "wrongful deeds."

Four decades later, we have made great progress. Our corner of the world, thanks partially to King's efforts, is a more tolerant and just place. But much work remains. We need to resist the twin lures of complacency and consumerism, young and old alike. We, too, need a new generation of "creative extremists," with grandiose dreams of changing the world, and an openness to heroes striving to make the world a better place, not just a more entertaining space.

CHAPTER 21

ADVOCACY 101:

HOW TO TALK ABOUT ISRAEL
ON CAMPUS AND ELSEWHERE WITHOUT
APOLOGIZING, CRINGING, CRYING OR YELLING

Unfortunately, the Palestinian uprising against the Oslo peace process has poisoned the atmosphere between Jews and Palestinians in North America as well. The renewed violence has triggered the most aggressive attack on the legitimacy of Israel and Zionism in a generation. Amid all the anger, it has become clear that, especially on college campuses, the bastions of political correctness, Israel and Zionism are Politically Incorrect.

When the violence first began, it quickly became apparent that the overwhelming majority of Jewish students were culturally, intellectually, and emotionally unprepared for the propaganda skirmishes that erupted on campus. Most young Jews are too distant from Israel and too conflict-averse to withstand the intensity of the anti-Zionist barrage. Culturally, most second, third, and fourth generation suburban Jews prefer analyzing, criticizing or ignoring Israel to defending it. Substantively, most Jewish students know more about Sharon Stone than they do about Ariel Sharon or the Palestinian stone throwers.

Palestinian terror, unfortunately, has targeted all Jews – wherever they stand politically. The jump in anti-Semitic incidents that coincided with the start of the violence, the terrorism unleashed against Jews on both sides of the Green Line, prove that, these days, you don't have to be a Sharon supporter to be called a "Zionist racist." Moderates who supported Oslo have a special responsibility to defend Israel. Our participation can help sift critics of Israeli policies from anti-Zionists who reject the Jewish state's right to exist at all. Moderates may also be able to blunt the polarizing tendencies that have made some universities resemble Jerry Springer sets rather than seats of learning.

POINTERS FOR DEBATING – AND NOT DEBATING

With that in mind, all supporters of Israel, from the left to the right, all Zionists, might want to consider some pointers for debating about Israel, formally and informally.

For starters, insist on ground rules. Not every argument must be met; not every distortion has to be corrected. If the terms of the debate will prejudice the outcome, sometimes silence is the best response. Activists need to clarify their goals and identify their audience, appealing to those who are undecided and ignoring close-minded antagonists.

Moreover, pro-Israel activists must demand intellectual parity. Do not debate Israel's right to exist unless the debate questions the rights of all nations to exist, from Switzerland to Swaziland. Similarly, before debating whether Zionism is racism, determine if the debate will also address the exclusionary character of all nationalisms, including Palestinian nationalism.

In short, while establishing boundaries, seize the initiative. At Harvard in the 1980s, Professor Alan Dershowitz would begin his debates with P.L.O. supporters by demanding that they first condemn the murder of schoolchildren, diplomats and Olympians. This demand often made the interlocutor defensive, and it reminded the audience that terrorism was immoral, regardless of the underlying motives. Similarly, today it is helpful – and morally necessary – to condemn terrorism against civilians. One can note that Israel has condemned the one band of Jewish outlaws that operates in the West Bank, the entire Jewish world recoiled in horror when two Jewish terrorists struck just before the August 2005 disengagement, while at the height of the violence, eighty percent of Palestinians polled cheered the suicide bombers who slaughtered dozens of innocents. One can also demand an affirmation of Israel's right to exist. Israeli governments of the right and left have recognized the Palestinians' national claims. Unless Israel's critics also recognize Jews' legitimate national rights, dialogue is doomed.

Meanwhile, don't get carried away with clever strategies and verbal acrobatics. Keep it simple – it will sound more "real" that way.

Intellectual integrity is important. Better to remain calm and reasonable, even if the other side is lying outrageously, as often happens.

The Middle East is a very complicated place. Israel, like all states, has its imperfections. It is easier, and more intellectually honest, to concede some imperfections, rather than claiming that every Israeli is always perfect – or that the Palestinians are all bad.

Still, it is helpful to accentuate the positive – to focus on critical differences. It is important to contrast Israel's offer of peace and a Palestinian state with the Palestinian response of violence and suicide bombings, and to contrast Israel's robust democracy with Mr. Arafat's corrupt kleptocracy. In February 2001, as the entire Jewish world braced for attacks upon Ariel Sharon's election, I preferred to write a newspaper article emphasizing the miracle that, amid all the violence, Israel continued to be the only country in the Middle East to empower its citizens with free elections.

Accentuating the positive also means focusing on other Jewish identity issues as well. One campus activist, remembering how shocked she was by the Arab barrage in Fall 2000, said, "So, of course, we dropped all the stupid stuff like *Shabbat* dinners and getting-to-know-you dances." Such "stupid stuff" remains essential. Student activists should not be simply Zionist zealots. They need to build their community and to nurture their souls.

While accentuating the positive, it also helps, as the old song goes, to "e-liminate the negative." Campus Jews, like other Jews, spent too much time on the defensive. In the first year, the Israeli army, the Israeli government, and Israel's supporters throughout the world often waited for Palestinian attacks, and then responded. By now, the other side's patterns are clear. On those campuses where Palestinians and leftists have intimidated Jewish students distributing pro-Israel pamphlets, Jews need to take pre-emptive action. Keeping a video camera or tape recorder handy, or turning to neutral students and professors to serve as witnesses, often inhibits aggressive partisans. If students do not demand civility (and, of course, if they do not behave civilly), the situation on campus will only deteriorate.

Finally, we all must learn, learn, and learn some more. Learning means more than arming yourself with useful facts and clever debating points. It is better for Jewish students to read for an hour about the history of the conflict than to contribute another sad chapter to the conflict by arguing with those who will not be convinced after ten hours of screaming.

These hints, of course, only skim the tip of the proverbial iceberg. But if students *I*nsist on terms; *S*eize the initiative; remain *R*eal and true to themselves; *A*ccentuate the Positive; *E*liminate the Negative and *L*earn, learn, learn, not only ***ISRAEL*** itself will benefit, we all will by building deeper ties with each other and with our homeland.

APPLIED KNOWLEDGE 1: ISRAEL'S SECURITY FENCE

Applying this approach to one of the latest assaults on Israel's good name, let's think about the attacks on the security fence Israel is building in response to Palestinian terror. Note we have already started playing the name game. Northerners know to call Abraham Lincoln's great war for union "the Civil War" while some Southerners still try calling it "the War Between the States" or "the War of Northern Aggression." The Palestinians scored a huge propaganda victory by naming their reprehensible turn from negotiating toward terror the "*el-Aksa Intifada*," the "uprising" to defend the mosque on what Jews call *Har HaBayit* or the Temple Mount. This label sounds romantic, indigenous, and blames the slaughter of innocents Palestinians unleashed on Ariel Sharon's September 2000 visit to the Temple Mount. Israelis should have agreed on a pejorative such as "Arafat's War" or the "War Against the Oslo Peace Process" rather than the vague sounding "*HaMatzav*," the Situation. Similarly, Palestinians rail against Israel's "apartheid wall" whereas Israel's supporters – refusing to succumb this time – call it the Fence or the Security Barrier.

In truth, the barrier is over 90 percent fence, meaning it looks like most borders in the world, except in places where hostile Palestinian settlements such as Kalkilya overlook Israeli towns. Moreover, the false apartheid analogy minimizes the evil nature of the South African Afrikaners' now-dismantled systematic racism while caricaturing Israel's ideology. Not only is there no Israeli or Zionist doctrine of Palestinian inferiority, but Israel has acknowledged Palestinian nationalism even as too much of the Palestinian national movement contains racist, anti-Semitic elements, and much of the Arab world practices a milder variation of an anti-Jewish, anti-Christian and often anti-Western apartheid!

The most important and relevant fact about the fence is that Israel only began building it after tens of thousands of Palestinian terror attempts and the loss of hundreds of Israeli lives. So…

• *Insist on terms* – not just the accurate label because it is more than 90 percent chain-link fence but start with the broader question: do countries have the right to defend themselves against violence?

• *Seize the Initiative* – let's ask: if every nation-state can and does create and defend its own borders, and if the United States can contemplate a fence to keep Mexican immigrants out and certainly patrol that border heavily, why can't Israel build a fence to keep terrorists out?

• *Remain Real* – acknowledge, yes, Palestinian farmers, students and commuters have been inconvenienced, and that is very unfortunate. But countless lives on both sides have been saved, and a semblance of normal life returned on both sides, thanks to the many attacks the fence prevented. How much inconvenience is one life worth? Ten lives? One hundred lives? The fence is an unhappy monument to the failure of Oslo, to the refusal of Yasir Arafat and the Palestinians to compromise. The fence is a daily reminder that Palestinians' deliberate, strategic turn toward terrorism killed the illusions of the left that Oslo would usher in an age of mutual cooperation. The fence also shows that Palestinian terror – and perseverance – also destroyed the delusions of the right that the Palestinians would quietly disappear. Echo the argument of the writer Yossi Klein Halevi that Palestinians' hatred of the fence should drive home in a non-violent way the cost of war, the price they pay in inconvenience and some territory for opting out of the peace process and embracing Arafat's terrorism.

• *Accentuate the Positive* – note how often the fence-line has been redrawn and the built fence has been moved thanks to Palestinian petitions and Israeli Supreme Court directives. What other nation in the Middle East follows the rule of law in that way? What other Western nation grants its judicial system so much input in the nitty-gritty of national security matters? And let's

• *Eliminate the Negative* – a fence is a passive, peaceful response to terror. If everything Israel does to defend itself, no matter how non-military it might be, is illegitimate, perhaps critics are really saying that Israel does not have the right to defend itself at all, which means, given the bloodthirsty nature of Israel's enemies, that critics are really saying Israel does not have the right to exist.

• Finally, most important of all, the best way to *Learn* about the fence, is to see it. When I stood on the edge of Jerusalem's Gilo neighborhood and looked across the valley to Bethlehem and Bet Jalla, I was shocked. The two Palestinian towns were so close. My guide noted that at least ten terrorists had simply walked across the valley and murdered innocents, and a ten-kilogram suicide belt had been found hidden halfway up the hill. My first question was not "How did Israel dare build this fence separating the Palestinians and the Israelis?" My first question was – and remains – "Why did Israelis wait two years before building this barrier to protect men, women, and children? What took them so long?"

APPLIED KNOWLEDGE 2: The Disengagement

With this difficult question of Israel's withdrawal from Gaza in August 2005, the argument turns confusing and three-dimensional, for critics have attacked Israel's actions from the left and the right, from the intensely anti-Zionist to the militant Zionist.

• *Insist on terms* – Does Israel ever get credit for doing anything right? One of the things that frustrated many pro-Israel supporters of the Oslo Peace Process was that after Israel brought Yasir Arafat back from exile, armed his "security" forces and relinquished control over most Palestinians in the territories, the world nevertheless pretended that Israel had made no concessions. As soon as Palestinians launched a war of terror and yelled "occupation," Israel was in the international doghouse.

Here is an opportunity to test for some basic integrity, let alone goodwill. Start off a discussion by saying, "I am willing to give credit where credit is due. I acknowledge that Yasir Arafat's successor Mahmoud Abbas has changed the tone and does not speak venomously about the Jews and Israel, and I appreciate that. Are critics of Israel willing to acknowledge just how bold a gamble and majestic a move the disengagement was, from the unprecedented willingness to relinquish territory the state secured in a war of self-defense, to the unilateral nature of the withdrawal, and including the humane way the Israeli soldiers treated the angry and resistant settlers?"

• *Seize the Initiative* – let's tell a tale of greenhouses. A group of Jewish philanthropists donated $14 million to purchase greenhouses from the Jewish farmers of Gaza. The idea was to donate functional Gaza greenhouses to the Palestinians. This gift covered 800 of the 1,125 acres the farmers of Gush Katif had cultivated, earning $75 million in 2004 and employing 3,600 people, mostly Palestinians. The hope was that these hothouses could generate an additional 3,000 nonagricultural jobs too. But, as the *Christian Science Monitor* of 25 October 2005 reported, "that hope was jeopardized when Palestinian looters damaged many of the greenhouses, stripping them bare, for instance, of computers that the settlers used to monitor crops. Irrigation pumps were stolen, electricity networks paralyzed, and protective sheeting for the hothouses were torn."

We are not even talking about the synagogues that the Palestinians torched when the Israelis withdrew. What kind of a political culture have the Palestinians developed which is so self-destructive? "If I start to destroy instead of building, there won't be a state," said Subhi Firwana, a Palestinian who worked in the greenhouses for eighteen years, who now may lose his job. How come most reporters ignored this burst of economic suicide? Why don't Palestinian actions invite the same scrutiny as Israeli actions? Doesn't this action prove that Golda Meir's challenge from decades ago remains true today: until Palestinians love their children more than they hate our children, meaning that until Palestinians are more committed to building their own state rather than destroying the Jewish state, peace will remain elusive.

And while we are at it, let's also tell a tale of Netiv Ha'Asarah, a farming community just north of the Gaza Strip. For decades, Israelis, Arabs and the international community accepted maps defining Netiv Ha'Asarah as within the uncontested, original, post-1949 Armistice borders of Israel, the so-called "Green Line." All of a sudden, on the eve of the disengagement, Palestinians including their leader Mahmoud Abbas, used a pre-1949 map to declare Netiv Ha'Asarah part of the Gaza Strip. Rather than pointing to this anomaly as proof of the enduring, humanizing, and compromise-oriented insight that the borders of the Middle East are fluid, this became the Palestinians' way of claiming that Israel would not be withdrawing from Gaza fully. Characteristically, the Palestinians reinforced their message with Kassam rockets and rocks. One month before the disengagement a mortar attack killed 22-year-old Donna Gelkovich as she sat with her fiancé. After the disengagement Palestinian mobs pelted the village with rocks as periodic rocket attacks vividly illustrated the difference between living directly on the border and even a few kilometers away. This last-minute, obscurantist twist played into many Israelis' fears that no matter what Israel concedes, Palestinians will always demand more, until there is nothing left to give.

• *Remain Real* – Acknowledge that the disengagement did not come easy, that there were heartfelt arguments both pro and con, that Israeli society experienced great strain in the months leading up to the disengagement, that no side was perfect. Among other excesses, too many of the settlers indulged in extreme rhetoric and flirted with both treason and violence, while the government was sometimes too heavyhanded in squelching dissent and did not do enough to resettle those evacuated smoothly and effectively. Acknowledging complexity, indulging in self-criticism, learning from mistakes, is what democrats and democracies do – and Israelis are certainly practiced in the arts of bashing each other and themselves.

• *Accentuate the Positive* – Amid this backdrop of tensions, doubts, and imperfections, the story of the actual disengagement becomes more grandiose, in fact. Israelis added a remarkable chapter to the noble history of liberal democracy in August, 2005. Before the disengagement, hundreds of thousands of Israelis protested, with far less violence than at most European soccer matches. Preaching non-violence, settlers invoked Martin Luther King, Jr., so often that some Israelis may think he was a rabbi, not a reverend.

In a remarkable, and under-reported, move, the members of many Gaza settlements held ceremonies handing their weapons to the Israeli army before the disengagement, even as many of those same settlers refused to pack. A week later, in one settlement, Israeli Army Radio reported that the remaining settlers prepared to congregate in their synagogue, wrap themselves in prayer shawls, and wait for soldiers to carry them out, to "create difficult images." Such antics, including the many people who shouted at soldiers while clasping their own hands from behind to avoid appearing physically threatening, were legitimate democratic moves – and represented a sophisticated, disciplined vision of civil disobedience.

Similarly, the Israeli Army and police selected their most mature members to evacuate resisting settlers. Teams of seventeen unarmed men and women – when else in history have security forces voluntarily disarmed? – approached each family. Officers instructed the soldiers to ignore insults, treat the families sensitively and pack the belongings, if necessary, respectfully. The security forces performed their difficult tasks with aplomb. One police officer told the *Jerusalem Post* that she helped peel carrots before escorting one family out, explaining that she approached the settlers as she would have wanted her own mother to be treated.

The Israeli media featured heart-wrenching images of people mourning their lost homes and, most especially, of soldiers hugging them – often crying with them. One soldier explained to an orange-clad, kippah-wearing boy, "I have no other country or people" – echoing the famous Israeli song about their country's challenges and beauty, *Ein Li Eretz Acheret*. The boy repeated it. The two embraced and wept. One young soldier said on national TV, "We've been asked to take all the sensitivity we've developed over our lives and put it to good use to help these people."

• *Eliminate the Negative* – All these moments proved that both the settlers and the soldiers understood that there were red lines they should not cross, that they remained fellow citizens – and fellow Jews – no matter their differences. Withdrawing from Gaza was a sacrifice for peace – or at least stability – the latest attempt on the part of Israelis to change the

Middle Eastern paradigm and lessen the tensions. This withdrawal was a dramatic, concrete step away from a major bone of contention between the Israelis and the Palestinians. What dramatic Palestinian concessions have we seen, either building up to the withdrawal or subsequently?

One of the enduring pathologies of this Middle East conflict is that the Palestinians are always demanding more and more concessions from Israel – true progress can come only from real compromises on both sides which entail mutual concessions.

• *Learn, Learn, and Learn some more* – To understand what occurred in the summer of 2005, people need to understand what happened in June 1967, when Israel seized Gaza from Egypt after Egypt violated international law by blocking the Straits of Tiran; people need to know about the 1977 Camp David negotiations, when Menachem Begin tried to return Gaza to Egypt, and Anwar Sadat resisted; people need to discover that whatever they think about "the settlements" in Gaza, they were developed on empty sand dunes and what had been Egyptian public lands, not on the ruins of Palestinian homes; people need to appreciate just what those 8,500 people built in those now-ruined villages, and just how much those people – and Israel – sacrificed in the hopes for some progress in Israel's quest for stability, legitimacy, and peace.

ACTION, NOT JUST ADVOCACY

Of course, when the arguments end, an enduring friendship with Israel must involve action as well as rhetoric. As a movement, Zionism always emphasized deeds over words. Yet the current conflict is so shadowy that many North American Jews have not known how to show that they do care. It might behoove us, as Jews, to follow the sad but inspiring examples that emerged after the tragedies of September 11.

The frustrating truth is that there was little Americans or their friends could really do in the wake of these vicious terrorist attacks either. Most who sought to volunteer at Ground Zero were rebuffed. The Red Cross quickly announced that blood banks were full. Undeterred, Americans – and good people throughout the world – expressed their support for the victims spiritually, politically, and financially. Candlelight vigils and makeshift memorials forged a worldwide community of mourners. Displaying the American flag demonstrated support for the grieving nation – and its eventual military response. And a flood of donations illustrated tangible support for the grieving families in the standard currency of our society. Within weeks, over a billion dollars was raised. Alas, the Israeli victims of terror – and their grieving society – have not benefitted from a similar outpouring of love and support from the Jewish world.

A MODEST PROPOSAL:
ADOPT THE FAMILY OF THE VICTIMS

Amir was a kibbutznik and a peacenik, a 33-year-old father of three. Vadim was a newlywed, a 35-year-old immigrant from Irkutsk. Ayelet, 28, had just moved to Jerusalem. Hillel, 36, was a rabbi, the father of seven. Shmuel, 42, was a doctor, the father of five. Hadas, 39, was the mother of four. David, Yelena, Yulia, and Koby were mere teenagers, aged 19, 18, 16, and 13 respectively.

These are ten of the Israelis who have been killed in over twenty thousand recorded acts of violence since September 2000. Amir Zohar, who had been born on Kibbutz Galon, was the community director of the East Talpiot neighborhood of Jerusalem, where he forged ties with the neighboring Arab town of Sur Bahir. A major in the reserves, he was shot by Palestinians near Jericho. Vadim Novich was also a reservist. He was one of the two Israelis lynched in Ramallah. Ayelet Hashachar-Levy, the daughter of a former Cabinet member, was one of the two Israelis killed by a car bomb in Mahaneh Yehudah. Rabbi Hillel Lieberman was the American immigrant who heard that a mob was desecrating Joseph's Tomb, and walked there, alone and unarmed on *Shabbat*, to protect the holy site. He was shot one hundred times. Dr. Shmuel Gillis was the senior hematologist at Hadassah hospital in Ein Kerem – he was "better than an angel," one of his Arab patients said. He was ambushed while commuting home from work. Hadas Abutbul, murdered on November 9, 2001, was a nursery school teacher. She, too, was ambushed while commuting. David Biri, 19, was a sergeant, the first victim of the war, killed by a bomb two days before Ariel Sharon walked on the Temple Mount. Yelena and Yulia Nelimov were two sisters waiting on line to enter the Dolphinarium disco. And Ya'acov (Koby) Mandell, the son of American immigrants, was brutally murdered, along with a buddy of his, Yosef Ish-Ran, on May 9, 2001.

Every one of us should "adopt" the family of one of the victims. Individually and collectively, in schools and in shuls, via our community centers and our organizations, we should reach out to the newly-orphaned, the newly-widowed. We should send cards and we should send money. We should send letters and our children should send pictures. We should envelop these unfortunate people – and the country that mourns with them – in one massive, long-distance group hug.

To make the ties personal, it is best to adopt one individual. It worked in the 1970s when we adopted individual Soviet Jewish prisoners of conscience. It can work again today. Let each of us learn about one victim, and the universe of love and pain he or she left behind. Let us learn about one set of needs, and see how we can help.

Of course, everyone reacts differently to trauma, and not every family wishes to be "adopted." But Israel is a small country and it is easy, through discreet inquiries, to find those who would appreciate the support. And the truth is that there are many, many families who do not wish to be abandoned either – and feel that Diaspora Jews have deserted them.

The various victims were as diverse in their origins and in their opinions as our community is, offering an array of role models from which to choose. Left-wingers can rally around the Zohar family, right-wingers can rally around the Liebermans. Or, in a true mark of *ahavat yisrael*, communal love, we can adopt those with whom we might not have agreed, but whose deaths we nevertheless mourn.

If indeed the Jewish world responds to this call, and there is a massive outpouring, the friends and neighbors of these grieving Israelis should help with the correspondence, thus further deepening the friendship.

A massive Jewish community response, on this person-to-person level, will have many beneficial effects. For starters, it is a true act of *tsedakah*, of righteousness, to offer comfort to those who mourn. Moreover, it will show the world that we Jews may be traumatized but we are not paralyzed.

Those who consider this proposal one-sided should also feel free to reach out to Palestinians who have suffered as well. Unfortunately, this crisis has created an us-versus-them siege mentality. Many rallying around Israel are condemning anyone who dissents and too many Jews and non-Jews who condemn Israel's actions today all too often categorically reject the Jewish state itself. We must learn to criticize and not delegitimize. Offering support to a fellow Jew in pain should not be a political act. The purpose here is to go beyond politics, and simply comfort fellow humans, and yes, fellow Jews, in distress.

Of course, there should be a fundraising component. We in the fleshpots of Babylon should offer financial help to these widows and orphans. But what we might call the "friend-raising" component is the most important element. Once again, we Jews have demonstrated our ability to fall back in love with Israel when it is under siege. We need, however, to forge strong friendships with individual Israelis, ties that will flourish in good times as well as in bad.

A MORE SWEEPING PROPOSAL: FIND BIG PICTURE, UPBEAT STRATEGIES

Here's a case study with a happy ending. Montreal's Concordia University, in particular, had become infamous as a center of unreason and discord. The situation at "Gaza U" had been one of unrelenting hostility to Zionism – and often Jews. Faculty members demonstrated the casual bigotry of the politically correct, injecting anti-Israel remarks into lectures unrelated to the Middle East and dismissing Jewish nationalism by referring to the Jewish "people" in quotation marks. Radical students, professing to build what the Concordia Student Union leaders of the time called "a community that is anti-racist, anti-patriarchal... and pro-queer" overlooked the fanatic nationalism, sexism and homophobia of the Palestinian Authority and the broader Islamicist movement. Palestinian activists sullied Concordia's name by intimidating Jewish students, harassing Hillel canvassers and importing a culture of threats and violence. These abuses culminated in the September 9, 2002 riot that prevented former Israeli prime minister Benjamin Netanyahu from speaking, followed by the Chanukah-time ejection of Hillel from the student government.

Concordia University functioned as an unhappy harbinger of what could happen on any campus where anti-Semitism masquerading as anti-Zionism festers. Even when Palestinian activists were not rioting – punching professors and kicking Holocaust survivors on that awful day – even when the anarchist-run student government was not stigmatizing Hillel, too many Jewish students felt scared at Concordia, a shocking failure for a modern university.

Fortunately, this tale has a less known but happier twist. Finally, Jewish students, the Jewish community and the broader community of Concordia students belatedly mobilized in the spring of 2003. Concordia soon became a model for how to respond to the epidemic of anti-Zionist bigotry afflicting too many of the West's most progressive circles.

Three important things occurred. For starters, Jewish students became better organized and more aggressive. Although a core group had been active for years, the September 9 riot galvanized many marginally involved students. When the student union attacked in December, Hillel struck back, launching an anti-discrimination lawsuit against the student government and its officers. As Israel, the United States and others have had to relearn these last few years, politeness and passivity in the face of aggression invites more attacks. The Hillel counteroffensive changed the campus dynamics, empowering the Jews and cowing the bullies.

The Montreal Jewish community backed many of these efforts generously. Legal expertise, public relations advice and, most important of all, moral support bolstered the embattled Jewish students.

At the same time, the pro-Palestinian hooliganism upset many non-Jewish students, who resented the chaos and worried about their university's reputation. In September 2001, the student union published a calendar filled with anti-Israel and anti-corporate ravings. Business and engineering students anxious about on-campus recruitment then mobilized. By 2003 a broader coalition of students who believed that a student government does not need a foreign policy but does need to represent student concerns ran a slate in the spring student government elections – and won, thanks to a higher than normal turnout by fed-up students. Zionists, especially in Canada, had failed to build many pro-Israel coalitions beyond the Jewish community, or even articulate a vision that associated support for Israel with support for democracy, civility, liberty and non-Jews' self-interest, making this achievement all the more valuable.

Most encouraging of all, Jewish activists at Concordia and throughout Montreal refused to despair. For years in Montreal, fueled by a happy combination of the birthright israel buzz, the broader Jewish identity agenda and superb communal leadership, many young Jews had been celebrating Israel, Zionism and Judaism, not just manning the barricades. Typical of this focus on identity building was the way the community responded after the riot. Borrowing the modern Israeli ritual of *hakafot shneyot*, a second round of Torah-parading after *Simchat Torah* ends, when music can be played and people can travel, the president of Montreal Hillel, Ariela Cotler, proposed a post-*Simchat Torah* march from

Concordia to McGill University to reclaim the streets for Jewish students.

The Concordia administration had foolishly banned all Middle East-related extra-curricular activities, so the *hakafot* were planned beyond Concordia's boundaries. The Montreal police, however, refused to permit such a parade at night – and instead offered a downtown square.

It was a marvelous redirection. When *Simchat Torah* ended, between 2,000 and 3,000 Montrealers – in a Jewish community of only 100,000 – transcended holiday burnout and descended on downtown Montreal. They were young and old, religious and secular. Rather than marching angrily, we sang and danced around the Torah scrolls, deep into the night. That celebration, that affirmation of Jewish unity, Jewish values, Jewish traditions, demonstrated peace, power and pride, while uplifting our souls.

Even as the situation calms down, that is the model to mass-produce. Even when we mobilize politically, even when we react to attacks, we need to celebrate Israel, embrace Zionism, delight in Judaism, build coalitions and nurture our community. That is the recipe for internal cohesion, external strength and individual satisfaction and salvation that the Jewish world needs, on campus – and elsewhere.

A THREE-DIMENSIONAL ROUNDTABLE: THE LEFT AND THE RIGHT STRUGGLE OVER THE "MATZAV," THE "OCCUPATION" AND THE LEGITIMACY OF THE STATE

Of course, not all facets of the conflict are clear, and the arguments are not limited to Jews and Arabs. Jews themselves are involved in a vigorous, sometimes invigorating, and sometimes depressing, debate about how we got here, what we are doing and where we are going. As a closing exercise, it might be useful to rehearse some of the arguments Zionists from the left and the right are having with each other – as well as with their Arab opponents.

For starters, it is important to debunk one of the central myths of this conflict – that our side is right, their side is wrong. As I have argued throughout this book, such an all-or-nothing, mutually exclusive approach to the problem is intellectually and morally untenable. While there are rights and wrongs here, and not everything is even-steven, it is misleading to romanticize one side and demonize the other, especially when the conflict will be solved – or reduced – only through some cooperation and compromise.

Having said that, it is worth contemplating the response to three levels of argument – about the current conflict, about the occupation since 1967, and about the very existence of the Jewish state.

LEVEL ONE – THE CURRENT CONFLICT: WHO STARTED IT – AND WHAT ARE THEY FIGHTING ABOUT?

It's confusing. According to most media reports Ariel Sharon started the current troubles when he walked on the Temple Mount surrounded by legions of security guards in September, 2000. To the Arabs, and to many leftists, it was a provocation, an insult to the Muslim holy shrine. To Ehud Barak, it was political theatre, directed not at him, and not at Arafat, but at Sharon's rival in the Likud Party, Bibi Netanyahu, with Sharon trying to assert himself as the champion of the Jewish claim to Jerusalem. Sharon and his allies on the right wonder why he would be the first Jew barred from visiting the Temple Mount, which, like all holy places in Jerusalem, is supposed to be open to all people.

Once again, we ask the historian's question, "Where do I begin?" Herb Keinon of the *Jerusalem Post* wrote an article arguing that all of Israel's wars, including this latest one, are one continuous fight over the right of the Jewish state to exist, suggesting this whole imbroglio started in 1948 with Israel's independence or 1947 with the UN partition or 1897 with the Zionist Congress, or four thousand years ago with Abraham. Many on the left would argue that the conflict began with the conquest of territories in 1967, or, perhaps, with the rise of the Gush Emunim movement, which pushed for many settlements in the West Bank and Gaza. Others on the right are more likely to date this conflict to the May, 2000 withdrawal from Southern Lebanon, which they believe sent a message to the Palestinians that the Hezbollah's approach – a terrorist war of attrition – would gain them more than the Palestinian Authority's approach – negotiating via Oslo. The conventional wisdom points to the failure of the July, 2000 Camp David initiative, which, depending on where you sit, either showed Israel's unwillingness to dismantle enough settlements and proved Oslo to be a farce, or confirmed Arafat's reluctance to sign any deal, no matter how generous, and proved Oslo to be a farce.

Of course, even as one identifies the underlying causes of World War I, one cannot ignore the archduke's assassination. Thus, one must concede that even if the Palestinians jumped on it as an excuse, the Sharon visit to the Temple Mount brought these tensions to a head. Still, that is a far cry from blaming Sharon for the Palestinians' apparently premeditated decision to try to achieve their nationalist aspirations via violence rather than negotiation.

In truth, even greater confusion lies over what everyone is fighting for. Many on the left believe this is a fight over the settlements, and over Israel's insistence on controlling critical roads, water-sources, and overpasses, making a Palestinian state untenable. These are the ones who would call this war *"Milchemet Shlom HaMitnachlim,"* the war for the peace of the settlers, wherein six million are held hostage to the whims of two hundred thousand. Others on the right insist that the Palestinians have shown that everything is a settlement, from Metullah to the Negev, from Tel Aviv to Jerusalem, and that the fight is over Israel's very right to exist. In this calculus, the strategic settlements are doing what they were supposed to do, serving as outposts, and as negotiating points, and two hundred thousand are carrying a special burden, and drawing much of the fire, from the other six million.

LEVEL TWO: WHO'S OCCUPYING WHO? WHO'S VICTIMIZED BY WHOM?

Here, as in so many parts of the conflict, your vocabulary betrays you. Leftists will talk of occupying the West Bank and Gaza; rightists of the liberation of Judea and Samaria. Moreover, rightists grumble that talk of "occupation" links Israel with Nazis and Soviets. It plays to the sensibilities and guilt of the world, from the Great Inversion wherein all non-Westerners are blameless. Historians remember:

a. that Israel entered the war with Jordan in 1967 only after Jordan attacked, and after King Hussein was warned to stay out of it.

b. that Israel relinquished vast amounts of territory and that by 2000 ninety-five percent of Palestinians were living under the Palestinian Authority's rule. No other country in history, after being attacked and then winning disputed territory, has ever voluntarily relinquished land. Israel did it in Sinai in the late 1970s, and did it again in the 1990s under Oslo.

c. In a land of fluid boundaries and shifting regimes, terms like "occupation" are relative. In 1948 the Jordanian Legion overran Gush

Etzion, a Jewish settlement on the outskirts of Jerusalem. For nineteen years the former inhabitants of Gush Etzion mourned their loss and prayed for their return. When they could return after the Six Day War, were they occupiers or rightful owners retrieving what was theirs? Isn't Zionism about a return to the land, about our historic ties to Hebron, where Abraham was buried, as well as Tel Aviv, which was created only in the twentieth century?

At the same time, the Left says, here history is irrelevant – demography counts. And regardless of the rights and wrongs, what do you do with a million and a half unfulfilled people – and what do you do about the brutalizing impact "occupation" has on Israeli soldiers, on Israeli society? If Zionism is more than just survivalism or land-worship, if it truly is democratic, humanistic, idealistic, how can the military rule continue?

Furthermore, leftists do not see the power disparity as some Western construct. They note that, in the West Bank, Israel has the armaments, the strategic passes, the choice land given to the settlers. And they compare the relative luxury of the settlers' lifestyles with the misery of most Palestinians, and feel both guilty and furious.

LEVEL THREE: THE BIG LIES

"Abraham was not a Jew.... The Jews never lived in ancient Israel…. There never was a Jewish Temple in Jerusalem…. Jews never had any connection to Jerusalem…. That is not the Western Wall at all, but a Moslem shrine."

These quotations unfortunately represent mainstream Palestinian opinions – not an extremist fringe. They are taken from a Palestinian Arab historian Jarid al-Kidwa, Palestinian television, the Palestinian Authority's Ministry of Information, and the first and last ones are from Yasir Arafat himself.

While leftists and rightists will quibble about how seriously to take this rhetoric, here our mythical Leftists and Rightists do join together. This negation of Jewish history is not only an insult and a threat to Jews – it is an insult and a threat to Christians as well. To deny the historicity of the Temple, to claim that only the Moslems have a special tie, is to wipe out the story of Jesus, and the start of Christianity.

In this context, it is worth remembering at least the following ten key dates – the last nine of which all mainstream historians conclusively accept – remembering that much more remains to be filled in. These dates trace the arc of the central Zionist narrative emphasizing the Jews' historic ties to the land, the theme of exile and redemption, and the tragic, frustrating, occasionally ennobling search for peace.

TEN KEY DATES:

c. 2000-1750 B.C.E.: *Lech Lecha* – Abraham Goes to Canaan

70 C.E.   Exile – The Romans destroy the Second Temple and exile many of the Jews, although some Jews will live in the Land of Israel continuously throughout the exile

1897   Zionism – Twenty years of pioneering culminates in the founding of the Modern Zionist Movement with the First Zionist Congress in Basel, Switzerland

1921   Transjordan Partition – Under the British Mandate, the area of Palestine is divided

1947   UN Partition – the area of Palestine is further divided, but David Ben-Gurion accepts the division to achieve statehood

1948   Founding of Israel

1967   Six Day War

1973   Yom Kippur War

1979   Camp David Treaty Signed with Egypt

1993   Oslo Peace Accords with Palestinians

I confess, I waver. Some days I see the Palestinians' plight clearly, understand their anger, recognize, as Ehud Barak did, that if I were a Palestinian I would be an activist, although I'm quite sure I would not be a terrorist. And as a Jew, I am proud of my upbringing and my heritage that allows me to see the side of the other, even if the other does not want to see my side. Other days, I see Israel's plight so clearly, I feel the pain caused by random deaths, endless hatred, a barbaric political culture, repeated attacks on the legitimacy of the state, and have no patience for compromise, no willingness to assume any risks for any elusive peace with a hate-filled people who will be satisfied only if Israel dies.

Polls indicate that the consensus in Israel is equally conflicted. When attacked, as they have been recently, the Israelis become unyielding, impassive, angry, and belligerent. But all they need is a word, a gesture, Sadat coming to Jerusalem, Arafat willing to sign the Oslo Accords, and they are willing to make huge risks, bear scary burdens, to keep the dove of peace flying in the air, hovering over all peoples who share a love for their mystical, magical, seething, yet deeply beautiful, land.

As an historian, I have learned that perceptions evolve based on real events as well as ideological trends. And things may be looking up. The Middle East analyst Barry Rubin hopes that the world may finally be evolving toward a "Third Paradigm" or framework for viewing the

Middle East conflict. The first paradigm from 1948 through the 1980s, viewed the conflict as one of Arab "aggression against a legitimate state," Israel. After the Lebanon War, the first Palestinian riots and Yasir Arafat's surprisingly effective propagandizing, the second paradigm became Israeli "oppression of a victimized people," the Palestinians. Now, thanks to the Palestinian rejection of the 2000 Camp David compromise, and the overlap between the Palestinian Wave of Terror and America's War on Terror, the new "Third Paradigm" recognizes "the impossibility of conciliating those who hold an extremist ideology and engage in terrorism."

Still, there is too much pain, on both sides. In September 2002, a suicide bomber on a Tel Aviv bus murdered six people, including Yoni Jesner, a nineteen-year-old B'nai Akiva religious Zionist from Glasgow. His parents donated one of Yoni's kidneys to Yasmin Abu Ramila, a seven-year-old Palestinian girl from East Jerusalem, who had been waiting two years for a compatible kidney. "I think the most important principle here is that life was given to another human being," Yoni's brother Ari said.

Three years later, Israeli troops mistakenly killed Ahmed al-Khabit, a twelve-year-old Palestinian boy who was playing with a toy gun as soldiers and terrorists clashed in Jenin. Ahmed's organs were transplanted into five Israeli children ranging in age from seven months to fourteen years, as well as a fifty-eight-year-old woman. "I have taken this decision because I have a message for the world: that the Palestinian people want peace – for everyone," Ahmed's father Ismail al-Khatib said. May the spirit of the Jesners and the al-Khatibs guide the leaders and citizens of this region. And even as we advocate passionately, may we do what we can to preserve the memories of Yoni and Ahmed, learning to see through others' eyes without being blind to reality and doing whatever we can to secure a real, lasting, and mutually respectful peace.

CHAPTER 22

LO NAFSEEK LIRKOD: WE WON'T STOP DANCING!

The beachfront stroll from high-tech Tel Aviv to the prophet Jonah's port city, Jaffa, passes Mike's Place, where a middle-class British Muslim poisoned by jihadist hatred murdered three music-lovers. It then passes the Dolphinarium, the disco where a killer later glorified by Palestinian Authority President Yasir Arafat slaughtered 21 teenagers and wounded 120. Today, Mike's Place still bops to the beat that made it famous. Outside the closed Dolphinarium a simple monument promises defiantly: "*Lo Nafseek Lirkod*," We Won't Stop Dancing.

We won't stop singing or dancing is indeed the right response, the spiritual reply to twenty-first-century terror. Israelis taught the world that lesson in so many ways as they persevered through an unprecedented wave of terror. While the military pursued its strategy of hunting terrorists in their home base, building a fence to keep them out, and mobilizing soldiers, security guards and citizens to stop potential mass murderers, Israelis simply chose life. Now, together with our Israeli brothers and sisters, we need to sing a new song of Zion, proud, assertive, affirmative and creative, one that not only defends our people and our homeland, but one that inspires and challenges us as twenty-first-century Jews, democrats and humans.

I am a romantic utilitarian. That means that yes, I have an emotional tie to the sights, smells, and stories of Israel and the Jewish people. That's the romance. But I am also practical. I need to exploit our good fortune of living in the era of the Third Jewish Commonwealth. I need to put the existence of the State of Israel to good use as an identity builder, a source of inspiration, a living breathing embodiment of our hopes and dreams. Rabbi Daniel Gordis recalls watching his grandfather cry tears of joy when Egyptian President Anwar Sadat visited Jerusalem in 1977. Gordis recalls the tears he himself shed when Israeli Prime Minister Yitzhak Rabin was assassinated 18 years later. Today, he regrets how long it took him to decode the message in those tears: "If there's a place in this world that can make you cry, isn't that where you ought to be?"

In Jerusalem, Rabbi Gordis delights in this "modern-day miracle's" historical depth and contemporary dynamism. When his 5-year-old says the Maccabees bombed the King David Hotel, Gordis rejoices that despite conflating stories 2,000 years apart, his son realizes that "This place isn't a city, or a country - it's a story. A story we tell and a story we live. A story about trying our one little place on the globe." Today, we as moderns, especially those of us lucky enough to be parents, need to learn how to use Israel as a tool. Israel roots us in this sweeping story and can give us a sense of mission, based on our shared commitment to the Jewish people. This vision should be accessible to both religious and less religious Jews, opening us all up to a country which is inspirational, spiritual, real, altruistic, enlivening and lyrical.

THE ZIONIST HEROES OF TODAY

Contrary to the many libels and smears surrounding it, the saga of Zionism has marked a proud chapter in the history of nationalism. *Medinat Yisrael*, the state of Israel, is a remarkable experiment in national rejuvenation – of building in *Eretz Yisrael*, the land of Israel, and reorienting and energizing *Am Yisrael*, the nation of Israel, meaning the Jewish people.

The early Zionists dreamed of a new Jewish commonwealth which would be a boon to humanity, not just to the Jewish people. Especially considering its small size and relative youth, the State of Israel has a pretty impressive track record so far. In the 1950s the kibbutz ideal offered a model of humane and freedom-loving socialism that contrasted with the oppressive Soviet-style Communism. By the 1960s the representatives of this young state were working with developing African societies less fortunate than their own. In the energy-stretched 1970s Israeli solar power offered alternative visions of how to live and consume. By the 1980s, *Tzahal*, the Israel Defense Forces, was already positioning itself as a world leader in search-and-rescue and in pioneering mobile medical units so that when there were earthquakes in Turkey, atrocities in Rwanda, bombings in Tanzania and Kenya, IDF soldiers were mobilized to save lives. In the 1990s Israeli technological, medical, and pharmacological miracles helped transform the world, shrinking the world through innovations such as ICQ an online chat technology, and Scitex which pioneered the world of computer graphics, while saving lives with cutting-edge brain research at Tel Aviv University, innovative emergency room techniques at Hadassah Hospital, and amazing cures developed in private labs. When in his early thirties, Scitex's founder, Efi Arazi, developed the relay system which beamed the video images of Apollo 11 from the moon to earth. Avi Katz, the talented illustrator whose work adorns these pages notes: "I always liked the idea that a vast American machine put a man on the moon, but a little Israeli brain let the world see it."

Israeli innovations, Israeli success, also prove that immigration can be a positive and creative force that fuels growth. It is noteworthy that in a country like the United States the first time an immigrant ascends to a particular position, people cheer. But Israel is such a melting pot that when Yitzhak Rabin became the first native-born prime minister, it was a cause for celebration. Israel has welcomed the surviving remnants of Hitler's Holocaust, the 800,000 refugees from various Muslim countries, 20,000 Ethiopians and one million Russians. Each time, it's been a win-win story, as Israel has offered desperate individuals refuge but also benefited from their skills, culture, and ambition.

Israel has been able to absorb so many immigrants because, as a capitalist country, it has enjoyed remarkable growth overall in the last half-century. As in the United States, Israeli society demonstrates how capitalism can harness individual skill for the good of the collective, as people enticed by the rewards at the end of the rainbow have helped build the modern, industrial, sophisticated society Israel is today.

Alas, as in the United States, that capitalist culture emerges as a social solvent, often undermining a sense of intimate community in the zeal to empower and energize individuals. Israel's story proves that free enterprise is good, but that it is not without its costs. The challenge of the 21st century will be to continue to build on the good while managing the costs.

These days, especially in Canada and Europe, it is far too fashionable to

dismiss Western values, American-style values, without really thinking about the alternatives. We live in a Manichean upside-down world which is hypercritical of Western mistakes and often blind to the drawbacks of other societies. We need to remind ourselves again and again that just because many people criticize us, just because we are in the embattled minority, does not mean that we are wrong.

To appreciate Israel's role as a Western, democratic, capitalist country, helping to build the world, even as it absorbs and enlists both immigrants and native Israelis, is to look at a fuller picture of Israel than what we usually see. This is not to say we should view Israel through rose-colored glasses. Rather, we should use a wide-angle lens.

At the same time, it is helpful to zoom in to appreciate the micro as well as the macro. Every day in Israel, without looking too hard, you can find the miracles of the everyday, the blessings of living in a country that remains intimate, old-fashioned and neighborly. The examples abound: the shopkeeper in Sderot who sends his kids to school with an extra sandwich for those who don't have, the friend fighting cancer who is accompanied to repeated treatments by friends skipping work – with their understanding bosses' blessings. You also find the miracles of modernity: the first Israeli astronaut orbiting the globe or the friend sticking with high-tech, working for Given Imaging, which applies guided-missile technology to develop a "camera-in-a-pill" that patients can swallow to photograph their innards.

These economic Zionists and social Zionists, cultural Zionists and religious Zionists, understand the power of community and of history. They bring added dimension to what they do by doing it in Israel, by contributing to a collective experiment in Jewish national rejuvenation. These real-life Israelis – not just the victims of terrorism and the soldiers – are the Zionist heroes of today.

NAOMI SHEMER'S LYRICAL LIBERAL NATIONALISM

Israel's greatest songwriter and poet extraordinaire, the late Naomi Shemer, taught the world – and Israelis themselves – to appreciate the Zionist miracle on both the macro and micro levels. Her lyrics, providing the basic soundtrack to Israel's history, evoke specific moments and transcendent ideals; many of her melodies invite swaying, and instinctive embraces of neighboring shoulders. She represented the broad, romantic, constructive sense of community that Zionism – and democratic nationalism at its best – nourishes. Her 1967 "Jerusalem of Gold" (*Yerushalayim Shel Zahav*) became Israel's "God Bless America," an un-official anthem offering the melody to the pop Zionism of tough sabras and sweet Jaffa oranges.

A great nationalist songwriter is more than just a poet, but must master language. In *Chorshat HaEkalyptus*, "The Eucalyptus Grove," Shemer evoked a timeless pastoral scene offering a symphony of the senses with just seven Hebrew words: "… the bridge, the boat, and the saltwort's fragrance on the water." A great nationalist songwriter is more than just a dreamer, but a visionary, promising individual and communal salvation. Following the brutal 1973 *Yom Kippur* surprise attack, Naomi Shemer again captured Israelis' mood. They craved peace without demanding vengeance. Saluting the Beatles, Shemer imagined "a white sail in the distance, facing a black and heavy cloud," saying "all that we shall ask: Let it be!" – *Lu Yihi*.

A great nationalist songwriter is more than just a historian, but must love the past. Recalling Solomon's Temple, marveling at the new state rebuilt with ancient stones, Shemer sang "a song older than wine, and sweeter than honey; a two-thousand-year-old song renewed each day" in *Shiro Shel Abba/Yibaneh*, My Father's Song/Please Rebuild. A great nationalist songwriter is more than just a nationalist, but must love community and humanity. *Anachnu Sheneinu MeOto HaKfar*, "We Two are From the Same Village," her haunting ode to eternal friendship begins. Inevitably, after "the battle that did not end… I saw how you were broken, and when the dawn rose over the hilltop, I brought you back to the village."

A great nationalist songwriter is more than just a philosopher, but must understand the human condition. Shemer's wisdom about *Hadvash v'haoketz, Hamar v'hamatok*, "the honey and the sting, the bitter and the sweet," created a communal cliché contextualizing the emotional rollercoaster of life in "our fledgling home." A great nationalist songwriter must be an idealist, a romantic, a populist, bonding with the people and capturing communal moods. Only an alchemist could spread the honey of dreams amid the toxins of life, transforming battlefield traumas into peaceful yearnings – while remaining popular.

Such sweet, quixotic populism transcends ugly politics and reflects a nation's soul, a people's aspirations despite life's complexities. Such noble democratic idealism reflects Western nationalism's roots in European romanticism and liberal democracy. Liberal democratic individualism balances nationalist collectivism, while nationalism's big-picture idealism checks liberal democracy's atomistic hedonism. Such constructive communalism has fed American and Israeli success.

Naomi Shemer's *Beit Halomotai*, her "house of dreams, on the crest of a hill," was joyous and welcoming. It eschewed hard choices and harsh realities. Another recently departed visionary optimist, Ronald Reagan, deployed a similar image, resurrecting the Pilgrim vision of a shining "city upon a hill." Unfortunately, Islamicist fanaticism has given nationalism – and religion – a bad name. Too many nationalist visions demonize others. Simultaneously, many intellectuals, indulging a hypercritical and hypocritical disdain for Western success, misconstrue nationalism, especially the American and Israeli-Zionist variety. Half a century ago, icons of the left celebrated their land, be it "from California to the New York Island," or "*Mimetullah ad Hanegev.*" A Woody Guthrie, a David Ben-Gurion, while steeped in unionism, in socialism, understood that loving the land, and the people, could mobilize good individuals to do great things together. Today, such patriotism is unfashionable, and frequently ceded to the right. This modern miserly caricature of nationalism as limiting, xenophobic, defensive, provincial, violent, imperialist and necessarily right wing is both historically inaccurate and politically foolhardy.

Naomi Shemer's oeuvre testifies to democratic nationalism's reach, miraculously uniting individuals building, reinventing, stretching themselves and their community. Her songs, like Ronald Reagan's and Bill Clinton's rhetoric, demonstrate the power of positive thinking, and the grandeur of communities rooted in affirmative ideals. One need not agree with the details of her politics to delight in her songs. *Yesh Li Yom, Yom Chag*, "I have a holiday every day… Halleluyah," Naomi Shemer sang. Her songs gave millions reasons to celebrate, new, unexpected holidays daily. That irrepressible joy, playing to the best of humanity, illustrates what democratic nationalism can be, if both left and right would let it be.

NEXT YEAR IN JERUSALEM: A PRICELESS OPPORTUNITY

Israel's successes, Naomi Shemer's songs, should lure those of who can to experience Israel, not simply as tourists, and not even as pilgrims, but as wandering Jews finally coming home. At seder time all across North America, families inevitably turn to the high school or college seniors at their table to ask the dreaded finishing up question: "So what are you doing next year?" Parents may be sufficiently well trained by their children to avoid the subject; relatives and family friends are less inhibited. Wouldn't it be great if, as in one of those ridiculous commercials in which two people discover the same cleaning solution, parents and children, deciding to harken to the words of the seder, stood as one singing, "Next year in Jerusalem."

College, law school, medical school or pre-graduate school anxiety can wait. Those all-important twenty-something years between high school and "real life" mark the perfect times to live in Israel, the Jewish people's homeland. Others should take an opportunity for an extended stay. With security stabilized, next year promises to be an extraordinary time for an Israel experience – as every year has proved to be for those who go, no matter what the politics of the moment happen to be.

To those of us disgusted with the demonization of Israel, the Nazification of Zionism, the politicization of all things Israeli, the Arafatian oversimplification reducing all discussions of Israel to the Palestinian problem, there is nothing more healing than visiting Israel. As the 100,000 18-to-26-year-old birthright israel visitors – and millions of others – have discovered these last few years, Israel is more than what you see on CNN.

Visiting Israel entails engaging Israel in all its multidimensional glory, delighting in an old-new land that counts history by millennia and not decades, experiencing a dynamic culture synthesizing cutting-edge Western values with Jewish traditions and Middle Eastern rhythms, and witnessing one of the youngest liberal democracies improvise sophisticated answers to bedeviling questions about church and state, minority and majority, terrorists and the terrified. Visiting Israel entails inhaling Jerusalem's spirituality, feeling Tel Aviv's beat, enjoying a symphony of the senses with the sounds, smells, sights and tastes of this exotic yet also comfortingly familiar land. Desert hikes, archaeological digs and Kotel prayers introduce visitors to *Eretz Yisrael*, the land of Israel. The novelty of navigating in a Hebrew-speaking culture, with all its achievements and idiosyncrasies, exposes them to *Medinat Yisrael*, the state – not just the government – of Israel. And their experiences with each other and with Israeli hosts link them to *Am Yisrael*, the Jewish people, living in Israel and abroad, building our homeland together.

For my family, summer times in Jerusalem have meant guaranteed sunny days, with appropriately sympathetic sighs for our rain-soaked friends in Montreal. It has meant attending Bar and Bat Mitzvahs in creative settings - a kibbutz, the Western Wall excavations, the Israel Museum and *Neot Kedumim*, a site on which every Biblical plant is cultivated.

Summer times in Jerusalem have meant sampling Ramah's Jerusalem Day Camp, with its charming spirit and beautiful values; the YMCA's sports camp, with Arabs, Jews and Christians united by a love of basketball and soccer; and the *Ein Yael* "Biblical Village," with its creative crafts, set in a 3,200-year-old farm.

And summer times in Jerusalem have meant distributing goodies to security guards – the often-overlooked invisible army protecting Israelis. One long, sweaty Friday morning was spent giving out wine and sweets to these unsung heroes while pondering with our nine-year-old daughter her question: "Why is it easier to make mischief than do *mitzvoth*?" Our seven-year-old son played the 17 songs of his Suzuki music "Book One," fiddling at a park overlooking the Old City. Our four-year-old scampered atop the Old City walls, joyfully confusing the Romans and the British, proudly pointing to every spot as being the place where Abraham prepared to sacrifice Isaac and where Solomon the Wise built the Temple. Our two-year-old daughter learned to say *bakasha*, a toddler version of the word *b'vakasha* meaning "please," while bastardizing with equal glee the song *Salaam*, with its hopeful lyrics, "Peace will soon come."

Summer times in Jerusalem have exposed us to some of the performance artists populating the city – the rabbi who hosts dozens at his home every Shabbat meal; the British teacher who delightedly introduces the uninitiated to *hasidic tishes*, the Friday-night gatherings where hundreds of Mea Shearim *hasidim* sing until 4 a.m. Summer times in Jerusalem have meant chanting with these *hasidim* one night; chanting with thousands of *Betar Yerushalayim* soccer fans the next night.

Summer times in Jerusalem have been about starlit concerts and dinners, about contemplating how to convey the beauty of Israel in a conversation with 40 Canadian birthright israel students and a dozen Israeli soldiers, who learned that they are not alone – and are fighting not just for their homeland but for the Jewish people.

The Jewish Agency's Education Department, along with the Israeli government, has launched MASA, a $100 million-a-year initiative to expand long-term Israel programs. This exciting initiative, building on birthright israel, recognizes great Jewish experiences including day schools, summer camps and free 10-day visits as gateways to sustained programs of studying and living in Israel, ideally for a year. Among many Orthodox Jews, the yeshiva year in Israel between high school and college has become the norm. The year has transformed thousands of individuals, as well as the Modern Orthodox community. Through the difficult years of Arafat's terror, participation in yeshiva programs held much steadier than other Israel experience programs. This stability reflected the Orthodox Jewish establishment's commitment to the Israel experience, as well as the fact that many of these kids' parents had spent similar years in Israel and understood the value.

For those contemplating a year in Israel, many choices abound, not one standard framework. MASA invites young Jews to taste Israel on their terms, be it studying at a yeshiva, researching at an Israeli university, volunteering on a kibbutz, programming at a high tech firm, saving fish in the Red Sea, working with the poor in the Galilee, helping immigrants acclimate in

Jerusalem, or digging through layers of ancient Jewish civilizations in the Judean desert. Israel offers marvelous opportunities for internships, for a Jewish peace corps, for a living breathing forum for *Tikun Olam* – repairing the world – as well as *HaGshama Atzmi* self-fulfillment.

This initiative could revolutionize Diaspora Jewry. Those of us who experienced Israel during this formative phase in our lives know how enriching and fun the year can be – the lifelong friendships formed, the broadened perspectives, the intensified Jewish consciousness, the expanded universe of Jewish living possibilities. In the summer of 2004, I spent time in Israel with nearly a dozen friends who had shared my year in Israel with me 25 years ago. Some live in Israel, most live in North America, but none regretted our Israeli "gap" year between high school and college. Thanks partially to that year, all lead more committed Jewish lives – and more honorable and value-oriented lives.

In this age of careerism, note that this unsystematic cross-section of Israel program alumni included some self-made millionaires and people who have succeeded in entertainment, academia, business and social work. No one's march to success slowed. Most appreciated that year as essential in making them who they are today as professionals, let alone as Jews and as human beings.

For thousands of years *Bashana HaBa'a* – Next Year in Jerusalem – was an unrealized hope. For decades, *B'shana HaBa'a* has risked being an empty vow. This year – for next year – let's make it a secret password into an inspiring, energizing, mind-transforming, soul-enriching, community-building, world-enhancing sustained Israel experience, whether you're in transition or not.

A CONCLUDING HOPE:
ZIONISTS UNITE AND TAKE BACK THE NIGHT

Moscow, April, 1985: The contents of my suitcase were already scattered across the customs counter. The burly uniformed Russian was pawing through it: pants, shirts, socks, underwear, seven pairs of blue jeans of various sizes, six cans of tuna, five American Jewish novels, four boxes of matzah, three cameras, two prayer books, and one embroidered bag holding a *tallit* and *t'fillin* – a prayer shawl and phylacteries. "I'm a student and I will be spending the Jewish holiday of Passover, here. You do have freedom of religion in the Soviet Union, don't you?" I asked, very politely. As he began rummaging through my knapsack, a taller, thinner man in plainclothes approached. "What are all those papers for?" he asked, pointing to fifty or so loose pages, filled with scribbles. Neglecting to mention the refusenik addresses written here and there in a code based on the first ten New York Yankee uniform numbers, characteristically camouflaging my Jewish identity in my American identity, I answered: "Those are my notes. I am a graduate student in American history and I have a big oral examination when I return home. Here," I continued, all innocence, without a hint of sarcasm, "would you like to read about Thomas Jefferson, he was a big believer in liberty?"

Silently but politely, the plainclothesman escorted me to the far end of the airport's customs area, ignoring my protests, refusing to answer my questions. "Please sit here," he said. Another uniformed guard approached and asked him a question in Russian. I heard the contempt in his voice as he spit out what sounded to me like: vyunah vyahlah pizhulsta pakleema followed by the one recognizable word "zeeoneist."

Twenty years after my Russian Passover, the Soviet Union may no longer exist, but "Zionist" remains a dirty word to far too many people. For too many others, even those for whom the word "Israel" triggers all sorts of warm glowy feelings, the word Zionist leaves them cold. At best, they view it as an elegant formulation of the clunkier "a pro-Israel person."

But Zionism once was and once again must be more than pro-Israelism; it must be a powerful and relevant response to the challenges facing Jews today. Zionism is the national liberation movement of the Jewish people. Zionism is a broad, complicated, diverse movement that can help fix what is broken in the contemporary Jew's identity. Zionism can help us navigate the complicated Jewish dilemmas so many of us face.

We need a new set of Zionist solutions to the unique problems generated by North American Jewish success. If Zionism cannot address modern North American hollowness, materialism, secularism, and superficiality, if it has nothing to say to our bored, spoiled, pampered youth, it is doomed to be a marginal movement, yesterday's news. If, however, by going back to first principles, by seeing how it was created, and where it started to falter, we can reconstitute and revitalize Zionism, we may indeed be able to find answers that help Jews and non-Jews alike. Only by going back into history with an understanding of our present needs can we begin to save Zionism to save ourselves. Only then can we bring pride and controversy, substance and edge, back into that word some spit out and too many others simply ignore – "Zionist."

TIMELINE

c. 2000 – 1750 B.C.E.: Abraham, Isaac, Jacob, the forefathers and the first Jews

c. 1750-1400 B.C.E.: First Exile – Slavery in Egypt

c. 1400-1250 B.C.E.: Exodus and Return Home, Moses receives the Torah at Sinai

c. 1250-1050 B.C.E.: Conquest of Canaan; Joshua leads, followed by the Judges

c. 1050-1000 B.C.E.: Samuel, the last of the Judges

1030-1006 B.C.E.: The reign of Saul, first Israelite King

1006-c. 965 B.C.E.: David rules, establishes Jerusalem as the capital

c. 965 to c. 930 B.C.E.: Solomon rules, builds the First Temple in Jerusalem

c. 925 B.C.E.: Division of the United Kingdom, North and South

721 B.C.E.: Fall of the northern kingdom to Assyria

586 B.C.E.: Destruction of the First Temple, many exiled to Babylonia

538 B.C.E.: Jews can return to Israel, many stay in Babylonia

520-515 B.C.E.: Jews rebuild Temple

c. 332 B.C.E.: Alexander the Great establishes Greek Rule throughout the Near East

c. 200 B.C.E.: Hebrew Bible standardized and divided into Torah, Prophets and Writings

168-165 B.C.E.: Maccabean Revolt against Antiochus (the story of *Hanukkah*)

63 B.C.E.: Roman Rule of Judea begins

37-4 B.C.E.: Herod governs Judea

30 B.C.E.: The great Rabbi Hillel becomes president of the *Sanhedrin* (until 10 CE)

19 B.C.E.: Herod's grand renovation of the Second Temple

29 C.E.: Jesus crucified by Romans in Jerusalem

70: Fall of Jerusalem, Temple destroyed, Yohanan Ben Zakkai escapes to Yavneh

73: Fall of Masada

132-135: Second revolt in Judea against Rome, led by Simon Bar Kochba

135: Hadrian renames Judea Syria-Palestina (Palestine), to minimize the Jewish tie to the land

c. 390: Jerusalem Talmud completed

c. 500: Babylonian Talmud completed

570-635: Mohammed founds Islam

638: Arabs conquer Jerusalem

1040-1105: Rashi, the great Torah commentator, lives in Troyes, France

1075-1141: Judah HaLevi, the Spanish poet, whose heart is in the East

1096-1099: First Crusade

1135-1204: Maimonides, physician, rationalist, innovator, teacher

1348-1349: Black Death devastates Europe, Jews blamed

1492: Jews expelled from Spain

1517: Ottoman Empire conquers Palestine

1534-1572: Rabbi Isaac Luria, Ha'ari, the great mystic of Safed

1555: Joseph Caro writes the *Shulchan Aruch* in Safed

1648-1649: Khmelnitski Revolt in the Ukraine – Jews massacred

1666: The false messiah Shabbetai Tzevi converts to Islam

1700-1760: the Baal Shem Tov, charismatic leader of the *Hasidim*

1720-1797: Vilna Gaon, rationalist leader of the *Mitnagdim*

1729-1786: Moses Mendelssohn, the Great *"Maskil"*

1791: 5 years after French Revolution, Jews declared full citizens

1806: Napoleon's *Sanhedrin*

1881: Pogroms in Russia

1882: BILU begins the *chalutzic*, pioneering movement to Israel

1894: Dreyfus Affair, French Jewish army captain framed

1896: Theodor Herzl writes *Der Judenstaat*, the Jewish State

1897: First Zionist Congress held at Basel

1903: Kishinev Pogroms – the subject of Chaim Nachman Bialik's *"Ir HaHareigah,"* City of Slaughter poem

1914-1918: World War I

1921: British partition of Jordan and Palestine, British Mandate begins

1925: Founding of Hebrew University

1939-1945: World War II and the Holocaust

1947: UN partitions Palestine. Arab guerillas reject the compromise and attack

1948: State of Israel proclaimed, seven Arab armies attack

1956: Suez Campaign, Israel forced to withdraw after capturing the Sinai

1967: Six Day War, Israel conquers the West Bank, Gaza, Golan Heights, the Sinai, and reunites Jerusalem

1973: Yom Kippur War, surprise attack

1975: UN declares Zionism is racism

1977: Sadat visits Jerusalem

1979: Camp David accords between Egypt and Israel signed

1982: Lebanon War

1993: Oslo Accords

1994: Peace with Jordan

1995: Rabin assassinated

May, 2000: Israel withdraws from Lebanon, UN sanctions border

July, 2000: Barak, Arafat and Clinton meet in Camp David

September, 2000: Palestinians riot against Oslo, launch terror war

February 6, 2001: Likud's Ariel Sharon elected Prime Minister

June 1, 2001: Dolphinarium Discotheque suicide bombing in Tel Aviv kills 21

August 9, 2001: Suicide bombing at Sbarro pizzeria kills 15, wounds 130

September 11, 2001: al Qaeda terrorists attack World Trade Center and Pentagon

July 23, 2001: Security Fence authorized as terror continues

March, 2002: 131 Israelis murdered, 30 killed at Netanya Seder Massacre

April, 2002: Operation Defensive Shield, Israel re-enters West Bank cities it left under Oslo

January 28, 2003: Sharon re-elected, Likud wins major victory

November 11, 2004: Yasir Arafat dies, Mahmoud Abbas succeeds him

August, 2005: Disengagement from Gaza

January 2006: A stroke incapacitates Sharon; Hamas wins parliamentary elections

For further elaboration see Menahem Mansoor, *Jewish History and Thought: An Introduction* (Hoboken, NJ, 1991)

GLOSSARY OF TERMS

Affluenza – "influenza" of the affluent – the ideological and psychological lethargy diagnosed by the *New York Times* in many of today's alienated suburban youth.

Al Naqba – the catastrophe; what the Palestinians call the founding of Israel in May 1948.

Aliyah – literally, ascent; the term for immigration to Israel, which is a step up in Jewish and Zionist terms.

Altneuland – literally old-new land; book Theodor Herzl wrote in 1902.

Am Olam – the Eternal People; a nineteenth-century movement filled with idealism about the Jewish immigration to the United States, a reminder of the ferment around that move as well.

Am Yisrael Chai – the Jewish people live, a popular affirmation and now classic song.

Ashkenazi – Ashkenaz is the area roughly in modern day Germany and France which was a center of Jewish living and learning a thousand years ago; more broadly, Ashkenazi refers to Jews of European descent.

Bereisheet – literally, in the beginning, Genesis, the first book of the Bible.

Bet HaMikdash – the Holy Temple, first built during Solomon's reign in the 10th century B.C.E.; then rebuilt 520-515 B.C.E.

Bilu – an acronym from the Biblical verse *bet ya'acov lechu v'nelcha*, (Isaiah 2:5) house of Jacob, arise and go forth, one of the early pioneering movements to Israel that sprang up in 1882 after pogroms.

birthright israel – modern program to send 18 to 26 year old Jews on a free trip to Israel as a way of building Jewish identity and ties to Israel (both words are spelled in lower case).

Bundism – Jewish movement founded in 1897 emphasizing secular, ethnic, and Socialist values.

Camp David – American presidential hideaway where Anwar Sadat and Menachem Begin succeeded in reaching an agreement in 1978, and where Yasir Arafat and Ehud Barak failed to come to terms in 2000.

Camp Tel Yehudah – national senior camp of Young Judaea, the largest Zionist youth movement in America.

Chalutzim – pioneers, the early Zionists who built the state's infrastructure a century ago.

Diaspora – literally, the dispersion, the term for Jews who live outside of Israel.

Dolphinarium – the Tel Aviv disco where a suicide bomber killed twenty-one young Israelis in June, 2001.

Emancipation – the movement in the 18th and 19th centuries to give Jews equal rights as citizens in European countries.

Enlightenment – a broad intellectual movement from two and three centuries ago to modernize Europe, which helped modernize European Jewry as well.

Entebbe – the capital of Uganda, where in 1976 Israeli commandoes rescued Jews held hostage in a terrorist hijacking.

Eretz Yisrael – the land of Israel, the Hebrew name for the homeland.

Galut – Exile, the pejorative term emphasizing that Jews outside of Israel are not simply dispersed but unsettled.

Gaza – a densely populated area bordering southwestern Israel and the Mediterranean Sea, captured from Egypt in 1967, largely ceded to the Palestinian Authority under Oslo.

Gevalt – a Yiddish expression of displeasure, literally, violence or force, meaning to raise a hue and cry, making Gevalt Zionism a reactive Zionism responding to attacks or crisis.

Golan Heights – elevated area bordering northeastern Israel, captured from Syria in 1967.

Green Line – the "old" border marking the line between Israel before 1967, and after.

Gush Emunim – literally, the Bloc of the Faithful; messianic settlers' movement that was very influential in creating many salvation settlements, and in energizing Religious Zionism.

Halachah – literally, the path to follow; Jewish law.

Hamas – literally, the committed, the zealots; radical Palestinian terrorist group responsible for many suicide bombs.

HaMatzav – literally, the situation, the euphemistic way many Israelis describe the anti-Oslo violence that began in September 2000.

Har HaBayit – The Temple Mount, literally, the mountain of the House, the House in question being the House of the Lord, the Temple in Jerusalem.

Hasmonean – the dynasty established by the Maccabees after the victory in 165 BCE we now celebrate each Hanukkah.

Hasidim – the devout ones; an eighteenth-century populist Jewish reformation movement in Poland emphasizing piety, intensity, joy and devotion in the service of God.

Hatikvah – the hope, the Jewish national anthem referring to the two-thousand-year longing for Zion.

Hezbollah – literally, the army of God; radical Arab terrorist group based in Southern Lebanon.

Intifada – Arabic for the uprising, what the Palestinians call the outbreak of anti-Israeli violence in the late 1980s, and most recently in September, 2000.

Jihad – Arabic word for holy war against infidels, non-believers.

Kabbalah – Jewish mysticism.

Kabbalat Shabbat – the welcoming of the Sabbath, the joyous ceremony on Friday night greeting the Sabbath bride.

Kehillah – the community, the formal communal organizations that ran Jewish communities in Europe and elsewhere for centuries.

Kibbutz – the collective farm settlements established a century ago that symbolized Zionism's radical reach and ambition.

Kotel – the wall, the Western Wall, the sole supporting wall remaining from the Second Temple.

Kwanza – an African-American holiday around Christmastime celebrating African roots and rituals.

Knesset – the Israeli parliament.

Lech Lecha – Go out, the start of the phrase in the Bible where God sends Abram to Israel.

Leil Shabbat – literally the Sabbath eve, Friday night.

MASA – Jewish Agency program encouraging and subsidizing twentysomethings to spend a year in Israel studying, interning, or volunteering.

Masada – the desert fort where Jews withstood the Romans and chose martyrdom rather than surrendering in 73 CE.

Maskil – an enlightened one, but quite literally a thinker.

Milchemet Shlom HaMitnachlim – the war for the safety of the settlers, what leftist critics of the Israeli government call the current situation.

Mitnagdim – literally opponents, the rationalist opponents of the Hasidim.

Mitzvah, Mitzvot – commandment or commandments, the good deeds and obligations dictated to Jews in the Torah.

Muezzin – cleric who calls Muslims to prayer.

Nigun – a wordless often upbeat melody; *nigunim* is plural.

Ohavei Tzion – lovers of Zion.

Oslo Accords – agreement negotiated in Norway in 1993 establishing a peace process between Israelis and Palestinians.

Palestine Liberation Organization – Yasir Araft's terrorist organization which pushed the Palestinian cause onto the world's agenda.

Palestinian Authority – the entity Oslo created to govern the Palestinians in the territories.

Partition – literally division, and a reference to the 1921 and 1947 divisions of territories between Arabs and Jews.

Pidyon Shvuyim – redeeming captives.

Pogrom – government-approved mob attacks against Jews in Russia and Poland.

Sanhedrin – the assembly, the ancient Jewish Supreme Court, which declined in the 4th Century C.E. and which Napoleon "reconvened" in 1806.

Sephardi – most literally Jews of Spanish origin, but it today encompasses mostly Jews of African and Middle Eastern descent.

Settlements – Israeli outposts established for civilians in the territories occupied since 1967.

Seudah Shlishit – the third feast, the last meal squeezed in as the Sabbath ends.

Shabbat – the Sabbath.

Shaliach – an emissary, a representative sent from Israel to work with Jews.

Shavuot – the Feast of Weeks, celebrating receiving the Torah at Sinai.

Shemot – literally, names, the second book of the Bible, Exodus.

Shulchan Aruch – the set table, the compendium of Jewish law edited by Joseph Caro in Safed in 1555.

Sinai – the large area to the south of Israel, captured in 1956 and again in 1967, and returned to Egypt, most recently after the first Camp David treaty.

Six Day War – 1967 war wherein Israel captured/liberated the West Bank, the Golan, Gaza, the Sinai, and reunited Jerusalem.

Talmud – the extensive commentary on the Mishna which is the commentary on the Torah.

T'fillot – prayers.

Tzahal – Hebrew acronym for IDF, the Israel Defense Forces.

UN Resolution 242 – resolution after the Six Day war calling for peace in exchange for territory.

UN Resolution 338 – resolution after the Yom Kippur War reaffirming 242 as a framework.

West Bank – the area to the East of Israel captured in 1967, also known as Judea and Samaria.

Wissenschaft – 19th century German initiative to study Jewish history scientifically.

Yerushalayim – Jerusalem.

Yerushalayim Shel Zahav – Jerusalem of Gold.

Yeshiva – seat of learning, a school where you learn Torah.

Yom Ha'atzmaut – Israel Independence Day.

Yom HaZikaron – Israel's memorial day.

Yom Kippur War – the 1973 Arab surprise attack which began on the holiest day in the Jewish calendar.

Zionism –Jewish nationalism.

SUGGESTED READINGS AND WEB SITES

ZIONISM:

Arthur Hertzberg, *The Zionist Idea: A Historical Analysis and Reader* (New York, 1997) – a collection of different Zionist thinkers, a bit heavy for first timers but my favorite book on Zionism.

Walter Lacqueur, *A History of Zionism* (New York, 1997) – a straightforward, if somewhat long, look at the history of Zionism.

Shlomo Avineri, *The Making of Modern Zionism: The Intellectual Origins of the Jewish State* (New York, 1981) – a shorter and more readable series of profiles.

Alex Singer, *Alex: Building a Life – the Story of an American Who Fell Defending Israel* (New York, Jerusalem, 1996) – an inspiring story of a young man who lived the Zionist dream.

Yossi Beilin, *His Brother's Keeper: Israel and Diaspora Jewry in the Twenty-First Century* (New York, 2000) – a secular, dovish Israeli politician offers his reading of modern Zionism and its relevance.

Yoram Hazony, *The Jewish State: the Struggle for Israel's Soul* (New York, 2001) – a counter to Beilin, offering a passionate denunciation of post-Zionism and Israeli ideological decadence from the right.

JEWISH HISTORY

The Bible – the all-time, best-selling classic – try reading it cover to cover – great stories your Hebrew school teachers skipped over, and the best possible grounding.

Haim H. Ben-Sasson, ed. *A History of the Jewish People* (Cambridge, 1976) – authoritative, but more encyclopedic than readable.

Martin Gilbert, *Jewish History Atlas* 2nd rev. ed. (London, 1976) – superb view of Jewish history from maps.

Howard Morley Sachar, *The Course of Modern Jewish History* (New York, 1990) – an excellent overview of what shaped the modern world. Or check out his latest which is a completely revised version, *A History of the Jews in the Modern World* (New York, 2005).

Mendes-Flohr, Paul R. and Jehuda Reinharz, eds., *The Jew in the Modern World: A Documentary History* (New York, 1980) – an amazing collection of documents.

Ron Rosenbaum, *Contemporary Anti-Semitism: Those Who Forget the Past: The Question of Anti-Semitism* (New York, 2004) – insightful essays by Harold Evans, Tom Gross, Simon Schama, Lawrence Summers, Ruth Wiesse, and others.

ISRAEL

Howard Morley Sachar, *A History of Israel: from the Rise of Zionism to our Time* (New York, 1996) – very thorough overview.

James Michener, *The Source* (New York, 1992) – don't be put off by its size. This is the classic first-trip-to-Israel historical novel, following the sweep of Israeli and Jewish history through the various layers of one archaeological dig.

Leon Uris, *Exodus* (New York, 1983) – the romantic view of Israel's founding, another classic historical novel.

Thomas Friedman, *From Beirut to Jerusalem* (New York, 1990) – somewhat dated, but still very interesting look at modern Israel.

Alan Dershowitz, *The Case for Israel* (New York, 2004) – a punchy, passionate, defense of Israel and the Jewish people. A very useful introduction to key issues.

Michael Oren, *Six Days of War: June 1967 and the Making of the Modern Middle East* (New York, 2003) – a well-written and authoritative look at the war which explains just how Israel occupied-liberated-conquered the disputed territories.

Itamar Rabinovich, *Waging Peace: Israel and the Arabs, 1948-2003* (Princeton, 2004) – a direct, interesting look at Israel's search for peace, quite well-balanced.

Daniel Gordis, *Home to Stay: One American Family's Chronicle of Miracles and Struggles in Contemporary Israel* (New York, 2003) – a lyrical, insightful look at life in modern Jerusalem, capturing both the terror and the joys during the difficult years. Originally published as *If A Place Can Make You Cry.*

Barry Rubin and Judith Colp Rubin, *Yasir Arafat: A Political Biography* (New York, 2005) – good, reliable overview of the life of the arch-terrorist.

OTHER SOURCES MENTIONED OR USED
(wherever possible the latest, in-print edition is listed)

Woody Allen, "Am I Reading the Paper Correctly?" *New York Times*, 28 January 1988, A27.

Benedict Anderson, *Imagined Communities: Reflections on the Origin and Spread of Nationalism* (London, 1983).

David Brooks, *Bobos in Paradise: The New Upper Class and How They Got There* (New York, 2000).

Phyllis Chesler, *The New Anti-Semitism: The Current Crisis and What We Must Do about It* (New York, 2003).

Alexander Cockburn, Jeffrey St. Clair, *The Politics of Anti-Semitism* (New York, 2003) – in this collection of skeptics, some trivialize the issue.

Abraham Foxman, *Never Again? The Threat of the New Anti-Semitism* (San Francisco, 2003).

Samuel G. Freedman, *Jew Vs. Jew: the Struggle for the Soul of American Jewry* (New York, 2000).

Theodor Herzl, *The Jewish State* (New York, 1989).

Moses Hess, *The Revival of Israel: Rome and Jerusalem, the Last Nationalist Question* (Omaha, 1995).

Michael Novak, *The Rise of the Unmeltable Ethnics: Politics and Culture in the 1970s* (New York, 1975).

Neil Postman, *Amusing Ourselves to Death: Public Discourse in the Age of Show Business* (New York, 1986).

Dennis Prager and Joseph Telushkin, *Why the Jews: The Reason for Antisemitism* (New York, 2003).

Robert D. Putnam, *Bowling Alone: The Collapse and Revival of American Community* (New York, 2001).

David Riesman, *The Lonely Crowd, Revised Edition: A Study of the Changing American Character* [abridged] (New Haven, 2001).

Philip Roth, *Portnoy's Complaint* (New York, 1969, 1994).

Barry Rubin, "The Region: A New Paradigm," *Jerusalem Post*, 14 Nov. 2005.

Michael Sandel, *Democracy's Discontent: America in Search of a Public Philosophy* (Cambridge, 1998).

Natan Sharansky with Ron Dermer, *The Case for Democracy: the Power of Freedom to Overcome Tyranny and Terror* (New York, 2004).

Avi Shlaim, *The Iron Wall: Israel and the Arab World* (New York 2000, 2001).

Michael Walzer, et al., eds. *The Jewish Political Tradition: volume one Authority* (New Haven, 2000).

Robert Wiebe, "Imagined Communities, Nationalist Experiences," *The Journal of the Historical Society,* 1 (Spring, 2000): 33-63.

Sloan Wilson, *The Man in the Gray Flannel Suit* (New York, 1955).

SOME USEFUL WEB SITES
(with special thanks to Justin Korda and the Canada Israel Experience Center)

birthright israel (http://www.birthrightisrael.com): Gateway to ten life-transforming days – and great content too!

Canadian Jewish News (http://www.cjnews.com): Weekly forum of Canadian Jewry.

Ha'aretz (http://www.haaretzdaily.com): The Hebrew language Israeli daily, translated into English.

Hagshama – World Zionist organization *(http://www.wzo.org.il)*: Great resource for Zionist Educational Resources.

Israel Defense Forces *(http://www.idf.il)*: Official Web site of the Israeli army.

Israeli Ministry of Foreign Affairs *(http://www.mfa.gov.il/mfa/home.asp)*: Excellent source for news and facts about Israel.

The Jerusalem Post (http://www.jpost.com): The English language Israeli daily.

The Jerusalem Report (http://www.jrep.com): Bimonthly news magazine focusing on Israel, the Middle East and the Jewish world.

Jewish Agency for Israel, Department for Jewish Zionist Education *(http:www.jajz-ed.org.il/index1.html)*: Israeli history and facts.

Jewish Telegraph Agency (*http:www.jta.org)*: The subtitle says it all: The Global News Service of the Jewish People.

The Jewish Week *(http:www.thejewishweek.com)*: Weekly forum of New York – and American – Jewry.

Masa *(http://www.israelexperience.com/Masa/English/)*: Gateway to long-term Israel programs, a useful guide to your many exciting options.

Mideast Truth (http://www.mideasttruth.com): A great collection of contemporary articles, updated regularly, staffed by "a small team of dedicated volunteers, from different nationalities."

FOR MORE INFORMATION ON HOW TO HELP OUT VICTIMS OF PALESTINIAN TERROR CHECK OUT:

The OneFamily Fund **(http://www.onefamilyfund.org)**: A grass roots not-for-profit entity established after the Sbarro Pizzeria bombing, when one Bat Mitzvah girl, Michal Belzberg, decided she could not indulge in a celebration while peers of her were suffering. The Website lists numerous ways we can support these victims including cards of condolences, walk-a-thons, bar mitzvah gift donations, and charitable contributions. They have already distributed over $12.2 million to hundreds of grieving families in need. Contact info is: Bynet Building, PO Box 45002, Har Hotzvim, Jerusalem 91450 – Tel: 011-972-2-571-4516; Fax: 011-972-2-581-7783; info@onefamilyfund.org

The Koby Mandell Foundation **(http://www.kobymandell.org)**: A foundation established in memory of Koby Mandell, the 13-year-old American-Israeli boy who was brutally murdered in May 2001 along with his friend Yosef Ish-Ran. The Foundation has a number of marvelous initiatives, including establishing Camp Koby, an enjoyable and therapeutic camp experience for survivors of terror and other trauma. To contact the foundation regarding tax deductible donations and other gifts email info@kobymandell.org. Or call: in the United States, 888-622-5629, in Canada 905-760-0073; in Israel 011-972-2-648-3758.

ACKNOWLEDGMENTS

In 2001, responding to the Mideast crisis, the book was shepherded quickly into print. I am most indebted to my publisher, Shlomo Shimon, the Executive Director of the Bronfman Jewish Education Centre in Montreal, for his energy, wisdom, savvy, and love for the Jewish people.

One of Shlomo's first ideas when he heard about the project was to sign on Avi Katz as an illustrator. The remarkable drawings that grace this work speak for themselves. Less obvious are all the other ways Avi's insight and spirit helped improve the final product.

I am indebted to many others who sacrificed parts of their summer vacation to help. The entire BJEC and Bronfman Israel Experience Centre staff has pitched in, creating a fantastic group effort, with special thanks to the BJEC Curriculum Development Department. The Silbiger family printing and layout wizards of Premco Enterprises did first-rate work, and were extraordinarily patient with a complicated and fast-paced project. Nina Assedo, Myer Bick, Marilyn Blumer, Dale Boidman, Tuvia Book, Danyael Cantor, Ariela Cotler, Julie Cusmariu, Gilbert Durocher, Leesa Fox, Micah Halperin, Helene Kaufman, Robert Kleinman, Don Levy, Lois Lieff, Ralph Lipper, Gil Mann, Avi Morrow, Marlene Post, Rabbi Reuben Poupko, Ruthie Saragosti, Evelyn Schachter, Sigalit Sretlit, Rabbi Chaim Steinmetz, Leah Strigler, Dan Troy, Dr. Tevi Troy, Craig Turk, Eli Valley, and Emanuel Weiner offered invaluable assistance. Eddie Shostak did an amazing job tracking down quotations. Alex Cowan did yeoman's work, assembling the index intelligently and efficiently, among many other kindnesses. People who read the manuscripts in whole or in part – but are in no way responsible for the opinions or content expressed therein, include Linda Adams, Rabbi Ron Aigen, David Cape, Dr. Karen Gazith, Rabbi Barry Gelman, Shai Korman, Lorne Klemensberg, Nancy Rosenfeld, Dr. Tevi Troy, and, especially, Don Futterman. Dan Troy, Justin Korda and Aaron Pollack offered helpful comments on earlier versions.

Some parts of the book first appeared as articles in *Moment* magazine, the *Forward*, the *Montreal Gazette*, the *Jerusalem Report*, the *Jerusalem Post*, the *B'nai Brith Magazine*, the *Raleigh News & Observer*, *The Jewish Week*, and the *Canadian Jewish News*. I thank Edie Austin, Mordechai Ben-Dat, J.J. Goldberg, Gershom Gorenberg, Richard Greenberg, Ronnie Hope, Brian Kappler, Wayne Lowrie, Josh Rolnick, Gary Rosenblatt,

Suzanne Singer, and Peder Zane for their skillful editing, which has taught me much, and for allowing me to retain copyright control.

The book has been underwritten with generous grants from the Bronfman Israel Experience Centre, the Jewish Community Foundation of Montreal, and FEDERATION CJA in Montreal. The financing came with no editorial demands or changes.

Although I am solely responsible for the content, on each page of this book I can detect the work of dozens of collaborators, friends, and teachers, who, over the years, have taught me much and honed my ideas. Four teachers in particular stand out. Dr. Steve Copeland, Mel Reisfield, Professor Elie Wiesel, and the late Professor Isadore Twersky z"l, shaped my understanding of Zionism, Jewish history, Jewish consciousness, and modern life. Similarly, I am indebted to thousands of students, especially Young Judaeans and birthrighters, who have listened to me, challenged me, and taught me so much over the years.

I wish also to thank Mr. and Mrs. Haim Avraham, and their lovely family. In June 2001 I met these brave people, whose son Benny was murdered along the Lebanese border – but whose fate was kept secret from them for years. The courage and faith they and the other families demonstrated have inspired me tremendously, reinforcing and stretching my Zionist vision.

Finally, this book could not have been written without the support and love of my family. All of us, on both sides of my family, share a deep commitment to Judaism and Israel. I am blessed to share these passions with my parents, Elaine and Dov Troy, my brothers, my various in-laws, my wife, and now my four children, each of whose names carry linkages both to Jewish ideas and to individuals with deep ties to Israel.

I am especially indebted to my wife and children. The time demands of writing this book – and community involvement throughout these difficult years – make this very much a collaborative Troy family enterprise. I thank them, especially my wife, my best friend, for joining me and assisting me in this endeavor. At times, the crisis seemed to get worse daily, but this book was written as an act of optimism not despair, and things have improved. We fervently hope that our children will grow up in a golden world of spring-like renewal, symbolized by the dove, a just world progressing toward peace rather than wallowing in war.

gt
February 2006
Sh'vat 5766

LIST OF MAPS

INDEX

Gil Troy is Professor of History at McGill University in Montreal. A native of Queens, New York, and a graduate of Solomon Schechter Day School there, he received his bachelor's, master's, and doctoral degrees in History from Harvard University. He was a member of Young Judaea, the largest Zionist Youth movement in America, for many years, and worked at Camp Tel Yehudah throughout the 1980s. His three other books concern American history: *Morning in America, How Ronald Reagan Invented the 1980s, Mr. and Mrs. President: From the Trumans to the Clintons*, and *See How They Ran: The Changing Role of the Presidential Candidate.* From 1997 to 1998 he chaired McGill's history department and in March, 1999 was promoted to full professor. Maclean's Magazine has repeatedly designated him as one of McGill's "Popular Profs," and the History News Network has called him one of America's "top young historians."

Troy writes regularly for the *B'nai Brith Magazine*, the *Canadian Jewish News* and *The Jewish Week.*

He has also published articles recently in the *New York Times*, the *Wall Street Journal*, the *Washington Post*, *Newsday*, the *New York Post*, the *Montreal Gazette*, the *National Post*, *Moment* magazine, and the *Jerusalem Post*, among others. He has appeared as a commentator on most major Canadian and American television networks. Troy is also the chairman of the Montreal birthright israel committee.

Avi Katz, Israeli artist, illustrator and cartoonist, was born in Philadelphia, PA, USA in 1949. He studied at Solomon Schechter Day School and Akiba Hebrew Academy, beginning his art studies at UC Berkeley before deciding to move to Israel in 1970, where he completed his studies at the Bezalel Academy of Art. Though best known as the artist of the *Jerusalem Report* since its first issue in 1990, he has also illustrated dozens of children's books – including the prize-winning *King Solomon and the Queen of Sheba, Princess Alopecia,* and *My Travels with Alex* – schoolbooks, and book covers, as well as newspaper and magazine articles. He has created comic strips, TV animation and multimedia titles and has exhibited one-man shows of his paintings and illustrations in Israel and the USA and participated in group shows around the world. He is currently working with Gil Troy on *Shalom Israel*, a history of Israel in text and pictures. Katz lives in Ramat-Gan near Tel Aviv; he is married and has three sons.